Series Created by Hans Höfer

MOSCOW

Project Editor: Wilhelm Klein
Introduced by Yevgeny Yevtushenko
Principal photography: Fritz Dressler
Updated by Chris and Melanie Rice

Editorial Director: Brian Bell

APA PUBLICATIONS

Houghton Mifflin

ABOUT THIS BOOK

As that great traveller Karl Baedeker once put it: "If ever a city expressed the character and peculiarities of its inhabitants, that city is Moscow." This book aims to capture the same characteristics, for not only is it *about* Muscovites, it is also largely written *by* them.

Taking advantage of the new freedoms being eagerly devoured by Russian writers, Apa Publications opted for a unique approach. The uniqueness lay in the daring departure from the customary guidebook practice of sending writers into a country or city to observe, explore and report their findings. Instead, we sought out expert writers within Russia, pairing their insights with Apa's proven expertise in producing an internationally renowned series of guidebooks. What is on offer, therefore, is not Moscow as filtered through the sensibilities of foreign observers, but Moscow as seen through the eyes of native writers. Their views are refreshingly outspoken. Reading this book is the next best thing to staying with a family in the city, sharing their joys and frustrations about the place they love.

Together with its companion volume, *Insight Guide: St Petersburg*, also edited by **Wilhelm Klein**, this book represented a milestone in East-West co-operation – but also, at times, a trial in patience. As well as coping with a worsening food supply, the radical independence struggles of some of the republics and the corresponding relaxation of government control, we had also to integrate the ongoing microchanges that are important for any city guide. Street names reverted to old designations, immigration and currency regulations were changing, and new tourist-related businesses were springing up all over the place. Life in Moscow changed more during the two years while the first edition of this book was being written than in the previous 70. It felt as if one was producing a guide to Peking in 1948 or to Saigon in 1975.

And Moscow has continued to change, ensuring that even this latest edition is a work in progress rather than a definitive guidebook. New street names keep on popping up, hotels and restaurants open and shut with bewildering speed, and the reins of political power are being tugged in many different directions.

But those are incidentals. What is exciting for the curious visitor is the sense of a city in the grip of revolutionary change, of people reinventing their lives day by day. Imagine the thrill of being in Moscow, for instance, on Christmas Day 1991, when for the first time in nearly 80 years the state actually marked the Russian Orthodox Christmas. By special decree, the Moscow Metro ran until after 2am to get the crowds home from the city's 160 churches. The legion of Santa Clauses were unusually merry that year, helped along with generous measures of vodka.

It was while publishing the German edition of the *Monthly Review*, an American neo-Marxist magazine, back in the 1970s that project editor Wilhelm Klein first gained an insight into the state of Soviet affairs. His ambition to get some of Russia's best writers to contribute to the present trio of books was realised when **Yevgeny Yevtushenko**, the country's most outspoken poet, agreed to participate.

Klein

Yevtushenko

Yevtushenko knows its history and creative background as well as anyone, and his introductory essay provides a mouthwatering appetiser to the treasure trove of art and humanity contained in the city.

With Yevtushenko's help, many other contributors were lined up. **Anatoli Blinov**, who wrote the history section of this book, is a journalist by profession. He worked as an aide to Valentin Falin, a Secretary of the CPSU Central Committee, and is co-author of the book *The Soviet Economy: an Insider's View*.

Igor Zakharov, who had written for an Apa's original guide to the Soviet Union (since replaced with *Insight Guide: Russia*), studied philosophy and wrote in this book about the "Private Life of Ivan the Terrible".

Vladislav Govorukhin, then a writer and editor at a prominent Moscow publishing house, spent more than a year assembling the details that form the backbone of this book: the Places section. He combed every important street and structure of Moscow and went time and again to research libraries to collect all those small details that bring to vivid life a city that, all too often, has been thought of as grey and uniform. Govorukhin has recently, like many Muscovites, gone into business on his own account and one of his successes has been the translation of a growing number of Insight Guides into Russian.

The chapters about Moscow culture, museums and architecture were co-written by **Elvira Kim** and **Olga Kalinina**, art critics and geographers by profession. The theatre and cinema

Govorukhin

Kim

scene were described by **N. Zorkaya** and **Andrei Karaulov**. Zorkaya is a leading Soviet film critic and Karaulov is a drama critic who has written several books about art and politics.

Yevgeny Filiminov is an expert on Russian tourism who had already contributed to the Insight's original book on the Soviet Union. For this book, he wrote the chapter on the Golden Ring.

The chapter profiling the undefeatable Muscovite was written by **Robert Tsfasman**, a typical Muscovite himself. He graduated from the Moscow University's philological department and later became editor-in-chief of the *Soviet Life Magazine*. He is author of numerous publications that have appeared in Russia and abroad.

This latest edition of *Insight Guide: Moscow* has been revised and updated by **Chris and Melanie Rice**. Based in London, they specialise in Eastern European affairs, visit Moscow frequently, and speak Russian fluently.

As with all Insight Guides, the photographs aim not only to provide a pictorial extension to the written words but also to capture the essence of the living, new Moscow, to show what it is like to be a Muscovite in the 1990s. Many of these pictures came from local photographers. To supplement them, Apa Publications sent an English photographer, **John Spaull**, to Moscow, and also called on the archive of one of Germany's top photographers, **Fritz Dressler**, who teaches photography at his native Bremen Academy of Art.

The final polishing of the book's text was carried out in Apa's London editorial office. Proof-reading and indexing were completed by **Mary Morton**.

Kalinina

Karaulov

Dressler

CONTENTS

<u>**Preceding pages:**</u> **St Basil's Cathedral, Red Square; Cathedral of the Annunciation domes, the Kremlin.**

TRAVEL TIPS

THE EMBRACE OF MOTHER BEAR

*The poet **Yevgeny Yevtushenko** on how to come to terms with Moscow*

According to one version, the Russian word for Moscow, *Moskva,* came from the Maris (a Finnish people) word *maska ava,* meaning "mother bear". Numerous attempts have been made to kill this mother bear, and many cruel bullets still drift around her body. But she has kept going and not become disillusioned with people. The expression "the hand of Moscow" used to inspire fear. Now this hand is held out to the rest of the human family, asking for support.

In the past we studied foreign languages purely as a formality, never imagining they might really come in useful. Now more and more young people are studying foreign languages not because they are forced to, but because they can't do without them.

But do make the effort to learn a little Russian, otherwise you will certainly lose out. After living in a police state for so many years, Russians tend to be suspicious of interpreters and are reticent in their presence. Muscovites like confiding, however, and sometimes their confidences may suddenly come gushing out like Niagara Falls.

I would advise you not only to stroll along the old Arbat and past the art and handicraft stalls in Izmailovo Park but also to visit the small picture galleries which are springing up like mushrooms after a shower of rain. I would advise you to go not only to the Bolshoi Theatre or the Circus – traditional haunts of foreign tourists – but also to the drama theatres and studios, where you will understand and feel much even without a translation. The expressive visual language of the Taganka and Leninskiy Komsomol theatres is easily understood, thanks to its tangible metaphors.

Do visit the Moscow Metro. I'm recommending it not just because it is beautiful but also because you will see for yourselves how many people are reading – not only newspapers and journals but also books by Gabriel García Márquez, Aba Kobo, Heinrich Böll, William Styron, and William Golding, and, of course, books of poetry. Moscow is a city of readers.

Visit the grave of one of the Muscovites' favourite heroes, the poet and singer Vladimir Vysotsky, and you'll see hundreds of fresh bouquets. Take a walk around Moscow's cemeteries where Muscovites come with a bottle of vodka on Sundays to converse with their deceased relatives and friends, and you'll gain a better understanding of Moscow's suffering but kind soul. Don't forget to stand quietly in one of Moscow's churches when a service is in progress; the heavy drops of wax from the candles in front of the icons will slowly mark off the passing of time, and the barely audible music will link you with all of Moscow's living and dead.

Preceding pages: the next generation no longer needs to lean on Lenin; the Russian Bike Show, organised by a Moscow biker gang, The Night Wolves; keeping in touch; busking on Moscow's Arbat; weddings are a big event. **Left**, 15th-century icon of the prophet Daniil.

THE MAKING OF MOSCOW

Yevgeny Yevtushenko describes the changing moods of Russia's legendary capital.

"Russia used to be run by St Petersburg and Moscow: now St Petersburg's role and the cultural period of the window cut through to Europe is over, now… but now the question is whether indeed St Petersburg and Moscow did run Russia… Was this really true? Certainly, not all Russia used to pour into St Petersburg and Moscow and gather there in crowds… and in actual fact, she ran herself, continually being rejuvenated by fresh influxes of new strength from her provinces and outlying regions…"

This is how Fyodor Dostoyevsky accurately defined the significance of Russia's two main cities: the two main knots of her history which are made up of the tightly interwoven threads of human destinies, political intrigues, threads of blood and tears, ships' and gallows' ropes, the tie that the great Russian poet Yesenin hanged himself with, the barbed wire over the walls of the Butyrka and Lefortovo prisons, and the skipping ropes children have such fun with.

A village turned capital: Moscow was the first primordial knot to be tied when Russia was in its infancy. In relation to Moscow, St Petersburg seemed a prodigal son, dressed in fancy foreign clothes and smoking tobacco, a son ashamed of his old-fashioned country bumpkin of a mother. Moscow is a village which has grown into a capital city, and even now, more than eight centuries after its foundation, it retains its village ways.

In no other world capital will you encounter such an obsession for home-made jams and salted foods. Muscovites are superstitious, as country folk tend to be, and fond of using home cures for common complaints. That's why on many window sills you will see spiky green aloe plants – supposedly the universal remedy for all ailments.

All the political news, all the rumours and all the gossip that have not been carried by the press spread like wildfire through the city as though it were no bigger than a village. When you visit Muscovites at home, they are as hospitable as country folk, and the entire contents of their refrigerators will be spread out on the table.

Every family has at least one dish of its very own invention but the stomach of a Muscovite, no matter how radical, is always conservative. Even the elitist intelligentsia prefers the traditional country fare that was eaten in the days before Peter I. Most Muscovites, for instance, adore roast duck stuffed with apples, meat dumplings (*pelmeni*), grated beetroot with garlic, pickled cabbage soup with dried mushrooms, freshly salted cucumbers, marinated tomatoes and honey-soaked apples. All this is what Ivan the Terrible ate and his gastronomic tastes were no different from those of his serfs.

There is also something rather countrified about the atmosphere in Moscow's leafy courtyards that nestle behind the box-like concrete apartment tower blocks. *Babushki* (grannies) sit on benches, their knitting needles clicking slowly, while runny-nosed children play at their feet; nearby, a local drunk snores peacefully on the shady grass, and old-age pensioners noisily bang down dominoes on a wooden table.

The heirs of the founder: The monument to Moscow's founder, Grand Prince Yury Dolgorukiy, stands in the very heart of Moscow, and hiding coyly behind his steed's bronze tail is the Georgian Aragvi restaurant. In nearby streets suave Caucasians with narrow black mustaches, who slink like mountain leopards after their blue-eyed, blond-haired prey, will tell you jokingly: "That man Dolgorukiy was no fool – he built Moscow around a Georgian restaurant…"

That is practically all there is to joke about in the history of Moscow's foundation. Grand Prince Yury was nicknamed Dolgorukiy (the Long-Armed) because of the greedy and single-minded manner in which he gathered lands, piece by piece, into his long arms. According to some legends, the lands of a boyar (as noblemen and landowners were then called) caught the Grand Prince's eagle eye. These lands included several villages, one of which, Vorobievo, was located on the site of the present-day Moscow University and on the same hilltop which brides and bridegrooms visit today to admire the view of the city. The boyar Kuchka himself lived in a house very close to what is today one of Moscow's best theatres, the Sovremennik.

Kuchka had the reputation of being proud and outspoken. Dolgorukiy finally murdered him and for a long time afterwards the site of

The following words of the monk Filotheus were cited in a 17th-century chronicle: "Two Romes have fallen, but the third stands, and there will be no fourth. Verily the town of Moscow is called the Third Rome, for a sign hangs over it, just as it did over the First and Second. And different though it may be, it shares the same destiny – bloodshed." Prophetic words. While the Slavs in Kiev were being baptised in the Dnieper River, in Moscow they were being soaked in the blood of invasions, rebellions and executions.

For some time St Petersburg became the official capital, but Moscow continued to be the national capital in the full sense of the

the murder was called Kuchkovo Field. Through this field ran Lubyanka Street, and here it was, in the infamous building also known as the *Lubyanka* and occupied by the secret police (known successively as the Cheka, NKVD, MGB and the KGB) that the long-armed heirs of Moscow's founder continued to torture and kill.

Yury Dolgorukiy decided to outwit boyar Kuchka's ghost and win him over by marrying off his son, Andrei, to the murdered man's daughter. That, however, didn't prevent Kuchka's sons from eventually killing the young man to avenge their father's death.

word. The straight thoroughfares of St Petersburg had nothing in common with the tortuous, uneven Russian preference for numerous dark back streets and blind alleys. Moscow's celebrated side-streets, which, unfortunately, are fast disappearing, embodied the psychological geometry of the Russian soul. Quite understandably, they were given names like *Krivokolenniy* (Crooked Knee) and *Krivoarbatskiy* (Crooked Arbat).

Moscow could not help but develop on the very site where it was first recorded in a chronicle of 1147, for, like a two-faced idol, it stood at the crossing of many ways with one face turned towards Asia and the other towards Europe. This was why, for many years, Moscow determined Russia's destiny, and why, even today, Westernisers and Slavophiles are still locked in their seemingly endless disputes. "Yes, we are Scythians, yes, we are Asians with greedy slanting eyes…" wrote the great poet Alexander Blok, even though he was a very highly educated European.

Foreign invaders: The Moscow princes received their royal titles from the Tatar khans and then, copying the khans' own wily tactics, gradually sewed together the fragmented patches of Russian lands. Over the next three centuries or so the Tatar overlords and con-

him with jubilant peeling bells and the city fathers would present him with the keys to Russia's capital on a silver platter; his hopes were soon dashed. Moscow rushed out of Moscow like water from a riverbed so that not a drop would reach the invaders' parched lips. Napoleon found himself in the position of a seducer who had succeeded in getting into a woman's warm bed, only to see her running away, laughing at him derisively.

But Napoleon's conquerors – and Hitler's victors in the 1940s – were rewarded with the same crass ingratitude. So accustomed did Russia become to constant humiliations that it could no longer become accustomed to

querors turned into janitors, waiters and steam-bath attendants…

Every Russian was born in Moscow because that is where Russia itself was born. Moscow stood like a fortress, barring the Tatar hordes' way to Europe and receiving all the blows and humiliations Europe might otherwise have suffered. However, no sooner had Moscow cast off its foreign shackles than it was clamped in the shackles of Tsarism. Napoleon hoped that Moscow would greet

Left, the *streltsi* on their way to execution. **Above**, the wooden Lenin Mausoleum in the 1920s.

freedom. It was the last country in Europe to abolish serfdom and, after the October Revolution, exchanged one state of servitude for another, far more terrible than Tsarism.

Then, after a short reprieve under Nikita Khrushchev, it exchanged the cult of Stalin's personality for that of impersonality. Yet it was in this officially stagnant but unofficially seething time that Moscow produced a young generation of poets who started gathering audiences in their thousands in public squares and palaces of sport. What's more, these audiences expected their contemporary idols to tell them the truth, which never appeared on the pages of *Pravda* (ironically, the Russian word for "the truth").

Eventually in 1962, *Pravda* published a poem against neo-Stalinism, the first of this theme to appear in our press. That poem was my own work *The heirs of Stalin*. The Moscow journal *Noviy Mir* was responsible for the earth-shattering publication of the first eye-witness account of Stalin's labour camps – *A Day in the Life of Ivan Denisovich* by Alexander Solzhenitsyn. And it was Moscow, the capital of the Party *nomenklatura* (the system whereby appointments to specified posts in government or the economic administration are made by organs of the Communist Party), that became the capital

the despairing gazes of all the exploited peoples of the planet were fixed. At the same time cars nicknamed "Black Ravens" were speeding round Moscow, packed full of innocent people who had just been arrested. The clanking sound of a lift at night used to be terrifying because the secret police could burst into anyone's flat with an arrest warrant at any time. But at school we kept on singing with all our hearts: *Industrious,/ Illustrious,/ Forever victorious,/ Moscow of mine,/ The greatest/ The greatest love of mine.*

I remember Moscow in 1941 when refugees drove their anxiously bellowing cows through Red Square and past the Bolshoi Theatre. I remember Moscow in 1944 when

of non-conformism in 1968; it was then that a small group of young people came out onto Execution Place, in former times the site of so many executions, to protest against the Soviet tanks in Prague. From then on, the human rights movement headed by Andrei Sakharov began to gain momentum.

Messianic ideas: France should be grateful to Moscow for not letting the French Empire expand: Napoleon turned back from Moscow just in time. I grew up in Stalin's time when the propaganda machine did its level best to give Moscow the image of a Messianic city; and the capital city of the world upon which

tens of thousands of German PoWs were led along the ring road. I remember seeing there a Russian woman who, submitting to the mysterious laws of female compassion, felt sorry for the people who had possibly killed her husband or brother, and feverishly began thrusting crusts of bread at them.

I remember that March day in 1953 when people crushed one another at Stalin's funeral and their breath was so dense you could see the shadows of the March branches quivering on it; all around lay piles of boots of every size and description which had been lost in the terrible scrum.

I remember a kiss under some tinkling spring icicles at Patriarch's Ponds (now Pioneer Ponds). I remember the day that Yuri Gagarin, the first man in space, flew into Moscow, and the public jubilation as though this heralded some unprecedented flight which still lay ahead of us all. And Boris Pasternak, you know, also believed in the future of this great city when he wrote of it:

For the dreamer and the night-bird
Moscow is dearer than all else in the world.
He is at the hearth, the source
Of everything that the century will live for.

Moscow, which once protected Europe from the Tatar hordes, has acted in the 20th

15th-century Konstantin-Yelena Tower, for instance, was once popularly called the "Torture Tower" because it contained a rack – a wooden instrument of torture on which prisoners could be made to confess to any crime. They were stripped to the waist and stretched on this horizontal rack with their hands tied behind their backs in such a way that their arms were pulled from their sockets. They were also tortured with a red-hot iron: three letters, VOS, standing for "Disturber of the Peace", were branded on their foreheads, and their nostrils were torn. Later, their corpses were flung onto the thoroughfare below to be carted away by relatives.

century as a shield for all humanity by defending it from fascism. But, internally, much blood has been spilled. The young tsar's record of 120 executions in one day of March 1697 pales in comparison with the one Stalin was to set in 1937 when he had approximately 3 million people arrested and killed.

If the atmosphere in the Kremlin seems daunting at times, this is no illusion – it is an awareness of horrifying historical fact. The

In 1606, the 6,000 rebels captured from Bolotnikov's army were executed in a conveyor-like manner: they were lined up in rows, struck over the head with a club, like cattle, and dumped under the ice of the River Yauza. When the so-called Copper Rebellion against the introduction of copper coins was put down in 1662, 19 people were hanged in Red Square and 12 had their arms, legs and tongues cut off.

A sophisticated method of torture was devised for Stepan Razin, the legendary peasant leader, who later became the hero of numerous folk songs. Razin withstood 100

Left, German prisoners-of-war being walked through Moscow. **Above**, crowds celebrate the failure of the 1991 coup against Gorbachev.

blows from a leather knout while on the rack; he rebuked his brother, Frola, on the execution block for groaning and not bearing the pain in silence. For three days icy water was dripped onto Razin's shaven head. On 6 June 1671 he and his brother were driven out into Execution Place (of which Mayakovsky was later to write somewhat flippantly: "Execution Place, so awful for heads to face").

Razin bore himself with extraordinary courage and, after crossing himself in the direction of the Cathedral of Basil the Blessed, lay down on the block himself. He kept silent when the executioner cut off his right arm, and did not utter a sound when the execu-

read" being burned in Red Square. During the Plague Riot of 1771, soldiers fired case-shot into the mob rushing towards the Kremlin with cudgels and demanding an end to the plague quarantines. Seventy-two of the rebels were beaten with leather knouts, had their nostrils torn, and were then dispatched to work on galleys.

Even the bell in the Alarm Tower, which had summoned the mob, had its tongue torn out, as though it was a living person, and then was exiled to Siberia. In 1775 the leader of the peasant revolt, Pugachev, after being betrayed by his fellows, was kept in a cage for two months to be jeered at and mocked by

tioner cut off his left leg to the knee. But when his brother shouted out, "I know the Sovereign's word" (which meant that he wanted to stay alive by revealing information of importance to the tsar), Razin, regardless of the blood gushing from his arm and leg, cried out to his brother, "Silence, cur!" At that moment the executioner cut off his head, stuck it onto a pole which, for a long time, stood in Red Square, the terrible rebellious power of its staring eyes striking horror in one and all.

Catherine II's accession to the throne in 1763 was marked by "lampoons unfit to be

the people, and then executed and his head stuck onto a wheel spoke.

The forerunner of Russian democratic journalism, N.I. Novikov, whose apartment entrance looked straight over Red Square, was sentenced to 15 years of imprisonment for an article against serfdom. Another to live at one time in this blood-stained square was Alexander Radishchev who received the death sentence for his book *A Journey from St Petersburg to Moscow*, a sentence that was subsequently commuted to 10 years' exile in Siberia. Radishchev's final words before committing suicide were: "Posterity will avenge me." His prediction came true as far as Tsarism was concerned but then history reversed itself in such a way that independently minded liberals like himself became the target of vengeance.

Another independent-minded person, Piotr Chadayev, suffered the tragic fate of being declared mentally sick because of his dissident views. The Tsarist government had already developed – on a modest, amateurish scale – the tactics of using psychiatric hospitals to treat dissidents. These same tactics were to be so skilfully re-introduced in the 1960s by the KGB head, Yury Andropov, who, for some incomprehensible reason, has

tween times had fallen apart, the link between Tsarism and socialism has proved to be the only convergence being secretly encouraged.

The formula of the former Chief Procurator of the Holy Synod, Pobedonostsev (who once pronounced the anathema on Tolstoy) was "Autocracy, Orthodoxy, National Identity". This was replaced at the First Congress of People's Deputies by the words of an Afghan war veteran. When he said: "Motherland, Power, Communism", most of the hall leapt to their feet, applauding, as though hypnotised. Practically all the elements of the Tsarist formula have remained intact except that Communism has replaced reli-

recently earned the reputation of being something of a progressive.

The revolution of 1917 knocked the two-headed eagles of Tsarism off the Kremlin's towers and replaced them with red stars. But have the hopes of the Russian intelligentsia been fulfilled with the merging of Russia's course with the civilised evolution of other peoples, described by Chadayev's heir, Sakharov, as a "convergence"? Whereas Shakespeare bitterly exclaimed that the links between

Left, Andrei Sakharov at a press conference. **Above**, a line-up of Russian leaders.

gion. The destruction of churches in Stalin's time has been explained as Communism's attempts to take the place of religion, as well as Communism's intolerance of such beautiful rivals as the stone and wooden churches.

In the 1990s the mania for Sovietising the names of towns and streets, so characteristic of the hungry, young and ambitious state brought into being in 1917, was replaced by a mania for de-Sovietising these names. In one way and another, the value of moral principles allied to politics is rising while that of mere politics, divorced from moral principles, is falling.

DECISIVE DATES

The region around the Moskva, Volga and Oka rivers was inhabited from pre-historic times by people who lived by hunting and fishing. They settled in the dense forest and used the rivers as their link with the outside world.

Swedish Varangians or Vikings crossed the Baltic and advanced southwest along the rivers setting up fortified trading settlements along the banks. Under the leadership of the legendary Rurik who had Byzantium in his sights, the Varangians established strongholds in Novgorod and Kiev. They mixed with the indigenous Rus population and created the first two Russian principalities in the north and south around these centres.

compels the Russian princes to pay tribute to the Golden Hordes (Mongols).

Towards the end of the 13th century the city, under the domination of the Mongolian hordes, becomes the capital of the principality of Moscow and gains in importance over ther towns of the principality of Vladimir-Suzdal.

1328: Ivan Kalita or "Money Bags" is designated Grand Prince by the Khan. He moves his residence from Vladimir to Moscow, where he sets about constructing his kremlin – fortress – built from sturdy oak trees. The first stone buildings, churches and living accommodation are constructed inside the city walls. Around 30,000 people live in the city and a number of fortified monasteries are built at the entrances to the city. To the east of the Kremlin walls, the trading and artisan centre, later to become known as Kitay-Gorod, develops into a sizeable district.

1147: The Prince of Suzdal, Yury Dolgorukiy invites his ally Prince Sviatoslav Olgovich of Novgorod to Moscow. This event is the first documented mention of Moscow. Recent archaeological excavations have unearthed evidence that at the end of the 11th century a settlement existed where the River Noglinnaya meets the Moskva around the Borovitsky Hill in what is now the Kremlin.

1156: Yury Dolgorukiy builds a defensive palisade around the Kremlin hill, covering an area equal to about one-twentieth of the present-day Kremlin. It provides the inhabitants of the surrounding area, including craftsmen and merchants, with protection from attack.

1238: Batu Khan, grandson of Genghis Khan, conquers Moscow and for the next 250 years until 1480

1368: Dmitry Ivanovich (Donskoy) extends the Kremlin with a new stone wall, which withstands two sieges by the Mongols.

1380: Grand Prince Dmitry defeats the Mongols in the Battle of Kulikovo on the Don. To avenge their defeat, the Mongols lay siege to Moscow two years later and burn it to the ground. Nevertheless the city soon recovers and becomes a symbol of Russian unity.

c 1400: The influence of the Golden Horde's yoke begins to wane. The now wealthy monasteries and boyars (nobles) enjoy prosperity and the first Russian artists, such as Feofan Grek (Theophanes the Greek), Andrei Rublev and Daniil Chyorny establish their reputations.

1462–1505: Ivan III completes the unification of the lands around Moscow. He calls himself the "Grand

Prince of Moscow and All Russia" and marries Zoe Paleolog, the niece of Constantine XII, the last emperor of Byzantium, who had been defeated by the Muslim Ottomans in 1453. Russia now succeeds Byzantium as the "second Rome".

At a time when the Renaissance was gaining ground in Western Europe, Ivan summons architects and artists, mainly from Italy, but also from the historic Russian cities of Pskov, Vladimir and Novgorod, to give the city the splendour worthy of a "third Rome". The period sees the rebuilding of the Cathedral of the Assumption and the construction of the equally beautiful Annunciation and Archangel cathedrals. The Kremlin is rebuilt in stone, as ironworks, foundries and studios are constructed along western European lines, trade links are developed and diplomatic relations with the rest of Europe established. The population increases to 100,000 and the area of the city now

c 1600: Boris Godunov builds another wall, which encircles the entire Kremlin and Kitay-Gorod in a defensive horse-shoe shape. The new parts of the city are named Belgorod (White City), as its inhabitants were relieved (whitened) of paying certain taxes. (These walls remained standing until the 19th century, when they were finally demolished to make way for the Boulevard Ring.) An additional, fourth concentric wall is built. This is now occupied by the Garden (Sadovoye) Ring. The newly created district is named Zemlyanoy Gorod.

Beyond the ramparts to the south and east, a chain of strongly fortified monasteries is established, including the Novodevichy and Danilov convents. Improved security allows trade and craft manufacture to flourish, with different quarters being occupied by different trades. The market in Red Square between the Kremlin and Kitay-Gorod emerges as the main

covers 5.4 sq. km (2 sq. miles). Moscow is one of the biggest cities in the world.

1538: The earth mound surrounding Kitay-Gorod, the district to the northeast of the Kremlin and home to craftsmen and merchants, is replaced by a brick wall.

1547: Two fires engulf much of the town.

1547–84: Ivan IV, or Ivan the Terrible, is crowned Tsar of All Russia. He defeats the Tatars in Kazan and Astrakhan. He commissions more new buildings in Moscow.

1563: Moscow's first printed book appears.

Preceding pages: the Novodevichy Convent. **Left,** Andrei Rublev's *St George with Border Scenes*. **Above,** Rublev's 16th-century icon *St Nicholas of Zaraisk*, commemorating a popular saint.

centre of commercial activity.

1612: Minin and Pozharsky liberate Moscow from the Poles and Lithuanians who occupied the city in 1610. 15 years later, the city which had been destroyed in the battles, is fully restored. Under the Romanov dynasty, which dates from 1613, cloth, paper, brick and glass-making factories are introduced. The carillon in the Spasskaya (Saviour) Bell Tower rings out over a city of 200,000 inhabitants.

1633: Moscow's first water main is built.

1671: Stepan Razin, now something of a folk-hero, leads an uprising of peasants in the Volga and Don regions and is later executed in Moscow as a warning to the inhabitants.

1689–1725: Peter the Great carries out a number of domestic reforms, including laws to improve sanitation, construction and the highways and also a system of recruits for regular army service.

After 1703, many officials, noblemen and clerics move to St Petersburg and, even though the "head" of government leaves for St Petersburg in 1713, the "heart" of Russia remains in Moscow. Many new industries are established in the city.

1755: Mikhail Lomonosov founds the city's first university. It is at around this time that architects such as Giacomo Quarenghi and Vasily Stasov begin to leave their splendid mark on the city.

1773: The contrast between the luxurious residences of the aristocrats and the abject misery of the poor who are still living in wooden huts is just as apparent in Moscow as in the rest of Russia and it is what lies behind the peasants' uprising initiated by the Cossack Pugachev. He represents some hope of relief from unremitting misery, but the uprising is put down

Armoury and the Riding School are built.

1816: Secret societies, such as the aristocratic revolutionaries known as Decembrists, are established with the aim of abolishing serfdom.

1825: The Bolshoi Theatre is re-opened after a fire in 1805 destroyed the first building. The Decembrist Rising is crushed by Nicholas I.

1851: Railway between Moscow and St Petersburg is opened.

1861: The abolition of serfdom is followed by a huge influx of landless peasants to the cities. By the end of the 19th century, Moscow's population has risen to 1 million.

1866: The Moscow Conservatory is opened.

1890: Electric trams are introduced.

1905: Moscow workers rise up against tsarism and the bourgeoisie. The October strike and the armed uprising in December by Moscow workers force the

by troops, Pugachev is captured, brought to Moscow in chains and publicly executed.

1786: On the edge of the city, a relief canal is dug parallel to the River Moskva, creating an island south of the Kremlin.

1787: Work starts on a water main to provide a regular supply of drinking water.

1812: Napoleon invades Russia and after defeating Russian forces at the Battle of Borodino, he occupies Moscow. Fire destroys two-thirds of the houses. Disruption of supplies by the partisans, hunger and continuing harassment from the Russian army force Napoleon to withdraw.

1813: The Commission for the Construction of the City of Moscow is set up, and a programme of rebuilding is launched. The Kremlin Great Palace, the

tsar to accept a parliament with limited powers.

1914: Russia enters World War I against Germany, but it brings untold misery to Muscovites.

1917: On 28 February, a second uprising wins the support of most Muscovites who want to see an end to tsarist rule. On 25 October (or 7 November), the socialist revolution sees the Bolsheviks under Lenin take power in St Petersburg.

1918: Moscow becomes *de facto* capital of Soviet Russia.

1920: By the end of the civil war, the devastated city's population has fallen to one million.

1922: Foreign troops leave Russian soil. Lenin declares the Union of Soviet Socialist Republics and Moscow is named as its official capital.

1924: Lenin dies. Petrograd is renamed Leningrad.

1925: The first Soviet truck is built in Moscow.
1926: The population rises to 2 million and the first five-year modernisation plan is implemented.
1933: Trolleybuses are introduced.
1935: A General Plan for the Development of Moscow along the lines of the old road system is drawn up. The ring and radial roads are to be retained. The banks of the Moskva are to be reinforced with granite. New bridges and a canal linking the Moskva with the Volga are planned. An 10-km (6-mile) stretch of underground railway opens.
1939: Non-aggression pact with Germany signed.
1941: Adolf Hitler unilaterally breaks the pact and invades Russia without declaring war. In October and November, two German offensives against Moscow are brought to a halt. In December, a Russian counter attack forces the Germans to withdraw.
1945: On 9 May, the Russians celebrate victory and

1980: Moscow hosts the xxii Olympiad. A second international airport opens at Sheremetyevo.
1986: The 27th Communist Party Congress agrees to a period of democratisation characterised by the policies of *glasnost* (openness) and *perestroika* (restructuring). The youthful party leadership under Mikhail Gorbachev catches the mood of the Soviet people, who are keen to see change.
1991: A failed *coup d'état* by hardline communists leads to the eclipse of Gorbachev, the collapse of communism and the disintegration of the USSR. A fragile federation of the republics known as the Commonwealth of Independent States takes its place under the leadership of Boris Yeltsin.
1992: The old street names are restored as Moscow seeks a new identity.
1993: Yeltsin wins nationwide referendum. In July the hardliners roll back on reforms, leading the president

the end of the war.
1947: The underground network is extended, and a new programme of domestic housing and administrative buildings is started.
1956: The 20th Communist Party Congress exposes Stalin's personality cult, restores some civil rights and rehabilitates millions of innocent Soviet citizens.
1961: On 14 April, Moscow honours the first Russian cosmonaut Yuri Gagarin. The motorway around Moscow is completed and the Palace of Congresses is opened in the Kremlin.
1971: A new General Plan for the Development of Moscow comes into force.

<u>Left</u>, Isaac Brodsky's *Lenin at Smolny*, painted in 1932. <u>Above</u>, Yeltsin at a pro-democracy rally.

to dissolve the Russian parliament in September and call new elections for December. The hardliners under Khasbulatov and Rutskoy occupy the parliament building until 4 October, when Yeltsin sends in the tanks to force their surrender. After the December elections – the first freely held elections in Russia since 1917 – the nationalist Liberal Democrats emerge as a formidable force in the new parliament.
1994: The reformer Gregor Gaidar resigns as First Deputy Prime Minister. Queen Elizabeth II pays her first historic visit to Moscow and St Petersburg.
1995: Dolls, Moscow's first strip club, opens with American dancers. President Bill Clinton visits the city.
1996: A business travel survey shows Moscow hotels are the world's most expensive after Tokyo's. Boris Yeltsin wins a second term as president.

People who live in Moscow have every reason to identify their city with the origins of Russian statehood. The many centuries of Moscow's history are, as it were, inseparable from the troubles and hardships that became the lot of the Russian people. Anyone wishing to visit Moscow and its historical highlights can rest assured that the impression produced by the Eastern Slav citadel upon the inquisitive visitor is certain to be a memorable one, especially since it is gener-

parts of principalities commanded by Chernigov and Suzdal overlords.

The year 882 brought the unification of the two largest cities in Rus, Kiev and Novgorod, to form the ancient state of the Eastern Slavs, the Kievan Rus, with its capital in Kiev.

The Prince of Suzdal: The 12th and the 13th centuries saw more and more Russian cities straying from centralised control. The ancient state was falling apart, a process which

ally conceded that an insight into a nation's past promotes understanding of its present life and mentality. Many things will thus be revealed in the character, aspirations and behaviour of the Russian people; and the veil over the "enigmatic Russian soul" will, perhaps, be lifted.

Historians say that the first settlements in the territory of present-day Moscow date to roughly the 3rd millennium BC. At the end of the 1st millennium AD, the Moscow Region was settled by Slavonic tribes called the *Vyatichi* and *Krivichi*. They did not remain independent for long: their lands became

was accelerated by the Mongol invasion. Several independent principalities emerged, of which the largest were the Vladimir-Suzdal, the Galitzko-Volynskoye, and the Novgorod republic.

The first mention of Moscow appears in the chronicles of the year 1147, when the Prince of Suzdal, Yury Dolgorukiy ("The Long-Handed"), the son of Vladimir Monomakh, invited his ally, Prince Sviatoslav Olgovich of Novgorod, to Moscow.

The Kremlin of the 12th century, where the two chieftains met, was a small fort, with wooden walls and towers and it protected an area with a perimeter of about 1,200 metres (4,000 ft). It was surrounded by the huts of peasants and craftsmen, who hid behind its walls in times of danger.

Razed by the Mongols: Early in the 13th century Moscow became the capital of a small yet independent principality. Racked by frequent wars, the land passed from one ruler to another. The invasion of the Mongol hordes nipped the town's growth in the bud. Weakened by internecine strife, the Russian

princes were helpless before the invading armies. Batu Khan took Kazan and went on to Kolomna in 1237. After Kolomna fell, it was Moscow's turn. The town was razed, the population was reduced to one-third, and many people were taken away as slaves.

In 1263, Moscow got a new prince: Daniil, the son of Novgorod's Prince Alexander Nevsky (the famous conqueror of the

Preceding pages: view of 18th-century Moscow. **Left,** icon of St Boris and St Gleb, 1340; the oldest mention of Moscow, 1147. **Above,** Mongols take Moscow in 1238.

Swedes on the Neva in 1242). Daniil was the first of the Moscow dynasty. He founded Danilov Monastery and Bogoyavlensky Monastery. By the year 1300, Moscow controlled Kolomna, Pereslavl and all the lands in the Moskva river basin.

Moscow consolidated its power in the struggle against its rivals during the reign of Ivan Kalita, Daniil's only surviving son. A shrewd tactician and no-nonsense politician, Kalita removed his political opponents with the help of the Mongols and added their lands to his realm. In Kalita's time, Moscow becomes the centre of the Russian church. The Assumption Cathedral, built there in 1326, was the first Russian church of stone and became the cathedral of metropolitans. Then came the church of Archangel Michael, the crypt of Moscow princes. After the old Kremlin was burned to the ground in 1331, a new one was built of sturdy oak. In 1326, Metropolitan Piotr moved his residence from Vladimir to Moscow.

A Kremlin of stone: The next ruler of Moscow, Dmitry Donskoy (1359–89) scored a number of victories over the Mongols. The heaviest blow that befell the invaders was delivered at Kulikovo Field in 1380. Prince Dmitry then built the first stone Kremlin (of white stone), together with additional fortifications and suburbs.

In the reign of Grand Prince Ivan III (1462–1505), Moscow conquered Tver, Novgorod, Pskov, and Ryazan. Politically, this completed the unification of the Russian lands around Moscow. The centralised Russian state was born. In 1480, it freed itself of the Golden Horde's yoke forever.

By the end of the 15th century, Moscow consolidated its international status: Ivan III married Zoe Paleolog, the niece of the last emperor of Byzantium. Russia was now regarded as the heir to the Empire of Byzantium. The two-headed eagle – the emblem of Byzantium – became the seal of Russia. Simultaneously, Russia established diplomatic relations with Western Europe – with Germany, Rome, Hungary and Poland.

THE PRIVATE LIFE OF IVAN THE TERRIBLE

Ivan IV, "the Terrible", (1533–84) inherited the throne of grand princes at the age of three. He considered himself the Deputy of Augustus, the Emperor of Rome. Perhaps it is for this reason that the regalia representing supreme power in Russia and Rome were similar, the famous *barma* (ceremonial shoulder-covers) and the *Monomakh* head-dress. Many historians have tried, for several centuries now, to portray Ivan the Terrible as an outstanding statesman, a brilliant mind worthy of respect and sympathy, a predecessor of Peter the Great. (For this, they forgive him all his atrocities). Yet the majority view him as a bloodthirsty tyrant.

Nikolay Kostomarov, the prominent Russian historian, observed a striking similarity between Ivan the Terrible and Nero, despite the differences of circumstances and environment. Like Nero, Ivan was corrupted in his childhood years. Both Nero under the guidance of Seneca, and young Ivan under the guidance of Silvester the monk, accomplished many commendable things. Finally, when both got rid of their mentors, they proceeded to out-Herod Herod in depravity and sadism.

In their cruelty, both favoured the bizarre, the mannered, the theatrical. Nero started out by killing his mother; Ivan did not kill his mother – she died when he was still an infant – but made up for it by killing his son towards the end of his life. Nero set Rome on fire, and then tortured innocent Christians, trying to make them confess to arson in his "court of justice"; Ivan razed Novgorod to the ground and killed many more Russian Christians than Nero had Roman ones. He, too, accused his victims of heinous crimes which he, the stern yet just arbiter, set out to investigate.

Nero went to Greece to fool around with the arts and sciences, leaving Rome at the mercy of his underlings; Ivan fled to Alexandrovskaya Sloboda, where he played the monk while his *oprichniki* (elite guardsmen)

Left, Ivan IV, after mortally wounding his son while in a rage.

plundered Rus. Both were greedy and self-interested. They devastated the provinces and harboured a particular hatred: Nero for heathen temples, Ivan for Christian monasteries. Nero boasted that he was the only Roman emperor who could reach the limits of arbitrariness; Ivan carried on about the enormity of his authority as a tsar.

Nero was a coward and did not have it in him to kill himself when the moment had come; Ivan did not have to save himself from what he did to so many others, yet he exhibited cowardice and faint-heartedness several times in the course of his reign. Nero took pride in his talents as a poet, singer and artist; Ivan never missed an opportunity to air his gift as a rhetorician, theologian, historian – in a word, he loved to philosophise.

Ironically, the Tsar of Muscovy was luckier in his respect than the Emperor of Rome. As far as we know, Nero's literary and artistic efforts were quickly forgotten. The tyrant of Moscow, on the other hand, is commended to this day for his "wit, humour, erudition, logic" and recognised as "the foremost writer of his time".

Other comparisons: Come to think of it, Ivan the Terrible can be compared to other monarchs, not just Nero. A curious picture awaits when we compare the Russian tsar's private life with that of the notorious polygamist Henry VIII. Here, too, Ivan excels: Henry had only six wives, while Ivan... well, let's count!

Knowing no restraint since his childhood years, spoiled by the boyars (nobles) whom he so ruthlessly executed in his later life, Ivan remained a priest at the altar of dissipation till the end of his days. Historians know of only two weeks when he led a life that can be called decent; the two weeks after he first married.

In 1546 the 16-year-old tsar married the youthful Anastasia Zakharina, who charmed him with her beauty and soft femininity. He had lost his virginity at 13; contemporaries say that he had several hundred lovers in the course of those first three years. And now, a week after his marriage, the boyars could not recognise their tsar: gone were rough-and-tumble practical jokes with bears and jesters, the obscene songs, the whores who filled every room of the palace... Ivan was notably courteous, helpful towards the needy. He even released many prisoners from his dungeons. This change was believed to come from the influence of his young wife. Alas, things returned "to normal" in the third week of his honeymoon.

Be that as it may, his first marriage lasted for 13 years, in the course of which Anastasia, who lived the life of a recluse, bore six children. Disease and the never-

whim of his young savage. Accustomed to unrestrained and bloody pastimes in her own land, the tsarina set the precedent of taking part in a four-hour mass public execution in Red Square. Drunken orgies in the Kremlin, in which the royal couple participated, were the talk of Moscow. Several causes are given for Maria's early death; many suggest that she was poisoned by her husband.

When Novgorod was taken and plundered, Ivan had 1,500 gentle girls brought to the city. The tsar chose Marfa Saburova-Sobakina, and, even though she started to pine away after the engagement, Ivan proceeded with the wedding. Yet Marfa died of

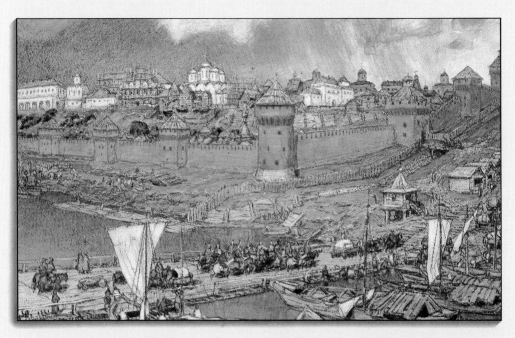

ending insults of her husband wore the tsarina out, and she died before the age of 30.

Orgies in the Kremlin: Ivan's second marriage was arranged in haste. Unsuccessful in Sweden and Poland, the Tsar's emissaries brought him back a bride from the Northern Caucasus. Kuchenei was a daughter of the Tsar of Kabarda. She accepted the Orthodox faith in Moscow, and was christened Maria Temriukovna; but, at first, she could not understand a word of Russian and could not make head or tail of what her husband said. This did not stop her from laying down the law in such a way that Ivan fulfilled every

unknown causes before the marriage was consummated. When her tomb was opened this century, Marfa lay pale, untouched by putrefaction, as if she had been buried yesterday, not 360 years ago.

The Orthodox Church allows only three marriages. Yet there was no law for Ivan. He continued his search for a bride, and chose the "common-born" Anna Kolovskaya. Being wild and passionate by nature (not unlike Maria Temriukovna), Anna tried to influence her husband by participating in all his orgies and supplying him with a steady stream of lovers. Even this did not enable her to retain the throne. Less than a year passed before Ivan divorced Anna and forced her to take the veil. She spent the following 54 years in a monastery dungeon.

Ivan's fifth marriage was a replica of his fourth. Seventeen-year-old Anna Vasilchikove spent several months in the Kremlin, after which she died under dubious circumstances. (Some say she died later, after having been forcefully deported to a monastery). In 1573 Ivan married Maria Dolgorukaya. This marriage, his sixth, was the most ill-fated of all: the bride, it turned out, had not been a virgin, and Ivan ordered her to be drowned.

His next marriage was something of a surprise: he chose a deacon's widow, Vasilisa Melentievna, a comparatively elderly woman with two children. The marriage conformed to the previous pattern in that it was short-lived, ending after less than two years because of his wife's untimely death. (There is, however, a contemporary testimony which says that Vasilisa was buried alive for "exceeding whorishness".)

Three years before Ivan's death, A. Nagoi,

Left, the Kremlin as it looked in 1584. **Above**, Ivan the Terrible.

the tsar's favourite boyar, gave his niece, the beautiful Maria Nagaya, to the ageing tsar. Even though the marriage was celebrated with great pomp, it ran contrary to all church rules, which made even many of the tsar's favourites consider it illegal. At the same time, Ivan made his son Fyodor marry Irina (the sister of future Tsar Boris Godunov) whom, shortly before, he had planned to marry. Ivan did not take his marriage seriously and willingly sacrificed the beautiful Maria for an opportunity to marry an English princess.

First, however, he tried his luck with Queen Elizabeth of England. When nothing came of this, Ivan sent his ambassadors to London, with the purpose of arranging his marriage with the queen's relative, Maria Hastings. Beside dynastic interests, this act had another goal: to lead Russia, plagued by a series of military failures, out of its total international isolation, and to serve as a prologue to a military union of Russia and England. He also hoped that, in the event of a palace coup (his lifetime pet fear) and forced exile to England, he would gain control of the Hastings principality, where he could live out his days with his sickly son. This plan, too, ended in failure: Queen Elizabeth rejected Ivan's proposals, citing "the bride's utterly shattered health."

The tsar's desire to see an English woman – any English woman – as his wife was so great that Ivan threatened, as Ambassador Bows wrote from Moscow to London, to take his treasury, go to England and marry one of the queen's relatives if she refused to find a suitable bride for him. To prove that he was not kidding, he exiled Maria Nagaya (who had just borne him a son) from the palace. The next time she would see him would be when his body lay in state.

On the eve of his death, on 17 March 1584, the tsar sent an envoy extraordinary to Sweden with an offer of marriage to a distant relative of the king, and an offer of unity to the king. The ambassador was informed the next day of the tsar's death, which had caught up with him suddenly over a chessboard. Even Ivan the Terrible's mighty health could not endure more than 54 years of such orgy-filled life.

ПЛАНЪ
императорскаго
столичнаго города
МОСКВЫ
сочиненной
подъ смотренiемъ
архитектора Ивана
Мичурина
въ 1739 году.

Москва ръка

After Ivan's death, the throne went to weak-willed Fyodor Ivanovich (1584–98). The actual power in the land belonged to Boris Godunov, the Tsar's brother-in-law. Godunov was by all accounts a talented politician. After Fyodor died without leaving an heir to the throne, Godunov was elected tsar (1598–1605). He relied on the church to keep the boyars (nobility) in line. When Russia got its Patriarch in 1598, the Russian Orthodox Church ceased to depend on Byzantium. The first Russian Patriarch, Job, was appointed by Godunov.

Impostors in power: Plots were hatching among the boyars (the nobility was outraged at Godunov's policies). In 1591, Tsar Fyodor's younger brother Dmitry, had died under suspicious circumstances. Some said Godunov had had him killed. These rumours were used by Sigizmund III, the King of Poland, who put "Tsarevich Dmitry" (it was announced that he had miraculously survived) at the head of an incursion into Russia. The first incursion was followed by a second, with another impostor in command. It was False Dmitry II who managed, with the support of several traitorous boyars, to take Moscow.

These events fuelled strong popular sentiment. Merchant Kuzma Minin and Prince Dmitry Pozharsky (there is a monument to them in Red Square) stood at the head of a popular army. The army, composed largely of peasants, defeated the Poles and liberated the capital.

Russia would come under attack from Poland and Sweden on several other occasions. In 1617, Vladislav, the son of the King of Poland, invaded Russia, while Gustav Adolf, the King of Sweden, besieged Pskov. After peace with these countries was restored, Russia was in terrible shape. Moscow had been ravaged beyond all recognition.

The coming of the Romanovs: The new Tsar

Preceding pages: Poles in Moscow during the Times of Trouble. Left, Moscow map from 1739. Above, the False Dmitry.

Mikhail Romanov (1613–45), the son of Metropolitan Filaret, was far from sure of himself and relied heavily on his closest aides, particularly on his uncle, Boyar Morozov. In 1674 Moscow was shaken by an uprising which became known as the "salt mutiny" (because of the draconian salt tax imposed by the government). As if that was not enough, Tsar Mikhail found himself with another uprising on his hands – the so-called "copper mutiny" was sparked by the ill-

judged devaluation of the new copper rouble which sent prices rocketing.

Peter I (the Great) became Tsar of Russia in 1672 and reigned until his death in 1725. He proved himself a great reformer and turned Russia into an international power. He also carried out innumerable domestic reforms. Peter introduced the system of recruits for regular army service and created the Russian fleet. In the last battle of the Northern War against Sweden, Russia won an outlet into the Baltic.

In 1702, Peter organised in Moscow the School of Navigation and the School of

Artillery. That same year, he ordered the construction of the Comedy Chamber in Red Square – Moscow's first public theatre. A special "beard" tax was levied on Raskolniks and other stubborn men who would not shave. The tax was extracted from them at the Spasskaya Gates where stuffed figures, suspended from the gates for all to see, were dressed in examples of the type of clothes that all were recommended to wear.

A time of reforms: Peter also introduced, as of 1 January 1700, the new calendar – *ad dominum*, and not "from the creation of the world" as before. Peter's challenge to ancient Russian tradition and lifestyle was all-encompassing, touching upon street processions and masquerades, with their *Papa Princes* and *Messrs. Cardinals* (merrymakers and jesters), costumes, and even upon styles of speech and writing.

remembrances of mutinies and executions, inveterate antiquity and the obstinate resistance of superstition and prejudice," as Alexander Pushkin wrote. "He left the Kremlin, which wasn't stifling, but which was too close for him, and departed for the distant shores of the Baltic Sea in search of leisure, space and freedom for his mighty and restless action... But Moscow, having lost its aristocratic glamour, blossomed in other ways: industry, with much support, livened and developed with extraordinary force. The merchants got rich and started to move into the palaces that the gentry vacated."

It was in Peter's day that the Kremlin

In 1712 Peter moved the capital from Moscow with its arrogant boyars to fledgling St Petersburg. Yet the tsar never stopped developing Moscow, and its significance as the country's economic and cultural centre did not falter. Moscow remained a stronghold of merchants and gentlefolk.

"Peter I had no love for Moscow, where, with every step he took, he ran into

became a fully-fledged administrative centre. The young monarch favoured the village of Preobrazhenskoye on the banks of the Yauza as his residence. He built a palace with a theatre, and a mock fortress (*Premburg*), used by the Preobrazhensky and Semionovsky regiments during their war games. In and around Moscow, aristocrats started building what can only be described as architectural masterpieces: Count Sheremetev's palaces (in Ostankino and Kuskovo), Prince Yusupov's Estate (Arkhangelskoye), Merchant Pashkov's Mansion (near the Lenin Library).

In 1755, the first Russian university opened in Moscow as the result of the efforts of Mikhail Lomonosov, the famous scientist. Students were taught in Russian. By that time, foreigners lived in the territory of Moscow in large numbers. They came either by the invitation of the Russian government, or on their own initiative.

Foreigners in the city: Foreigners were approached with caution and, frequently, with distrust. The clergy tried to drive a wedge between its flock and the aliens, who were forbidden to hire people of the Orthodox faith as domestics. The general desire was to keep Catholics out of Russia, because

majority. The German Settlement was mainly inhabited by West Europeans; the other three settlements were occupied by Poles, Lithuanians and Greeks.

Understandably, diplomats were treated differently. A foreign ambassador was an extraordinary phenomenon back in 15th-century Moscow. It is noteworthy how totally un-Russian were the stiff, mechanical ceremonies of greeting in the court of the Russian tsars. In Moscow, for example, a fine line was drawn between the three grades of ambassadorial rank: the highest honours went to the *great ambassador*; then came the *envoy* and then the *messenger*. Moscow re-

Catholic "propaganda" was considered especially dangerous. Moscow merchants and craftsmen regarded foreigners as unwanted competitors. Foreign citizens were not allowed to buy palaces in Moscow and, as a result, special settlements for foreign subjects appeared in the city. The largest was the German settlement on the tributary of the Moskva river, the Yauza. It is interesting to note that all Europeans were called "German" because the Germans constituted the

Left, Peter I. **Above**, Count Sheremetev (left) and Mikhail Lomonosov.

ceived embassies with proper splendour and solemnity.

It may well be that these ceremonial receptions took root in the Russian character, producing the respect generally felt today in Russia towards any foreigner. The schism of Orthodoxy, which occurred in the 17th century (certain clerical parties opposed Patriarch Nikon in connection with an up-dated comparison of Biblical texts in Russian with the Greek originals), was destined to become an anti-feudal flag for many generations.

During the short reigns of the great reformer's successors – his grandson, Peter II and his niece Anna – Moscow again became the capital and a scene of palace coups. It was here that the mighty Menshikov (Peter the Great's crony) was defeated and exiled.

It was here that the conspiracy of the Golitsyns and the Dolgorukiys, who wanted to force the Empress to share her power with the aristocracy, was uncovered and punished. And it was here that Biron, the Duke of Kurland, Anna's favourite, started out on his reign of tyranny, which was to last almost a decade. Empress Anna built a new wooden palace, the Annenhof, in the Kremlin, and a summer palace in Peter's former retreat on the Yauza.

cemeteries beyond the Kamer-Kollezhsky Val (the *de facto* border of Moscow at the end of the 18th century, 37 km (23 miles) from the centre: the Vagankovskoye, Danilovskoye and Kalitnikovskoye cemeteries. The territory of the Kremlin was cleared, and the old marketplace was burned to prevent the spread of disease.

In Catherine's time Moscow continued to grow. In 1775, the Empress divided the city into two parts; everything inside today's Boulevard Ring was to be considered Moscow proper, and everything beyond its limits was to be the suburbs. Numerous stone mansions went up; streets were paved and lit by

The "quiet" palace coup of 1762 heralded the dawning of the age of Catherine II, a native German princess. Her years on the throne (until 1776) are described by historians as "the era of enlightened absolutism". Keeping reforms down to a minimum, the Empress (it was Peter who had introduced the title of emperor in Russia) tried to reconcile serfdom, which continued to hold Russia in its vice-like grip, with budding bourgeois relations.

The plague: In 1771, the plague struck. Over 57,000 died. It was forbidden to bury the dead within the city limits. Hence the

oil lamps by night; a water-works was installed. Embankments appeared along the Kremlin section of the Moskva river, across which several bridges were built. It was even planned to rebuild the Kremlin. The population boomed, reaching 275,000 by 1811 – almost double the figure of 75 years earlier.

The golden age of the gentry: Free from the burdens of state service, the aristocrats mostly thought about their careers, built many residences in and out of town, amused themselves lavishly, drank and fornicated. The Empress herself, as her contemporaries attest, was a great lover of amusements.

Clubs became centres of the Moscow gentry. The English Club was founded in 1772, the Assembly of the Nobility in 1783, the Merchant Assembly in 1786, and the German Schuster in 1819. "Moscow", a contemporary wrote, "is a remarkable haven for people with nothing to do but blow their wealth away, play cards, and pay endless visits..."

Napoleon in Moscow: The year 1812 brought the French intervention. Inspired by his victories in Europe, Napoleon's "Great Army" invaded Russia and pressed towards Moscow. "Once I take Moscow, I'll smite Russia through the heart," he believed. On 6 August, the French took Smolensk. Moscow out fighting in order to preserve the army. People started to leave Moscow.

The fire of 1812: Meanwhile, Napoleon approached Moscow and waited for "the boyar deputation" to give him the keys to the city. But no one came – Moscow was empty. Soon after the French occupied it, the city perished in a terrible fire, the cause of which is still unclear to this day.

The fire lasted for six days. It was made all the stronger by a gale-force wind. "I myself remained in the Kremlin until the flames surrounded me," Napoleon remembered. "I then left for Emperor Alexander's country palace a mile or so from Moscow, and it may

plunged into panic, and many noble families hurriedly left the city. The Russian army retreated, avoiding a decisive battle. Then, on 26 August, battle took place near the village of Borodino. Napoleon's army, which was numerically stronger, received such a devastating blow that it never recovered. The military council of the Russian army meeting in the village of Fili near Moscow (Kutuzov's House there is now a museum) decided to surrender the city with-

Left, Napoleon and Alexander I meet in Tilsit in 1807. **Above**, the Battle of Moscow, 1812.

give you an idea of the force of the fire when I tell you that it was painful to put your palm against the walls or the windows which faced Moscow – to such an extent were they heated up. The sky and the clouds appeared to burn, it was a majestic and the most terrifying sight humanity had ever seen!"

Napoleon left Moscow, where no food remained. He ordered the Kremlin blown up. The vanguard of the Russian army stormed into the city, but managed to save only a few structures. The "Great Army" started running. Napoleon suffered defeat after defeat.

Moscow was rebuilt, of course. Reconstruction was accompanied by the rapid growth of trade and industry. The leading industries were textiles, metal processing, tobacco and perfumery.

It is noteworthy how the merchants and the fledgling Russian capitalists imposed a ban on foreign imports, yet continued to export their own goods. Moscow merchants and trade companies developed ties with the Ukraine, Transcaucasia, and the Volga Region. Freight turnover grew after the first railroad to St Petersburg was opened in 1851. As the Moscow market expanded, the city saw the rise of its first families of businessmen – the Prokhorovs, the Novikovs,

of truth arrived in December 1825, when the revolutionaries came bearing arms to depose the tsar – and were christened "Decembrists". Nicholas I was brutal to those who rebelled against him in St Petersburg's Senatskaya Square. Five officers were sentenced to death, and countless others condemned to forced-labour camps and exile in Siberia. The wives proudly accompanied their outcast husbands.

The second half of the 19th century saw the decay of serfdom. Hired labour, which was finding increasing use at factories and plants, proved to be several times more efficient than slave labour. And so, in February

the Guchkovs.

Alexander I (1801–25) continued to suppress peasant movements. A liberal in word, Alexander was cruel and reactionary in deed. The atmosphere of general discontent spawned the revolutionary movement in Russia, which was mainly directed against monarchy and serfdom. Intellectuals from among the aristocracy founded several secret societies, aiming to overthrow the tsar.

The secret societies: In 1817, one of the first such societies appeared in Moscow – "The Union of Prosperity", which united officers and civilians of noble ancestry. The moment

1861, Alexander II issued a manifesto which declared serfdom null and void. The country entered the era of capitalism.

Moscow's industry was growing at a rapid pace. Capital was concentrated in the hands of several giant companies. These were owned either by merchant dynasties, or by peasants who got rich (as, for example, Savva Morozov, the famous patron of the arts). There was progress in transportation as well. By the 1860s, Moscow was connected, by highways, to eight major cities. In 1899 the city got its first tram line and in 1902 its metro project.

The Moscow of that time is quite accurately described by Vissarion Belinsky, the famed literary critic: "There are many eating-places in Moscow, and they are always crawling with the kind of people who only drink tea there. These people drink up to fifteen samovars a day; they cannot live without tea, they drink it five times a day at home, and as many times on the town. Where but in Moscow can you work at the office, engage in trade, write novels, and publish journals for no other reason but your own amusement and recreation? Where, if not in Moscow, can you carry on so much about your labours, present and future, become

out several progressive reforms. It gave greater elective rights to big business and pushed through agrarian reform, which essentially eliminated communal land ownership. Now it was the peasant who owned his land. In recent years, progressive economists have been turning to the programme of the "reactionary minister" Stolypin in search of the rationale that could save the present beleaguered economy.

As Russia plunged into World War I, its economic crisis got worse. The provinces, particularly Central Asia, were swept by a national liberation movement. The army seemed ready to turn on the government.

famous as the world's most active person — and do absolutely nothing?"

An example for today: In 1906, Piotr Stolypin became head of the Russian government. Stolypin, who served as minister of internal affairs before his appointment, had all deputies from the social-democratic parties arrested and dissolved the Duma (parliament). Yet the Stolypin cabinet also carried

Left, Nicholas II, the last tsar, with wife and officers. **Above**, the Tsar's four daughters, Olga, Anastasia, Tatyana and Maria, who were murdered together with their parents.

Things got too hot to handle. The various political parties proposed different ways to deal with the crisis. Some demanded that the power of the tsar be limited and that the scope of democratic freedoms should be broadened; others questioned peaceful methods and called for a *coup d'état*.

The uprising finally started in St Petersburg, and was supported in Moscow. The workers and soldiers from the Moscow garrison took over all government offices. Power passed to the "Committee of Social Organizations" and the Soviet (Council) of Workers' and Soldiers' Deputies.

In April 1917, Vladimir Ilyich Lenin returned to Russia from Finland, where he had been hiding from the Provisional Government, and began preparing for the socialist revolution. On 25 October, another armed uprising racked Petrograd, and the Second All-Russia Congress of Soviets declared Russia a Soviet Republic. The first Soviet government – the Council of People's Commissars – was headed by Lenin.

The revolutionary forces took almost a week to gain victory in Moscow. It was only after reinforcements arrived from Petrograd, Vladimir and other towns that the revolutionaries shelled the Kremlin and won the day. The old power structures – the Senate, the ministries, the Synod – were abolished. Industry and banks were nationalised. The state was separated from the church. Because the country remained at war with Germany, the old army could not be immediately disbanded. In January 1918, the Lenin government issued a decree on the creation of the worker-peasant Red Army and Fleet.

Government returns to Moscow: After peace was made with Germany, the Germans occupied the Baltic region and Finland. Because they were in a position to threaten Petrograd, Lenin moved the government to Moscow, which, on 11 March 1918, once again became the nation's capital.

From 1918 until 1921, the republic fought for survival – not just at the fronts, but in the capital itself. In June 1918, the left-wing Socialist-Revolutionaries, hoping to provoke another war with Germany, had assassinated the German Ambassador, Count Mirbach. There was then an armed uprising. To fight the counter-revolution, the All-Russian Extraordinary Commission (forerunner of the KGB), was set up, headed by Lenin's comrade-in-arms, Felix Dzerzhinsky.

The killing of the Romanovs: Most leaders of the White Guard armies, which pressed towards Moscow and Petrograd, fought Soviet

Left, monument to the worker and the woman collective farmer. **Above**, V. I. Lenin.

power under the banners of monarchy – they wanted to restore Tsarism. Because of this, to do away with the apple of discord once and for all, the last of the Russian Emperors, Tsar Nicholas II, was executed with all his family in the summer of 1918 in Yekaterinburg in the Urals (now Sverdlovsk).

In December 1922, four republics – Russia, Transcaucasia, the Ukraine and Byelorussia – founded the Union of Soviet Socialist Republics. The original plan for the formation of the

new state, drawn up by Josef Stalin, envisaged autonomy status for the union republics; but in reality there would be infringements upon their rights. Lenin chose another form of unification – a voluntary alliance of independent republics with equal rights.

On 30 December 1922, the first congress of Soviets of the USSR adopted, on Lenin's principles, the Declaration and the Treaty on the Foundation of the USSR. In the summer of 1923, the first Soviet constitution was ratified. The constitution granted each republic the right to free secession from the union, and gave any socialist republic the right to join the union. Union authorities were placed in charge of foreign policy, economic planning, matters pertaining to borders, war and peace, the armed forces, and so on. Each union republic had a constitution of its own.

In the early 1920s, the cohort of Lenin's aides was increasingly dominated by Josef Stalin, who spearheaded the struggle against Trotskyists, right-wing opportunists and nationalists. He became General Secretary of the party's Central Committee and, once firmly established after Lenin's death in 1924, began to eliminate his political rivals.

Stalin unchallenged: Stalin gave *carte blanche* to the secret police, headed by the

political adventurer, Lavrentiy Beria. Beria's reign of terror resulted in the suffering of thousands. The years of Stalin's regime crippled the development of self-consciousness, freedom of thought and the sense of dignity of the Soviet people.

In July 1938, Japan invaded Soviet territory in the area of Lake Khasan. The invasion continued into Mongolian territory with the aim of capturing Mongolia, cutting the Trans-Siberian Railway and occupying the Soviet Far East. The attack was repelled, but the threat of aggression remained.

At about the same time, Stalin concluded a non-aggression pact with Hitler, which the foreign ministers of the two countries signed in August 1939. Today, it has been proved that there was an additional, secret protocol to the Molotov-Ribbentrop Pact, which would have divided continental Europe into Russian and German spheres of influence.

But the pact could not keep the Germans at bay for long and, on 22 June 1941, they invaded Soviet territory without declaring war. Stalin, caught after a recent "purge" in the army without the greater part of his commanding officer corps, refused to believe, despite numerous intelligence reports to the contrary, that Germany would attack so soon after signing the treaty.

The defence of Moscow: Moscow was the goal set before the group of German armies involved in the operations code-named "Centre". Powerful fortifications were erected on the approaches to Moscow to stop the Wehrmacht's drive. Blocking the most probable lines of attack were some 24,000 anti-tank "hedgehogs" and over 1,500 km (930 miles) of mined timber barricades.

The entire nation rose to protect Moscow. High Command HQ sent reinforcements from its strategic reserves – divisions from Siberia and units from Northwest and Southwest fronts. Army General Georgiy Zhukov, commander of the Western Front, was put in charge of Moscow's defence. The Germans were stopped on Moscow's threshold. For the first time in World War II, the Führer's armies suffered a major defeat. The Blitzkrieg was over, yet there were still four years before the triumphant spring of 1945.

The post-Stalin years: When Stalin died in 1953, Nikita Khrushchev was elected first secretary. He ushered in the *thaw*, as it is called today. Khrushchev's most commendable achievement was his elimination of the legacy left by Stalin. He presided over the improvement of living conditions and promoted international contacts. Being virtually uneducated, Khrushchev was incapable of devising a working strategy for political and economic development; he also committed numerous errors of a subjective nature during his term in office (1953–64).

Economic blunder: His failure to assess the political situation and errors in foreign policy finally bore bitter fruit: after a quiet palace coup, Leonid Brezhnev was installed in power in 1964. During his 18-year rule, Brezhnev proved strong-willed, yet managed to disappoint the aspirations of his patrons: "he changed his spots", concentrated enormous power in his own hands, and surrounded himself with a host of admirers. Economic blunders and the death throes of democracy were hidden behind self-congratulation, hypocrisy and triumphant rhetoric. The gap between word and deed, the arrogant irresponsibility and nepotism finally led to total corruption of the party apparatus and, ultimately, to chronic economic crisis in the USSR.

president. The planned centralised economy gave way to a regulated market. Enterprises were given new rights. A land act was passed providing for active land ownership by individual producers.

It was never Gorbachev's intention to abandon Communism, but the effect of his *perestroika* movement was to break up the entire Soviet empire. Faced with gigantic political, economic and social upheavals, the people were in no sense thankful to Mikhail Gorbachev – indeed, he was as reviled at home as he was lauded abroad – and it was left to his ailing successor, Boris Yeltsin, to cope with almost insuperable problems.

Perestroika at last: The turning point in political development within Soviet society came with Mikhail Gorbachev's *perestroika* campaign of April 1985. Essentially, it was a turning away from the concept of the Soviet people's victorious march towards Communism, which had been endorsed for decades. The power in the land was returned to elective bodies – the Soviets of People's Deputies. The country also got a powerful

Left, Stalin's preferred image of "Uncle Joe". **Above**, the monument to Felix Dzerzhinsky, founder of the KGB, is toppled in 1991.

Subtle change: What was the best aspect of the new Moscow, a satirical novelist was asked. "The Soviet system has collapsed," he said. And the worst thing? "The Soviet system *hasn't* collapsed." And in a sense it was true that, while everything had changed, nothing had, because many of the same politicians and officials were still active. What's more, capitalism quickly became equated with individualism bordering on anarchy. It was as if a fledgling motorist, having just passed a driving test, had climbed behind the wheel of a Lamborghini and decided to test it to its limits.

Just across the river from the Ukraine Hotel is Free Russia Square and an unremarkable building with a marble facade and gilded clocktower. Now known as Government House, it is better known by its former ironic soubriquet, "The White House". In the autumn of 1993 this was the scene of a dramatic confrontation between the Russian parliament and its president, Boris Yeltsin.

When Yeltsin ordered parliament to dissolve after he accused the deputies of obstructing his reform programmes, about 200 of them barricaded themselves into the White House. The stalemate quickly escalated into violence, in the course of which more than 150 Russian citizens lost their lives. The world's media reported the amazing scenes: snipers firing on unarmed demonstrators from the roofs of buildings on Novy Arbat, protestors setting fire to cars on Smolenskaya Ploshchad, the erecting of barricades outside the Council building on Tverskaya Ulitsa and parliament supporters storming the mayor's office before laying siege to the TV centre at Ostankino. Finally on 4 October the army, which had remained loyal to Yeltsin, bombarded, then stormed the White House and arrested the rebel deputies in what had become Russia's second attempted coup in the space of two years.

A comparison with the situation in 1991 yields a number of ironies. Then, it was Yeltsin who was under siege in the White House championing democracy while the Soviet President, Mikhail Gorbachev, was under house arrest at his holiday home in the Crimea. Yeltsin's staunchest supporter at that time, Vice-President Alexander Rutskoy, now found himself under arrest as the leader of the parliamentary opposition. While Yeltsin had, in 1991, claimed the moral high ground by condemning those who resorted to violence to achieve their ends, two years later the President himself had blood on his hands.

In the short term, Yeltsin's authority was

Left and right, pro-Yeltsin demonstrators in Revolution Square.

strengthened by the events of 1993 and by the end of the year he was able to introduce a new constitution which gave the president sweeping powers. But disillusionment with his economic reforms as well as with his handling of political events had negative long-term repercussions. The rise of the nationalists under the leadership of the maverick Vladimir Zhirinovsky was both an indication of deep-seated dissatisfaction with Russia's loss of world-power status and a reflection of the

regional and intra-national conflicts that were erupting right across the former Soviet Union, most alarmingly in the Caucasus.

Even more remarkable was the strong performance of Gennady Zyuganov's Communist Party in 1995's parliamentary elections, only five years after it had been outlawed and held responsible for decades of economic decline and political tyranny. Yeltsin's fortunes were by now at such a low ebb that many Russian commentators were surprised by his decision to stand for a second term in 1996.

His victory over Zyuganov after a second ballot was due to a number of factors. First, there was the series of timely endorsements from western leaders (accompanied by dark hints that a defeat for Yeltsin might lead to drastic reductions in Western aid). Then there was the equally timely dismissal of a number of his unpopular advisors, including Alexander Korzhakov, paving the way for the appointment of Yeltsin's formidable nationalist opponent, Alexander Lebed, as security chief. Finally, there was the collusion of the Russian media in securing his re-election, particularly telling after the first ballot.

But Yeltsin's triumph was soured by revelations about the 65-year-old's parlous state of health which, by late 1996, had deterio-

rated to such an extent that open-heart surgery was carried out. The prospect of a "lame duck" presidency and of acrimonious public clashes between would-be successors (Lebed and the prime minister, Viktor Chernomyrdin) was potentially damaging for Russia.

Yeltsin's continued low ratings in the opinion polls, despite his election victory, were due mainly to the perilous state of the Russian economy and the fearsome impact of privatisation – especially the freeing-off of price controls – on the average Russian citizen. Yet Yeltsin could justifiably point to Moscow as the success story of the post-Communist era.

The transformation of the city had come about precisely because of the government's free market policies, which encouraged foreign investment on an unprecedented scale, drawing Russian capital in its wake.

Moscow now has a thriving stock exchange and chamber of commerce and is the location of more than 65 international and as many national banks. The powerful oil and gas industries – the key to Russia's future – also have their headquarters here. Meanwhile, the face of Moscow has changed beyond recognition following a construction boom the like of which has not been seen since the 1930s.

Flying into Sheremetyevo, one can't help but notice the growth of new satellite towns and private housing estates on the northern fringes of the city. Old Moscow hands will be more struck by the proliferation of shopping malls close to the historic centre, even on Manezhnaya Ploshchad in the shadow of the Kremlin. Across the road two pre-Revolutionary hotels, the National and the Metropol, have been returned to their former glory, and Western advertising hoardings compete for the attention of passers-by on old Communist thoroughfares like Novy Arbat.

Thumb through the pages of any modern business directory and you'll find the addresses of dozens of business centres, financial consultancies, translation services, commercial radio and TV stations, investment companies and real estate agencies. Even on a small scale, the entrepreneurial spirit is alive and well in Moscow – symbolised by the corrugated metal kiosks you'll see outside metro stations selling everything from cut price vodka to shoelaces and make-up.

The chief beneficiaries of the boom are the "new rich", ironically in many instances the same people who ran things in "the bad old Communist days". Two prime examples are Viktor Chernomyrdin, and Oleg Boiko, the son of a Moscow factory director who became head of the National Credit Bank and sponsor of the Democratic Choice Party.

There is, however, an entirely new breed of entrepreneur, the "Children of the Wild Market", twenty-something self-made millionaires – hungry, fiercely competitive and ready to employ any means, not eschewing violence, to get their way (there are more millionaires in their twenties in Moscow than in any other city in the world). Typical of this generation is Sergey Mavrodi, perpetrator of the MMM share scam, who became a deputy in the State Duma despite being prosecuted for fraud and tax evasion.

This new, wealthy elite spend conspicuously, they have a penchant for fast cars (the current status symbol is a BMW), spend their evenings at night clubs or at the gaming tables, hob-nob with actresses and fashion designers, fill their houses with antiques, take their holidays in the Bahamas and send their children to private schools. If you feel you can run with these people, the place to head for is

lated as "broke". Their ranks include doctors, scientists and university lecturers, whose wages have fallen hopelessly behind the cost of living which continues to spiral out of control. For this reason, you're as likely to find a trained medic selling kebabs from a stand in Gorky Park as anyone else.

Factory workers and government employees – those who have managed to hold onto their jobs – are in a similar predicament, as many of them have not been paid at all for periods of up to six months. To add to their misery, thousands of these Muscovites still live in Kommunalki, communal apartments in which kitchen and bathroom are shared by

the "Up and Down Club" where membership will set you back $10,000 and an additional $570 each time you show up. If you're not quite in that league, try Maxims Restaurant in the National Hotel where you can easily run up a bill well in excess of $200 a head.

According to one survey, 13 per cent of Muscovites would like to see these conspicuous spenders behind bars. This isn't surprising when 40 per cent of the population classed themselves as *bezdenezhniki*, roughly trans-

several families and where living conditions are often unsanitary.

If these casualties of Gaidar's economic miracle might be deemed the "walking wounded", up to 800,000 Muscovites (around 8 percent of the total population) are the "terminal" cases. They include the flotsam and jetsam of society, the homeless, refugees, impoverished pensioners, drunks and down-and-outs and, saddest of all, abandoned children. Alarmingly, the gap between rich and poor is widening by the day.

The crime wave: There is an even greater enemy of social cohesion which threatens to

Left, vodka consumption is high. **Above**, the rich can afford to eat well at the Café Budapest.

undermine the very existence of the body politic. Organised crime has its roots in the "stagnation" and endemic corruption of the Brezhnev era and so far all attempts to tackle it have failed. In 1994 Yeltsin himself acknowledged as much – "organised crime has us by the throat," he declared while committing his government to a total crackdown. Huge resources were placed at the disposal of the law and order agencies, from the Federal Counter Intelligence Service to the special troops (OMON) and even, it was rumoured, the American FBI. The results were not impressive and the mob was quick to respond – early in 1995, Vladimir Listev, a fearless investiga-

Every business from the kiosk or hot dog stand upwards has to pay protection money but the mafia's favourite target is the wealthy Russian businessman who can be kidnapped and held to ransom. This has paved the way for private security to emerge as a boom industry, employing up to 800,000 Russians. The market leaders in this field organised an Arms Fair in the "Soviet Wings" Sports Palace on Leningradskoe Prospekt where the body guards (including women) competed in kick boxing, martial arts and target shooting.

Perhaps with one eye on the presidency he is said to covet, Moscow's tough mayor, Yury Luzhkov, announced yet another clamp-

tive journalist and TV presenter, was gunned down on a Moscow street.

Organised crime has a stake in every illegal dealing, from money laundering and racketeering to extortion, drug trafficking, bank robberies, prostitution, kidnapping and contract killings (currently running at 500 a year). There are up to 100 gangs operating in Moscow alone, each one controlling its own turf, from the specially lucrative Tverskaya Ulitsa to Izmaylovskiy Park. Russia's mafiosi are predominantly southerners – Georgians, Azerbaijanis, Daghestanis and Chechens, many living illegally in the capital.

down on organised crime in the capital. "Wipe out the gangsters... we have to annihilate them," he announced in a wave of publicity. Initially, though, he did little more than set up a new elite police unit, closed down a few casinos and began deporting homeless refugees "back to where they came from." In striving so hard to create the capitalistic opportunities of a New York City, Moscow had also acquired the concomitant endemic problems.

Above, a broker gets to grips with the market in the Commodities and Raw Materials Exchange.

CAPITALISM AND CHAOS

In the old days, no-one was even permitted to sell flowers at a street corner in Moscow. Suddenly, as the USSR mutated into the CIS, the pendulum swung to the other extreme and everybody could sell whatever they wanted, wherever they wanted. Stalls appeared, on the steps of the best hotels, with underpants displayed alongside cases of champagne.

It was typical of Moscow that the approach to change was immoderate. Maria, a widow, was horrified to find that the spring bulbs she planted on her husband's and mother's graves had been dug up and sold. Someone acquired a supply of fashionable shoes, and so potential customers balanced inelegantly on one leg on the pavement to try them on. Beggars held out a pleading hand, asking for a dollar or a mark. Who needed roubles any more?

Attitudes to visitors changed, too. Once, foreigners were still special, respected, treated as honoured guests for whom only the best would do. All this became *passé*. Foreigners now get cheated the same as anyone else by restaurant owners and taxi drivers.

The economic crisis hit the old-age pensioners hard. Some regulars at the soup kitchens preferred not to drink their glass of tea there, but to take their tea leaves home for later or for breakfast, along with the teaspoon of sugar that went into each glass.

Take Klava, for instance: her wages as a cleaner are so low that she spends all her weekends and holidays earning a little extra by going out to cook or wash windows. Yura, on the other hand, is so sick of the whole situation that he prefers to go fishing instead of getting on with his interior decoration.

Whether such changes are for the best is another matter. The successful establishment of a Rolls-Royce dealership in Moscow made a droll headline in the West, but it symbolised the widening gap between rich and poor in Russia, recalling that early owners of the world's most prestigious car included Tsar Nicholas II. (On the other hand, it may be worth noting that Rasputin's killers used a Rolls-Royce to dispose of his body in St Petersburg's River Neva.)

The sense of injustice in a city where hundreds of women have become street vendors selling soft drinks or children's clothes to visitors finds an outlet in the letters columns of *Pravda*. One reader recounted details of a new year party at which "the wine flowed in rivers and the food was all prepared in the manner of the court of Peter the Great. Peter the Great! And so here we are, being asked to endure hardships of our present life in the name of a bright future while the moneybags cannot think of enough ways to get rid of their cash."

Getting to grips with the tenets of capitalism is

Right, as prices soar, an old woman offers to sell her puppy and kitten to buy food.

difficult for some. One Muscovite visiting the West, for example, interpreted the well-stocked shops as a sign of economic failure "because people can't afford to buy the goods." Children, on the other hand, having fewer preconceptions to shed, often come to terms with the new realities with frightening speed. Soon after McDonald's opened on Tverskaya Ulitsa, gangs of 10- and 12-year-olds started to save well-off customers the trouble of queueing at the perpetually busy restaurant by collecting the orders and delivering them to their cars, adding a service charge that increased sharply as the winter temperatures plummeted. The local mafia, which controls this patch, took a percentage of the children's earnings (which were said to exceed Boris Yeltsin's).

Whether such children grow up to become tomorrow's entrepreneurs or tomorrow's gangsters is a

moot point. "The main problem," says a Moscow University sociologist, "is that the authorities have simply resigned themselves to the idea of children roaming the streets. The average policeman or apparatchik considers them to be criminals-in-waiting and treats them accordingly. Once they have cut their ties with their families, there is no way back from the gutter, despite the fact that, in their heart of hearts, many street children would like to go back to a more secure life." An even bigger problem, though, is that many people see the rising crime rate as an inevitable concomitant of capitalism. As Aslambek Aslakhanov, chairman of the Russian parliamentary commission on crime, put it: "A whole class of people have appeared who understand democracy as being able to do whatever they want." ∎

Patriots are few and far between in Moscow. There is much cantankerous complaining and masochistic backbiting when Muscovites talk about their native town and themselves. Everyone seems to have a grudge against something. As with all generalisations, there is the risk of oversimplification: still, it seems worth making the effort and try and sum up the life of the typical Muscovite of today.

Traditionally, the native of this city is something of an intellectual – an engineer, doctor or librarian with an average income. He lives, as we often say, "on his salary alone", and often borrows money from colleagues or friends. Haunted by the housing problem throughout his life, he lives, at best, in a cramped co-op built with his scanty savings, or in a room in a "communal apartment" in some shaded sidestreet of old Moscow. "Communal apartments" (in which several families share the kitchen and the bathroom) still give shelter to something close to a million people, most of whom are true-blue Muscovites.

The dream of owning a car: The average Muscovite clearly cannot afford a car. Spiralling inflation during the early 1990s has rendered the roubles of the average earner all but worthless. Many ordinary citizens dream of having a car, but the honeymoon of the lucky owner is usually short-lived: garages are practically non-existent.

This lends the owners of brand-new Ladas the sensitivity of a watchdog. They have been known to rise many times during the night to peer through the darkness – is someone out there fiddling with the doorlock of the compact?

Then there is the nightmare of spare parts. These are usually acquired through dubious characters at exorbitant prices (the state-run car industry is still in the Middle Ages). The

Preceding pages: Western values are ushered in by fast food. **Left**, *Walking Down Tomorrow's Street*, painting by Jury Pimenov, 1957. **Above**, for the young, symbols have become decoration.

list of woes has expanded recently and now includes fuel problems – the lines at petrol stations are, at times, several miles long. The only advantage Moscow has over a Western European city is that there are no parking difficulties. But problems are on the horizon: however slowly, the number of private cars is growing.

A broad outlook: Whatever the problem, people find ways to remedy the situation. The vintage Muscovite is a person with a

broad outlook and diverse interests. You won't catch him locked in an artificial little world, in the circle of everyday problems. He reads all the latest bestsellers, stands for hours to see avant-garde exhibitions and storms the ticket counters of international film festivals. In politics he is knowledgeable, radical and has become fervently anti-totalitarian.

Today, he is free to do what he likes: liberty has come to the land, democracy forges ahead, and he willingly takes part in meetings and demonstrations or even in the creation of new parties. This in a city where freedom of thought was traditionally punished with labour-camp sentences, exile to Siberia or, at best, banishment from the country – the past fate of the cream of Moscow's intelligentsia.

The typical Muscovite: Moscow is a town of celebrities. There are hundreds of people whose names are known at home and abroad: the ballerina Maya Plisetskaya and the poet Andrei Voznesensky, the cantatrice Yelena Obraztsova and the playwright Mikhail Roschin, the renowned economist and Presidential-Council member Shatalin and the historian Yury Afanasiev – a list that could be continued. There are also thousands of the

show how Muscovites lived in past centuries, how they dressed, how they looked."

The gap between Moscow and the provinces has dramatically widened over the last few decades, encompassing food products and consumer goods, creature comforts, entertainment and spiritual interests. In the minds of millions of people – particularly the young – the myth that "you have to leave your hole and go to Moscow to see some real life" predominates.

Migration from the provinces: In the meantime, Moscow is growing. Nine million live where there were 7 million 20 years ago. This has almost nothing to do with natural

less well-known, who are, in their own way, no less interesting. They are the people who form society's "fertile layer". Most of them are rather eccentric; then again, as the old adage has it, "queer fish make life brighter".

All his life, the Muscovite Yury Mazurov, a man in his sixties, has been collecting postcards dedicated to Moscow and he now has close to 13,000. It is by far the largest collection in town. You won't find some of Mazurov's prized cards even in the largest museum collections. "For me, postcards offer a glimpse of long-gone corners of the city, a remembrance of my early years. They

increment, because families are small (two children are a rarity, most often, there is a single child in the family, and sometimes even none at all). The main factor behind the population growth is the migration of out-of-town manpower. This, naturally, creates many problems, all of them formidable in their scope.

National sentiments: Like any megapolis, Moscow is a melting pot, a kaleidoscope of faces, languages, accents, religions. Russians form the traditional majority. There are many Ukrainians, Tatars, Armenians and Jews. Until recently, racial tensions were non-existent, despite a certain amount of officially approved discrimination. Jews, for example, found it difficult to attend colleges.

Today, when there is a broad awareness of mismanagement on the political level, social consciousness exhibits a paradoxical increase in nationalism, which sometimes acquires ugly forms. There are several reasons for this. Democratisation has fostered an awakening of national self-consciousness experienced even by Russia, the largest nation in the former Soviet Union, which, it transpires, has worse living conditions than most of the other republics. And as the living conditions have continued to deteriorate, as

nationalities who are made scapegoats. Hence the black-shirted toughs from the notorious Russophile pseudo-patriotic society *Pamyat* ("Memory"), who shout anti-Semitic slogans and paste leaflets full of malicious slander against Jews in the streets. They enjoy little support, yet they certainly manage to poison the atmosphere.

Foreigners in the capital: Foreigners occupy a special niche in cosmopolitan Moscow. Previously, foreign tourists, businessmen and scientists attracted by some international symposium or other, and members of endless delegations, stood out in the crowd – simply because they were differently dressed.

people have perceived that so many outside influences have eroded the country's independence and dented their pride, it is not altogether surprising that the ultra-nationalist rhetoric of Vladimir Zhirinovsky should have found so much support.

Unfortunately, the majority of Russians lead such a difficult life, and the crisis facing society is so formidable, that blind anger mounts and causes people to seek culprits. More often than not it is the people of other

Not so today: Muscovites, particularly the young generation, now wear the same kind of clothes as the foreigner (one cannot help wondering where all these chic items come from, considering the country's endless deficits). Yet foreigners are still easy to recognise by their untroubled, carefree expressions (the average Muscovite zooming through the rough-and-tumble of the street crowd usually has the resolute, tense expression of the Marathon runner).

Traditionally, foreigners have been treated with special deference, a quality which dates to olden times. When Peter the Great set out

Left, Mongolians living in Moscow. **Above**, the youth icons of the West were readily adopted.

to fashion a European nation out of medieval Russia, he borrowed a great deal from the Germans, who shared an entire quarter of Moscow with other foreigners. Yielding to the tsar's pressure, Moscow and St Petersburg aristocrats adopted the German way of life. Later, in the reign of Catherine the Great, Russian aristocrats started to emulate all things French.

Something of the sort is also going on today – with America as the standard this time. Indeed, the young generation is thoroughly Americanised – but only outwardly. Here and there, in the crowd, one sees T-shirts with logos of American universities (worn for the most part by people unable to make head or tail of these universities; they probably wouldn't know where to find Moscow University, either). American rock music blares from portable stereos and youngsters show off their American slang, distorted by hideous pronunciation. Many have a working knowledge of English, which is usually just good enough to direct the lost foreigner to the Cosmos Hotel. They may even accompany them there. People, worn out as they may be by everyday trivia, are still hospitable and amiable.

Hospitality: Moscow has always been known far and wide for its hospitality and willingness to welcome people from distant lands. Even in the days when it wasn't safe (to put it mildly) to associate with foreigners – until very recently, by the way – Muscovites ignored these restrictions. Today, when Russia is well on its way to being a more open society, no one is surprised when children from the US or France, who come to Moscow under educational exchange programmes, stay with the families of their Russian peers rather than in hotels. There are also adult tourists and businessmen who, driven by a catastrophic lack of hotel rooms, rent apartments or rooms from Muscovites.

Every foreigner who has spent at least one evening in the company of a Moscow family will speak of the hospitality and amiability of the hosts – with a twinge of surprise at their uncanny ability to stack the dinner table with foodstuffs and exquisite bottles, considering the emptiness of the stores. But that secret must never be revealed to the guest.

A run-down service industry: It is a pity that a visitor's favourable impression of Moscow can be jeopardised by the various blackguards he encounters in the service industry – extortionist cabbies, slow-coach bellhops, untidy and somewhat rough-mannered waiters. Yet don't rush to judge Muscovites by these people, because Muscovites suffer from them in the same way that visitors do.

During the long, long years of stagnation behind the iron curtain, official propaganda hammered home the idea that Muscovites lived in what was, for all practical purposes, the best city in the world – clean, green, safe and inexpensive. International observers

painted intimidating pictures of New York ghettos, Bangkok's poisonous fumes, Parisian prices, and lonely old men dying of hunger in unheated rooms somewhere in London. Moscow, by contrast, it was implied, was just a breath away from becoming a "model Communist city".

Problems of pollution: In the meantime, the former city fathers delivered speech after self-congratulatory speech – and destroyed the economy step by step, undermined the capital's infrastructure, and stole whatever they could lay their hands on (they were particularly partial to works of art from

Moscow museums). Today, when many of yesterday's secrets have been revealed, it is clear that Moscow is not doing well at all. Half the population lives under what experts in the field call "ecological discomfort". In plain language, this amounts to air pollution (car exhaust fumes and toxic industrial emissions), water pollution, excessive noise and vibration levels, and so forth. Members of the medical profession insist that at least every fifth Muscovite who falls ill is the victim of ecological hazards.

It also transpired that there are, in the capital, tens of thousands of old women and men who eke out an existence on a tiny

years. Municipal authorities and trade unions usually regard families with many children as privileged and, for such families, the waiting is cut to a minimum. But for newly-weds whose children are still unborn, they have no choice but to crowd the apartment of one of their parents.

Demand is, as with many other things, way ahead of supply. "Looking-to-rent" ads abound, while "To let" signs are practically unknown. This naturally drives prices up. There is a positive "but" to this situation. It may not be easy to get an apartment, true, but, once acquired, it is very inexpensive to maintain. Rent is still low, especially by

pension with no one to care for them. Although raised in 1992, this pension was never enough to cover anything but the most basic of commodities. Now that the prices of goods have skyrocketed, the situation for the old and infirm has become even more desperate.

Housing: We have already touched upon the housing problem. To get a better, larger and more comfortable apartment from the state, Muscovites have to wait for several

Left, an Orthodox monk and nun collect money in the street. **Above**, fresh produce for sale in the Central Market at Tsvetnoy Bulvar.

Western standards, although most people would love to pay more in order to live more decently.

What the municipal authorities are doing now is selling state-owned housing into private hands. Many will find this change a welcome one: "At last, my own apartment, to do with as I see fit!" It can then be sold or bequeathed in a will. Until recently, when an elderly mother died, her son, registered in his wife's apartment, could not keep his late mother's place.

Social services: There has been much talk in the press about the fact that free social services, which have traditionally been hailed as a triumph of socialism, are not necessarily a blessing – there is a darker side to the matter. Free housing – after years of waiting. Free – but hopelessly retarded – education. Free – yet impotent – medicine.

The doctors who work at outpatient clinics are overworked beyond the limits of human endurance. At times they don't even have the time to examine their patient properly. Hospital equipment is obsolete. There are shortages of the most elementary drugs. Naturally, the doctors do everything they can for the patient, but a surgeon's skills are not enough when it comes to post-operative nurs-

Daily chores: Let's try to follow the average Muscovite's day. Let it be a woman, because women have more responsibilities than men, and hence lead a more eventful life. On her way to work, she brings her youngest to the kindergarten, of which the child is sick and tired. But she thinks that the ingrate is lucky to have been admitted into a kindergarten of such favourable repute, with kind instructors and even a course in the basics of esthetics.

Meanwhile her oldest is on the way to school. Under his shirt, tied to a string around his neck, there is the key to the apartment – he will return home before his parents come back from work. Both parents are proud to

ing, and there is a hopeless shortage of hospital attendants since private nurses are unheard of.

But the people of Moscow do not give in to the gloom. They are patient, since they have never been pampered. Remembering the post-war years, when decent going-out clothes were a rarity and everyone lived in overflowing "communal apartments", they remark: "before, we were poor, but life was happy and people were more friendly to each other." Muscovites are also saved by their sense of humour and briskness of character, a devil-may-care good-naturedness.

see their son in a prestigious "special" school with "enhanced study of the English language". After he leaves – who knows? – he may be admitted to the still more prestigious Institute of International Relations. Then it's plain sailing to the diplomatic Olympus. And who cares if the future Talleyrand loves to fiddle with all kinds of machines rather than reading Shakespeare in the original? In Moscow, as elsewhere, parents decide for their children.

With the youngest safely in kindergarten, our mother storms a bus (filled to overflowing), which takes her to the metro. There she has her first good luck of the day – some well-mannered young man surrenders his seat, giving her the opportunity to read. For the 20 minutes or so it takes to reach her destination, she might read a literary journal with a previously banned novel by one of the recent past's non-persons.

The reading room metro: If you look closely, you'll see that the entire underground carriage resembles a reading room on wheels: many people don't find any other time to read – and so the underground system comes to the rescue. The underground, by the way, is clearly a feather in Moscow's cap: it is clean, pretty, and efficient – trains arrive

ancient adage about a penny saved is likely to produce a smile of condescension on the modern Muscovite's face.

Taxis aren't expensive, but are difficult to flag down. It's easier to pay a private owner more to take you to your destination.

Arriving at the office, our heroine greets her colleagues, takes out her cosmetic bag and starts to work on her face. There is no time for that at home, but at work you can always spare the required few minutes. The other women in the room are doing the same thing – an occurrence to which their male colleagues have long since become accustomed. In any case, the men don't have time

every minute in peak hours. It is also cheap compared to metros in the West, and you can go as far as you like with any number of transfers – stay there all day if you want to.

Buses, trolleys and trams are also cheap. Surface transport, however, is much less reliable than the subway. In winter passengers shake from the cold waiting for delayed buses at the stops. The public transport fares are increasing almost by the week, but that's hardly a problem – a rouble isn't money. The

Left, in a Moscow high-rise apartment. **Above**, the Moscow Metro.

for such trifles – they are on their way to the smoking room.

Shopping: During the lunch hour, the women hastily grab a bite and start to "distribute assignments". One is delegated to the nearest dairy store, another to the bakery, a third to a vegetable store. Each buys for three. This saves time, because the employees of neighbouring institutions aren't sitting idle – they are already standing in line.

After work, the first thing to do is to fetch her child from kindergarten. Once home, she thoroughly questions her elder son about his progress at school. Her husband has not been assigned any household chores because, after work, he and a friend stopped off for a drink on the way home. He is therefore unnaturally gallant. Trying not to breathe in the direction of his spouse, he sets the table with elegant movements. Over supper, between answering the children's interminable questions, the adults speak about almost everything, from troubles at the office to global problems, giving the highest echelons of power the dressing-down they seem to deserve. Before, parents tried to avoid discussing these things in front of children — God knows what they might tell at school, and then trouble would follow. Today, no

scandalising and cleverer than what Moscow has to offer. As for the women, they rarely watch any programme to the end — there is cooking and laundry to be done. The men have it incomparably easier, even if they condescend to do the dishes.

There are, of course, elements of diversity: entertaining at home, going out, movies, theatres, and so on. But this gives rise to new problems. It isn't easy to get a ticket to a good theatre. A large proportion of the audience of the world-famous Bolshoi is made up of hard-currency paying foreigners.

Political life: The years of *perestroika* and **glasnost** and the subsequent political and

one is afraid of anything any longer – a sure sign of society's recuperation.

Television: After supper, *Novosti* (a national news programme) is a must. The programme has become very interesting in the past few years, because it covers life in Russia without colouring it pink and life in the West without painting it black. After watching the news programme, some choose a movie, others a sports programme, and still others a televised discussion of the day's problems. It is interesting how Muscovites prefer TV programmes from St Petersburg: more often than not, they are sharper, more

economic reforms have turned life in Moscow around, largely ridding it of its habitual patina of bleak indifference. Life has become politicised. Formerly off-limits to TV viewers, parliament sessions are now broadcast live. The man in the street is tired of being a cog in the soulless clockwork that is managed from the top. Everyone openly states his mind on each and every issue, and argues in favour of his platform.

During one of the last May Day parades in Red Square a group of demonstrators addressed the country's leaders from on top of the mausoleum and demanded their resignation. It was not a very tactful thing to do but it is significant that no one touched the rebellious loudmouths.

According to some estimates there are over 40 political parties and movements in Moscow alone. Previously, the word "party" could only mean the Communists. Today, it applies to the social-democrats, the greens, the so-called liberal democrats, the anarcho-syndicalists, all of whom have their own platforms, programmes, ideologues, organisations and newspapers.

At one end of the city, there is a small gathering in support of Yeltsin and his market reforms, against the return of conserva-

and disputes are still a regular occurrence. People form tight circles around those who engage in debate. When either runs out of wind he immediately gets help from the lookers-on. A grey-haired Stalinist faces a cocky student ("We fought with Stalin's name on our lips!" – "And he sent you to the labour-camps!"). An Azerbaijani and an Armenian argue over Nagorny Karabakh. A co-op worker proves to his state-employed opposite that he works more and harder than him and that there is nothing shameful about his comparatively larger income. "They are selling Russia out to the West!" comes the tortured scream from somewhere else.

tive hardliners into the ranks of government. Meanwhile, others have assembled at the other end. They are much more aggressive and passionate. "Look what the market economy has done to us," shouts a man. "Made fortunes for the shady wheeler-dealers at the expense of the working class. Who needs this return to capitalism?"

In the centre of Moscow, in Pushkin Square, (where *Moscow News*, *perestroika*'s most popular newspaper, has its offices) meetings

Left, a choice of indoor and outdoor shopping. **Above**, an Earth Day concert in Gorky Park.

Nevertheless, there has been a marked decline in the number of people arguing and demonstrating on the streets. Many Muscovites are simply disorientated by the endless rhetoric of the politicians, in whom there is now a general lack of trust. The promises haven't been delivered and they now just want to get on with their lives as best they can.

Revival of old values: Russians cannot work like the British or the other developed nations. They are more accustomed to taking everything apart than to building with patience and care. But, as they say, "New is well-forgotten old." These "new old" things in Moscow include a revival of religion (even the word "renaissance" would not be too lofty here) that official ideology had helped everyone "forget".

Churches are hopelessly crowded on religious holidays. Many young people in the churches look quite up-to-date and incongruous amid the ever-present old women. There is little, if any, reason to believe that it is a foppish desire to stand out that brings them here. Having lost the ideals that were hammered into their heads, young people are groping for a truth, for a way towards self-improvement.

Moscow is a Russian city by its origins,

and it is not surprising that the overwhelming majority of its churches belong to the Russian Orthodox Church. There is also a Catholic cathedral, a synagogue, a mosque and a Baptist prayer house. Few churches, however, are functional (they were all open before the revolution), yet with each passing year, more and more long-neglected churches which previously sheltered obscure offices or served as warehouses are being reinstated. St Basil's on Red Square has been given back to the church, as has the Assumption Cathedral in the Kremlin. And the Kazan Cathedral, missing for so long from the Red

Square landscape, has now been rebuilt. There are even plans to reconstruct that most famous victim of Stalinist zeal, the Cathedral of Christ the Saviour.

The church is a particularly active philanthropic institution. It does not limit its activities to generous donations to charity. Priests and parishioners visit hospitals and houses for the aged, they bring comfort, consolation and help to those who are unable to help themselves. Charity (aid to orphans, invalids, the poor) is also quite popular among atheists. It is another sign of "the new old", a revival of Moscow's golden tradition. In the days of yore, aristocratic ladies never disdained to lend a helping hand to homeless tramps. For us it would be a sin to neglect the less fortunate, if we really are to attain "humane socialism".

Since we mentioned the aristocracy, we should also say that it has been decided to revive Moscow's Assembly of the Nobility. The first meeting was attended by those descendants of noble families who had, by some miracle or other, survived the era of class struggle. The function of this "new old" association is not clear as yet, but our aristocrats now have a leader – Andrei Golitsyn ("Prince" Golitsyn), a well-known graphic artist who can trace his genealogy back to the 14th century.

New sights everywhere: Life really has become much more interesting. Before, could there have been, openly on sale, literature that was secretly photocopied and, at great risk, smuggled into the country? Could one have bought, with no trouble at all, tickets to a Western movie which our vigilant critics (who were allowed to attend the Cannes Festival) dismissed as talented yet hopelessly escapist and appealing only to man's base nature?

Even a simple walk can be fun. Take that vintage Moscow street, the Arbat. Picture galleries right on the pavement, concerts by street musicians, poetry, often bad, yet amusing and invariably imbued with great pathos by our homegrown authors, Krishna freaks, punks, and other picturesque groups of young people united by something you never knew existed. Fortunately, there are not many junkies among them.

It is easy to see signs of material stratification in our society – those very contrasts that our press used to criticise so much in the West. Above and over the surface of the Sadovoye Ring a suspicious-looking *nouveau riche* flies in his Mercedes; below, in the tunnel pedestrian crossing, an old woman stands, trembling hand outstretched in the beggar's pose. Beggars, by the way, have grown more numerous lately – they seem to feel that the cops won't hassle them any more and that the passers-by have become kinder. There are also a growing number of street urchins in Moscow. This is no new phenomenon: children have worked on the

Moscow girls who dream of leading exciting easy lives regard these ladies of the night with malicious envy: an income such as theirs will forever remain a dream for a girl who keeps her virtue. The only way to make money and remain morally pure seems to be to win, on a regular basis, beauty pageants and modelling contests, which have become very popular.

Growing crime has caught everyone unawares. For some, freedom and democracy have tended to be interpreted as a licence to commit crime. Those papers that publish police chronicles report as many as one or two murders every day – and rising. If it is

streets at various stages in the country's history. But new tricks are learned all the time and the young entrepreneurs have become so ingenious that they can easily earn more than a doctor or professor.

The reverse side of the new times: Hotels are besieged by prostitutes (hard currency only). Our home-grown adventurers look at them with a twinge of sadness – they know that without dollars in their pocket, it is futile to hope for such exquisite female company.

<u>Left</u>, Moscow's flamboyant nightlife. <u>Above</u>, the Moscow marathon is an international event.

any consolation, most are committed in the traditional Russian manner – over a bottle. There is organised crime, too. The gangsters have smart cars, two-way radios and firearms, which are sometimes used in shootouts between rival mobs. It is then that the chance passer-by gets to see Chicago gangsters in action – and not on the screen.

Admittedly, the ordinary Muscovite has nothing to fear from the Mafia. The mobsters target the wealthy: co-op officials, collectors of paintings and antiques, certain joint-venture employees, and assorted dealers of the "shadow economy". Nevertheless, anyone's chances of being mugged or beaten up are improving. Recently, private detective agencies have come to the aid of those who want personal safety for a moderate fee. If the militia can't cope with criminals, then, say the cynics, the criminals themselves are all too eager to give you a hand.

The black market: Progressives are embarrassingly ready to admit that the country's life is poisoned – there is no other word for it, they say – by increasing numbers of speculators who make hefty profits thanks to shortages of the most basic goods. Habitual smokers gladly pay six times the official price for a packet of cigarettes.

from supporters of the right-wing Vladimir Zhirinovsky, few Muscovites would advocate a return to "the good old days". Many put their faith in General Alexander Lebed, who promised to clean up the rackets, and were critical when Yeltsin sacked him from his post of national security chief in 1996.

There is a variety of things good and bad in Moscow. Visitors from abroad usually experience the brighter side of life; ordinary Muscovites often draw the short straw. But the winds of change are getting stronger. The power in the city has increasingly moved to people of a new type – the progressive, independent thinkers and intellectuals.

The profiteers sell whatever there is to sell – from vodka to furniture suites which cost many thousands of roubles. The country's only hope, it seems, lies with the market economy, which should in the end take care of the shortages. But at what price? This is evidently a question that increasing numbers of Muscovites have been asking as they have seen their living standards plummet and the value of their wages dwindle by the week. In many quarters there is now an atmosphere suggesting that things have happened too abruptly and that what is now needed are rigid controls on the economy. But, apart

In the early 1990s, Moscow's high-profile mayor, the prominent economist Gavriil Popov, set out, with the aid of their political allies and the most active sector of Moscow's population, to turn the town into a real "model city". But the problems soon seemed overwhelming and his successor, Yuriy Luzhkov, took a much tougher law-and-order line. The legendary long-suffering nature of Muscovites, it seemed, would still be needed for the foreseeable future.

Above, many of the expensive tourist hotels offer shows in their dining rooms.

THE JOY OF BATH-HOUSES

In a small passageway at Okhotny Ryad, in a section of the former Marx Avenue, you will find Moscow's Central Bath-House, once known as the *Khludov Public Baths*, which are still the most popular in the capital, along with the Sandunov Public Baths, not far away, in First Neglinny Lane.

The Russians have always believed that taking a bath cures all ills. There is an old saying which runs as follows: the bath makes you sweat to get tough and to get slim.

The old tradition of taking a bath is an involved, multi-stage ritual. The bath-house itself consists, as a rule, of several premises, with the sweat-room coming first. It is not the cleanliness or exquisite workmanship of the interior, but the design – better or worse – of the sweat-room that generally prompts Russians to choose one particular bath-house in preference to any other.

The temperature in it is not high; it is lower than that of Finnish saunas, and usually in the order of 60°–80° C (108°–144° F). But the humidity of the vapour makes you think it approaches 200°F. You enter the sweat-room, as a rule, with your head covered and long mittens on, equipped with a well-made and well-dried switch of oak or birch twigs. Before you enter the sweat-room, you must soak your switch in hot water to prevent the leaves from falling off when you strike with it.

The most respected man in the sweat-room is the one who knows how to handle the furnace: when to raise steam and how much, and what to feed the furnace with. Every sweat-bather has a formula of his own which he sticks to. Some like mint or eucalyptus added to the steam while others pour beer on the furnace. The heated-up and blazing bodies are properly whipped with switches.

You may shudder at the sight of a pair of husky fellows lashing their defenceless victim, seemingly more dead than alive. The latter, however, instead of pleading for mercy, smiles gratefully. Having got themselves to the point of half-fainting, with their legs about to give way, they then rush out to dip into icy water or, in winter, to dig into a snowdrift.

After a few spells in the sweat-room, you

Right, cleansing the body and the soul.

start the actual process of washing in a special wash-house where stone deck-benches and shower-baths are at your disposal. With a few simple gadgets, like a tub, wash-cloth and soap, you wash off what is still sticking to your body and soul.

Russian baths are big, as a rule, roomy enough for some 50 persons to wash at a time. Everybody willingly rubs anybody else's back and so hard, in fact, that the skin seems to be about to peel off. After washing most people prefer to relax in a lounge, a big hall with rows of benches and separate small compartments. You seldom go to a bath-house alone. It is common for a group of friends to do so in order to discuss all press-

ing and world problems in good humour and wash themselves at the same time.

It is also customary for bathers to drink all kinds of beverages to regain the moisture lost while sweating. Some prefer beer, others drink tea and still others treat themselves to various herbal potions. You may also enjoy a massage, a haircut and a pedicure.

In Russia you learn the tradition of going to public baths from childhood: fathers take their sons along and mothers take their daughters to initiate them into all the mysteries of the washing process. In short, you can hardly claim to be a Russian if you don't go to a bath-house. ∎

Александръ Пушкинъ

THE MANY FACES OF MOSCOW CULTURE

You will have a hard time finding a Muscovite who doesn't consider him or herself to be at least a trifle more educated or the tiniest bit more cultured than "the rest of 'em" – that is, the unfortunate millions sentenced by fate to live outside the capital. Even janitors and cabbies look down, with heartfelt pride, upon their colleagues from the provinces. Not very modest, perhaps, yet you will find many capitals similarly afflicted. Some praise it as "enhanced awareness of personal predestination". Others dismiss it as "common bigotry". Both are probably wrong.

Since time immemorial, Moscow has been a Mecca for the enlightened and the industrious. The monasteries boasted impressive libraries and the first book was printed here in the mid-16th century.

During the Middle Ages the city became a haven for the fine arts. Rubbing elbows with Greek painters helped Russian artists to establish the foundation of what was later to become the Moscow school. The earliest records of musical life date to the 15th and 16th centuries (the Tsar's Choristers); by Peter the Great's time, no festival or celebration could be held without music. Roughly in the same period, the first travelling theatre troupes of clowns and circus performers appeared in the land of the Russians. Russia, then, was far from "lost in ignorance and the darkness of cultural self-isolation".

Poets and writers: Moscow's books and magazines taught Russia "to speak and write in Russian," wrote poet Piotr Vyazemsky, a friend of Alexander Pushkin. In fact, it is difficult to think of even a lesser writer or poet who was not connected with Moscow in one way or another. Moscow was home for Pushkin, Mikhail Lermontov and Fyodor Dostoyevsky. The Taganrog-born Anton Chekhov experienced such an enormous creative upsurge here that he proclaimed himself "a Muscovite for eternity". Mikhail Lomon-

osov, the peasant son from the distant White Sea, came to Moscow and, a quarter of a century later, founded the university that still bears his name. "The oldest and the best university in Russia" gave literature many first-rate talents: Nikolai Karamzin, Vasily Zhukovsky, Alexander Sumarokov.

As Alexander Herzen pointed out, when Peter the Great demoted the city from its rank of Tsar's Capital, it nevertheless remained the capital of the Russian people.

Even though the cream of high society and the royal court resided in St Petersburg, Moscow managed to cling on to its cultural traditions. Away from rigid censorship and the stern eye of secret-police watchdogs, it became a breeding-ground for progressive thought and a haven for free-thinkers.

Pushkin, the great love of the literate: On 8 September 1826 Alexander Pushkin was conveyed from exile in Mikhailovskoye to the Kremlin for an audience with Tsar Nicholas I. The poet was allowed to live in St Petersburg and in Moscow – under constant secret surveillance. The secret police did not

Preceding pages: __tradition translates into the electronic age.__ __Left__, __Alexander Pushkin as a child.__ __Above__, __Kandinsky's *Improvisation*, 1911.__

let the poet out of their sight. Pushkin's arrival in Moscow became a major cultural event celebrated by all. He brought *Boris Godunov*, written in exile, to Moscow. The first public reading of the play was on 12 September 1826. He was given a stern dressing-down from Benkendorf, the chief of the secret police, for reading the play without first submitting it to the censors.

Pushkin led a cheerful, if dissipated, life in Moscow. He was a frequent guest in the salon of "the queen of Muses and beauty", Zinaida Volkhonskaya. Here, he met Adam Mitskevich the Polish poet; here he first laid eyes on his "madonna" – Natalia Goncha-

Mikhail Lermontov returned to Moscow from exile (imposed by Nicholas I for his poem *On Pushkin's Death*) in 1837. "Moscow is my native land, and will forever remain so for me: I was born there, I suffered there, and was too happy there!" he wrote.

On 25 February 1852, Moscow saw an extraordinary funeral procession as hundreds followed the hearse from the University to the Novodevichy Cemetery. It was in this way that Moscow paid its last respects to Nikolai Gogol. His popularity proved that he was loved and respected.

UNESCO pronounced 1981 Fyodor Dostoyevsky Year. The century of his memory and

rova. He described his later life in Moscow as "married and merry". Memorials to Pushkin in Moscow consist of more than just the old houses and estates where the poet lived or which he visited. Pushkin's name was given to a street, a square, and an embankment, a museum and a theatre, a metro station and a library. He is still with us: he stands in bronze in the middle of Pushkin Square, high up on the pedestal, in a relaxed pose with a noble bearing, his face thoughtful and a little sad while, down below, crowds boil over at meetings as if excited by the poet's freedom-loving verses.

his 160th anniversary was celebrated throughout the world. Moscow is his native city. Here, in the courtyard of No. 12 Dostoyevsky Street, he spent his childhood. Dostoyevsky travelled a lot, yet always returned to Moscow with joy.

Another literary Atlas, who was born in Yasnaya Polyana, also found acclaim in Moscow. "Any Russian looks at Moscow and feels that she is his mother," Leo Tolstoy wrote in *War and Peace*. Tolstoy's attitude to Moscow was contradictory, changing several times in his lifetime. He loved the city for the way everything Russian was concentrated and because it reflected so many centuries of history.

Anton Chekhov started his literary career in Moscow. In 1884 he graduated from the university's Department of Medicine, and found himself increasingly attracted to literature. Soon afterwards, the sign Doctor A. Chekhov disappeared from his front door, even though he joked that medicine was his "lawful wedded wife" and literature only his "mistress". In the last years of his life, Chekhov rarely visited Moscow, but he retained his ties with the Khudozhestvenny Theatre which staged his plays. *The Seagull* – that symbol of a Chekhov play – became

nature and brilliant talents. During the 19th century the city became a kind of a poet's workshop for all of these writers, a place where they polished their personal techniques.

The early 1960s saw the rebirth of an old tradition – "poetry nights". As fresh voices rang out, new problems were brought before the public eye. Yevgeny Yevtushenko, Andrei Voznesensky, Robert Rozhdestvensky, Bella Akhmadulina, representatives of the new generation, spoke about World War II, the future of the nation, and the role of the individual in the transformation of society. Yet the spiritual handcuffs and hy-

the theatre's emblem.

Vladimir Gilyarovsky was a contemporary of Chekhov and his bosom friend. A connoisseur of the epoch, he somehow did not fit into the mould of his contemporaries. Alexander Kuprin wrote that he could more easily imagine Moscow without the Tsar Bell or the Tsar Cannon than without Gilyarovsky. He was picturesque in everything – background, appearance, manner of conversing and, despite his childlike air, he had a multi-faceted

Left, Mikhail Lermontov and Fyodor Dostoyevsky. **Above**, Anton Chekhov and Leo Tolstoy.

pocrisy of the epoch, now habitually referred to as the "stagnation", precluded the solution of those acute social and political problems which they raised in their poems.

Glasnost at last: Today, theatre posters once again carry the names of Gorky, Chekhov, Bulgakov, Mozhayev and Voinovich. People line up in front of bookstores and theatres and bring flowers to Pushkin's monument. There is now little doubt: a kind of a cultural turnabout is at hand. As *perestroika* brought dogmatic discipline crashing down, as the long-awaited Press Bill finally brought freedom of speech to the land, the reader was flooded by a torrent of literary publications churned out by all and sundry – state-owned, co-operative and even private companies. Independent information and telegraph agencies sprang up.

Desk-drawer writers and émigrés: Writers had gained their freedom at last, but an anti-climax soon followed. Ask any prominent publisher, and you're likely to hear that contemporary Soviet literature is rapidly losing moral and spiritual ground. Time will tell if this is true. Yet one thing is unmistakably clear: the 1990s are giving many grey-haired literary veterans a second youth. Writers such as V. Dudintsev, D. Granin, A.

Pristavkin, F. Iskander, V. Rasputin and Ch. Aitmatov – who for years wrote, as they say, "for the desk drawer" – have taken advantage of the changing times to make everything they wrote in the years of stagnation available to the reading public.

There are also double-edged publications on socio-economics and history by the grandees of 20th-century Russian literature: Ivan Bunin, Vladimir Nabokov, Andrei Platonov, Mikhail Bulgakov, Varlam Shalamov, Vasily Grossman and Alexander Solzhenitsyn. In addition, there are the *émigrés* – G. Vladimirov, V. Voinovich, V.

Aksyonov, I. Brodsky. The poor Russian reader, trained (or brainwashed) to take in mainly "trustworthy" and "permitted" facts, has suddenly been drenched by a Niagara of scandalous disclosures concerning the top leadership of the country, past and present. There are Utopian novels. There are even books about intimacy between the sexes! In a word, "non-party" literature is booming.

They say that the Muscovite has one undisputable advantage over the Westerner – the unique ability to read everything that turns up without a thought for more important things. But the pace of life has become so incredibly fast that there is no time nowadays even for that.

Painting: Moscow has been famous for its "masters of all arts" since the old days. The 15th century was blessed by the genius of Andrei Rublev. There's a museum dedicated to his work in the territory of the former Andronnikov Monastery, where the artist lived out his final years. In the 17th century, Simon Ushakov, an artist and engraver, organised a kind of an academy of arts in the Armory Chamber. The 18th century heralded a breakaway from medieval religious themes (mainly represented in icons) to secular subjects and, first and foremost, to the portrait. We have Peter the Great to thank for this – it was he who invited Western masters to Russia.

In the mid-1860s, Ivan Kramskoi became the leader of the 14 rebels – progressive artists who formed the Company of Travelling Artistic Exhibitions. At this time Ilya Repin was a frequent visitor to Moscow, where he painted several portraits. It was there that the artist befriended another titan of Russian culture: Leo Tolstoy.

The most poetic pieces of Russian national art came from Vasily Vasnetsov, who painted scenes from folklore, heroic epics and lyrical fairy-tales. Today there is a museum in the artist's fairy-tale house built according to his sketches.

A new phase in the development of Russian art was opened in the early 20th century by Konstantin Korovin, Vladimir Serov and Mikhail Vrubel. Korovin's work is "a feast for the eye". Attracted to the bright side of life, the artist neglects everything that interferes with harmony. Serov was a master portrait painter and an accomplished graphic artist. He was also one of the best-loved professors among the students of the Moscow Art School.

Passing by the freshly restored Metropol Building, you will no doubt notice the panels on the facade. Their author is Mikhail Vrubel, a master of monumental and easel painting, a graphic artist, sculptor and architect. In his imagination, he tried to enmesh the entire world of beauty, of all centuries, of all peoples and of all the arts, a concept totally in keeping with the times he lived in.

The new century evoked new images and

heroic, the falsely pathetic, the parade-like, the thoughtless sense of "well-being". A great many works of this period astound with their triviality and uniformity.

The early 1960s brought large exhibitions. Most significant was the retrospective exhibition of Moscow artists which, unfortunately, was trampled underfoot by the party leadership and the old men from the USSR Academy of Arts. It was a lethal blow to progress, after which many artists had no choice but to flee the country.

A new brand of artists: Today's generation of artists knows nothing of war. Their work reflects a different era, marked by a protest

brought new names – Kasimir Malevich, Vladimir Tatlin, Alexander Rodchenko, Vasily Kandinsky, all of whom tried to find the language of the "new era", the "revolutionary epoch". And the world of their art has opened for Muscovites in the last few years.

The first decade after the war brought, together with reconstruction of the war-ravaged economy, the worst period of Stalin's cult marked by the degeneration of lifestyle and, in the arts, a striving for the pseudo-

Left, the writer, Aitmatov. **Above**, Repin's painting *Cossacks Writing a Letter to the Sultan.*

against rigid unification of purpose. It is based on diversity of plots, the desire to cover new spheres of life and philosophical problems, such as art and outlook, the human being and the planet, the artist and the world, life and time. Many of these works still have a hard time getting to people, being exhibited, at best, in Arbat Street or in one of Moscow's parks. Some representatives of the new generation were more fortunate: their works were sold at Moscow's first Sotheby's auction. Some bureaucrats "responsible" for art are still trying to puzzle out how that happened.

Russian music tantalises, attracts, enthralls. It evokes the olden days – and the modern era. Aeons ago, it sprang from the deft fingers of the *gusli* (psalters) players (who also sang and told tales), the throats of the merry *skomorokhi* (travelling circus actors), the deep chest of the peasant ploughing his land.

"Song is the soul of the people" is the adage that great Russian composers have endorsed on more than one occasion. In a way, Russian folk songs spawned Russian classical music, the music of Glinka, Dargomyzhsky, Mussorgsky, Rimsky-Korsakov and Tchaikovsky. Moscow, naturally, was always a center of Russia's musical life. It gave the world Alexander Aliabyev (1787–1851), the author of the famous romance, *Nightingale*, Alexei Verstovsky (1799–1862), and Mikhail Glinka (1804–57). One of the fathers of the musical scene was Mikhail Rubinshtein (1835–81), an outstanding conductor and a brilliant pianist. He put together the first music classes in Moscow, which were later reorganised into the original Russian conservatories.

Tchaikovsky's career: On 1 September 1866, Arbat Street filled with carriages as the cream of Moscow's intelligentsia gathered for the opening of the Conservatory, an event that coincided with the beginning of Pyotr Tchaikovsky's extraordinary career. Tchaikovsky led a singularly eventful life in Moscow – professorship at the Conservatory, friendship with people like playwright Alexei Ostrovsky, actor Piotr Sadovsky (who lovingly called the composer *oriole*), and the charming, talented Italian primadonna Desiré Arto. Then, of course, he worked in Moscow on such greats as *Swan Lake*, the *Symphony No. 4*, and *Eugene Onegin*.

In 1990, Muscovites celebrated the 150th anniversary of Tchaikovsky's birth. The jubilee coincided with the annual international contest bearing his name and the pride of the repertoire of the young contestants remained the great maestro's *First Piano Concerto*.

Left, Pyotr Tchaikovsky. **Above**, Mikhail Glinka.

Moscow is also the birthplace of Alexander Skriabin (1871–1915), the pianist and composer who was fated to write a new page in the history of piano music with his emotion-filled symphonies. The last thing the Skriabin Museum, near Arbat Street, resembles is a museum. In the museum-apartment, where the author of *A Poem of Ecstasy* and *Prometheus* spent his last years, everything has been preserved intact. There are sheets of music, manuscripts, and Skriabin's philo-

sophical essays. There is also the apparatus Skriabin designed to enhance the effects of his music with flickering light.

The new times produced new names: Isaac Dunayevsky, Tikhon Khrennikov, Rodion Schedrin, and Dmitry Shostakovich. Isolated from the outside world in the 1950s and the 1960s, Soviet music went its own way, drawing on its roots in search of profound links between the past and the present. This direction, Soviet *avant-garde*, is associated with the names of A. Shnitke and S. Gubaidullina.

Jazz and Soviet rock: Musical life in the

1960s would have been nothing without jazz, which had to fight a long and uphill battle to come into its own in this country. The first international jazz festival of the USSR was organised in Moscow.

The early 1970s gave us our first rock and pop musicians. Both types were frowned upon by the powers-that-be – both the performers and the listeners were accused of following Western trends and leading an "alien" way of life. Contemporary music, thank heavens, combines every known type of folk, classical and pop music.

Cultural-exchange programmes with Western countries are growing, and rock 'n'

hall in the Scientists' House, the Beethoven Hall of the Bolshoi, the Olimpiisky on Prospekt Mira, halls in Izmailovo and Luzhniki – it's simply impossible to name them all.

The concert hall named after Tchaikovsky has a perpetual exposition dedicated to the composer of *Swan Lake*, along with a collection of bow instruments by Russian and foreign masters. The pride of the collection are 14 Stradivarius violins, seven instruments by Amati and eight by Gvarneli. In accordance with tradition, these instruments are made available to outstanding performers on tour in Moscow.

There's a place in Moscow which music

roll fans will probably recognise the names of such popular groups as Mashina Vremeni, Park Gorkogo, DDT, Chyorny Kofe and Rock Hotel, and individual performers such as Alla Pugacheva, Vladimir Kuzmin, Zhanna Aguzarova, and Valery Leontiev. There are also the young hopefuls – Alexander Malinin, Katia Semenova, Alexander Yegorov and Yelena Sysoyeva.

Abundant music halls: Moscow has many concert halls, with music to suit any taste: the Column Hall and the Oktiabrsky Hall in the House of Unions, the Major and the Minor in the Conservatory, the Tchaikovsky Hall, the

lovers hold especially dear: the Gniesinykh Institute. Created as a music school in the late 19th century by Yelena Gniesina, the institute has educated several generations of Soviet musicians, composers and performers. There's always music in the building the latest work of a modern composer, a simple folk ballad, finger-breaking jazz passages, pop songs, you name it.

Ballet: Ballet came to Russia in the 17th century, and the first troupes appeared in the 18th century. Over the centuries, Russian ballet-masters created undisputed masterpieces, and after World War II troupes such as the Bolshoi set new standards with their innovation and disciplined energy. Today, the rating of Russian ballet is so high that there is hardly a ballet theatre in the world which does not stage ballets by Russian composers (mostly *Sleeping Beauty* and *Swan Lake*). Russian ballet is Anna Pavlova, Mikhail Fokin, Kasian Goleizovsky, and Galina Ulanova. Sergei Prokofiev said about Galina Ulanova, "She is the genius of Russian ballet, its intangible soul, its inspired poetry." Ulanova became a teaching choreographer with the Bolshoi.

Crisis at the Bolshoi: The troupe of the Bolshoi has had no shortage of stars such as pany for more than 30 years. The new economic realities hit the troupe hard, its members complaining that their creativity was being stifled by the need to perform endless variations on "greatest ballet hits" for coachloads of Western tourists. To make matters worse, the theatre's fabric was crumbling and needed heavy investment.

New rhythms: There is more to dance than ballet, of course. New times bring new rhythms. Hence the steady popularity of Boris Sankin's Rhythms of the Planet Dance Ensemble, which, as the name implies, dance every dance imaginable. Be sure to see a performance of the plastic drama theatre

Vladimir Vasiliev, Yekaterina Maksimova and Nina Timofeeva, and the Bolshoi's school of choreography has produced talents such as Maya Plisetskaya, Igor Moiseev and Nadezhda Nadezhdina. But the Bolshoi's international reputation went into decline in the 1980s and, by 1994, a tour of England had to be cancelled because of poor ticket sales. In 1995 its artistic director, the acclaimed but tyrannical Yuri Grigorovich, was forced to resign after running the com-

Left, inside the Bolshoi. **Above**, the Bolshoi's company in performance.

headed by Gedriavichus. Lovers of contemporary ballroom dancing can both admire the intricate *pas* of classical waltz, rumba or fiery lambada and test themselves in dancing schools, or numerous community centres.

In the evenings and on weekends, young people flock for modern rhythms to discos in Gorky Park, Sokolniki, the Palace of Youth, cafés and disco bars; elderly people find themselves more attracted to wind orchestras which, appearing more and more often in the streets and squares of the city as buskers seek to make a living, remind them of the days of their youth.

The city's theatrical centre is Teatralnaya Ploshchad, where three theatres form a semicircle: the Bolshoi, still one of the world's best opera/ballet theatres, the Maly Drama Theatre (founded in the early 19th century), and the Central Children's Theatre. Just around the corner is the Khudozhestvenny Theatre (founded in 1898) and, a little further up Bolshaya Dmitrovka Street, Moscow's second music theatre, named after Konstantin Stanislavsky and Vladimir Nemirovich-Danchenko.

Perestroika didn't leave theatres untouched. The Khudozhestvenny Theatre split into two after a scandal in which the stars backed director Oleg Yefremov and the lesser-known members of this oversized troupe broke away to form their own Khudozhestvenny Theatre (named after Gorky, and not Yefremov's Chekhov). To avoid confusion, remember that the real Khudozhestvenny is on Kamergersky Pereulok. The new theatre is on Tverskoy Boulevard.

The new wave falters: Not far away, in Bolshaya Nikitskaya Ulitsa, is the Mayakovsky Theatre, headed by director Andrei Goncharov, who has managed to maintain his reputation for two decades. As perestroika shuffled off all notions of leftist and official art, the playwrights of the new wave (as they were called in the 1970s) seemed to lose touch with reality. Meanwhile, the radicals – Mikhail Shatrov and Alexander Gelman – occupy orthodox positions. Gelman accepted the nomination to the CPSU Central Committee at the precise moment that thousands were leaving the party – people such as foreman Potapov, the character in the play *Protocol of One Meeting*.

Nowadays, there are no "angry" or "pro-reform" theatres: it is each for himself. Sovremennik, the popular theatre on Chisto Prudny, seems to prefer classical plays by Chekhov, Bulgakov and Olby, even though more recent productions have been based on books that were banned before *perestroika*.

Left, traditional drama still finds an audience.

Galina Volchek has come forth with a bold production of E. Ginzburg's *Hairspin Route*, about Stalin in 1937, while actor Igor Kvasha has turned to the prose of Voinovich.

Moscow's most popular theatre is the Leninskiy Komsomol Theatre, headed by Mark Zakharov. It's probably the only place where finding a spare ticket is always a problem. There used to be many such theatres in Moscow. Today, when everyone bemoans the years of Brezhnev's stagnation, few seem to recognise the stagnation that resulted from *perestroika* – a stagnation more formidable than ever, particularly in the arts. Mark Zakharov battled against this trend. Even in the 1970s, he fought the "official patriotism of the epoch", and produced what he wanted to stage, not what the minister of culture and his circle desired. For this reason, his plays from the 1970s are still in the repertoire: *Til and The Star of Joaquino Murietta*, for example.

A recent addition is Ostrovsky's *Wise Man*, and *Mourning Prayer*, a play based on a collection of stories by Sholom Aleikhem. It is a real masterpiece, marked by Yevgeny Leonov's inspired acting. Leonov, who had just recovered from a severe heart attack, conveyed a painful, heartfelt understanding of his character *Tevie the milkman*.

Ten minutes from Chekhov Street, in Triumfalnaya Ploshchad, is the Aquarium Garden, where director Pavel Khomsky staged *Jesus Christ Superstar* for the Mossoviet Theatre. Everything that Europe and America marvelled at 25 years ago is now in Moscow. Better late than never. The theatre also offers another fine play – Piotr Fomenko's production of Albert Camus' *Caligula*. Seemingly dealing with the long-gone past, the play nevertheless discusses many of the moral issues of the Gorbachev epoch.

Then there's Merezhkovsky's old *Pavel I*, the play describing the last two days of the emperor. Not for nothing did Pavel Heifits produce this for the Soviet Army Theatre at this particular moment. The play shows a court unhappy with the emperor's reforms and his desire to make Russia a truly European country with the best army in the world.

When the once-powerful Yegor Ligachev came to see the play, the actors joked that they taught him to arrange palace coups. According to Heifits, Pavel I dies because his reforms are not needed by the people or by his closest supporters, who prefer to live as they'd always lived – merrily fornicating, thinking of nothing, and letting the devil take the country.

There are several hundred theatres in Moscow – as many as in New York. Around 50 are state theatres, and the rest are small studios which eke out an existence in basements, garrets and even apartments. Unfortunately, almost all are professionally incompetent and more often imitate theatre than create something artistically valuable. Yet they include such world famous troupes as A.Vasiliev's School of Dramatic Art and V. Beliakovich's Theatre on Yugo-Zapad.

Avant-garde Russian cinematography: Can we speak about Moscow movies? Is there a breed we can call the Moscow moviemaker? Emphatically, yes. They can easily be spotted: they are good-natured, hospitable, slightly worried and always in a hurry. And with good reason – the movie locations map covers many different studios, movie theatres, clubs and concert halls.

Moscow moviegoers have traditionally been appreciative, but recently their enthusiasm has turned increasingly to foreign films, and the latest blockbuster is almost certain to hail from Hollywood. The new freedoms, which have proved such a stimulant for newspapers and television, have not had the same effect on film production. During the first half of the 1990s, the number of films made in Russia plummeted from around 300 a year to fewer than 50.

Many cinemas closed too, though Channel One, Russia's public television channel, began filling the gap to some extent by showing new Russian films, accompanied by interviews with their directors. A booming video trade also sprang up, with cassettes on sale at almost every street kiosk. Again, most of the videos featured American movies, but popular first-run Russian films such as Sergei Bodrov's *Prisoner of the Mountain*

(1996), in which two Russian soldiers are held hostage by an old Chechen chieftain, went quickly to video.

The appeal of the American product was not lost on the newer film makers, and movies such as *Vse Budet Khorosho* (*Everything Will Be OK*) were every bit as packed with contemporary fairy-tale myths as any Hollywood feel-good fantasy.

Whether old values will survive is not yet clear, and many traditional film makers like Nikita Mikhalkov, director of *Burnt by the Sun*, deplored the new trends. "I mistrust the 'new democrats' who want to reject everything from the past without recognising what was positive," he said. "That is what happened after 1917. Russia has now to look back and discover what was good in its past and rediscover its roots."

Its cinematic roots were certainly distinguished. Movies were first shown in the city in 1896, and nearly all the 2,000 films released between 1908 and 1918 were produced there. After the revolution, the city's production included such innovative masterpieces as *Battleship Potemkin*, *Mother* and *The Descendant of Genghis Khan*.

Moscow became the seat of the country's highest cinematographic authority – Goskino, which was simultaneously the buyer and the supplier of films produced in accordance with state plans. During the years of "stagnation", bureaucratic pressure mounted, and the movie producers of Moscow suffered the worst of it because they were so near. The conflict escalated and finally flared up at the 5th congress of the USSR Cinematographers' Union in May 1986. The democratic election of an alternative leadership for the Union heralded the beginning of a new period – "perestroika in action". Conservatives such as Mikhalkov and Sergei Bondarchuk were ousted by the liberals whose loyalty went to adventurous directors such as Andrei Tarkovsky (known in the West for *Solaris*).

The Union began taking new initiatives. Over 250 previously banned films were released. Many new artistic associations were set up: ASK (American-Soviet Cineinitiative), the society of friends of cinematography, the Christian association, the association of women cinematographers, and so on.

Newly formed guilds in all moviemaking professions proclaimed it their goal to protect the rights of union members.

Art and politics: Hot-headed, excited people come together in the House of Cinematography near the Union building. They are the members of the capital's professional movie club. There, in the two viewing halls (Bolshoi and Bely) and in the adjacent cosy cafés that are linked by a monumental fresco by Fernand Leger, new films are shown. The ritual of presentation, when the entire team comes out on stage, has developed into a cult.

The schedule of the House is crammed with events. *Perestroika* brought frequent younger sister of America's Oscar and Europe's Felix. The presentation borrowed heavily from its older siblings, turning into a glamorous affair with beautiful girls bringing out the fateful envelopes containing the jury's decisions. The envelopes were opened, and the statuettes awarded by Russia's most famous poets, singers, and ballerinas. It became a morale-boosting festival of talent and good luck.

The House is always under siege. Sometimes the militia has had to lend a helping hand when there were too many people trying to crash the gates and see one of their superstar heroes or heroines. Recently, the

meetings in which universal problems were discussed. In the run-up to the New Year, the House turns into a forest of green fir trees, under which groups of people sit down to celebrate. The *Kapustnik*, a stage-show dedicated to topical issues, is famous across the country and is, as a rule, always filmed.

The award of the Nika: In 1989, a new ceremony was conceptualised as a yearly event – the award of *Nika*, the professional prize of the Soviet Cinematographers' Union. Nika, the Greek winged goddess of victory, is the

Above, actress Tamara Aculova and stagehands.

House got its first rival – Kinotsentr, a young institution in an old Moscow district, not far from the mayor's office, the Zoo and the pretty church of John the Baptist. The monumental edifice made of rosy tufa incorporates an entire complex of large and small cinema halls, a museum, offices and co-ops, an exhibition hall and a restaurant.

During the International Festival, which takes place every odd-numbered year in July, the entire square in front of the movie centre becomes a unique world of cinematography, decorated with banners and flags. It's a good omen for Russian cinema's future.

If one was to describe the architecture of Moscow in one word, one might call it multi-style. Is this necessarily a criticism, though? Some people argue that Moscow does not have a face of its own (as does St Petersburg, which was mainly built at the same time). Moscow, which is nearly nine centuries old, has a great deal of intermingled styles, which tend sometimes to diminish the initial impact made on the visitor by a city that seems positively to encourage preconceptions. Yet, the more one looks, the more one can see a cunning plan behind it all, which reconciles many things (irreconcilable at first sight) into a general cohesive scheme.

The first wooden structures which remotely resembled a fortress appeared on Borovitsky Hill in the times of Yury Dolgorukiy in the second half of the 12th century. In the 14th century, Ivan Kalita built a real town, which was called Kremlin. The main churches in Sobornaya Square also date to that time. Late in the 14th century, during the reign of Prince Dmitry Donskoy, the wooden walls of the Kremlin were destroyed by fire, and resurrected in white stone (limestone mined near Moscow).

Real work on the Kremlin started only under Ivan III, who hired Italian masters for the somewhat intricate job of combining the originality of ancient Russian architecture and the perfect finish of Renaissance cathedrals. By the beginning of the 16th century, the Kremlin ensemble and the merchant quarters to the northeast of the main walls were largely completed.

Gradually, Red Square was cleared of all houses (to prevent fires) and became the main marketplace of the city. Behind it, three streets fanned out: Nikolskaya, Ilyinka and Varvarka. In 1535–38 the space between them, Veliky Posad, was sealed off with another thick wall. The area was called *Kitai*, which meant "middle fort".

Preceding pages and **left**: onion-shaped towers crown Moscow's churches. **Above**, the entrance to the Economic Achievements Exhibition.

Medieval architecture: In those days, the place to settle down was at the junction of Moscow's three rivers – the Moskva, the Neglinka and the Yauza. Hence the historical settlements Zaneglimenye, Zayauzye and Zamoskvorechye. Within the limits of to-day's Boulevard Ring, there were wide streets: Volkhonka, Znamenka (*Kalinin Prospekt*), Tverskaya, Petrovka, Lubyanka, Soliyanka, Mjasnitskaya and Maroseika. In the late 15th century, all the residential quar-

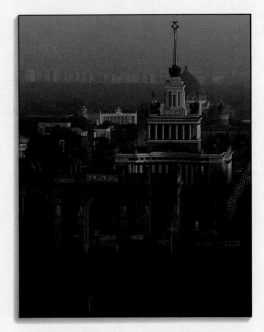

ters within the limits of these streets were surrounded by a whitewashed brick wall and included into the so-called *White Town*.

Finally, the growing capital got another, this time wooden, circular wall in 1591, complete with an earthen wall and moat (it was 16 km/10 miles long). The town within these new limits was called *Skorod*. The new wall had gates (*zastava*), from which new roads ran. To the southeast and the southwest of Kaluzhskaya Zastava, there were two roads – Bolshaya Kaluzhskaya (Leninsky Prospekt) and Shabolovka; to the east of Semyonovskaya Zastava – Taganskaya; to the northeast of Vladimirskaya Zastava – today's Entusiastov Highway. Beyond the gates, there were settlements, estates and monasteries, of which several stand to this day – Andronnikov, Donskoy, Simonov Monasteries and the Novodevichy Convent. In this way the city grew in accordance with the typical Russian radial-circular layout which is still adhered to in our day. The main characteristic of medieval architecture in Moscow is the tent-domed church (these had cupolas in the form of a multi-faceted pyramid with a cupola on top). Of those which still stand, the most characteristic is the Ascension Church in Kolomenskoye.

Church (also known as the Menshikov Tower, 15a, Telegrafny Lane), which combine the strict lines of a tiered tower and secular decor, making one think of European rococo.

Peter's reforms turned architectural development in Moscow full circle. The spotlight was claimed by public buildings. For instance, whole sectors of the city were given to rectangular layouts that appeared chopped up into squares – Nemetskaya Sloboda, Lefortovo on the Yauza. Wooden streets gave way to pavements, cemeteries were removed from the city limits, and several orchards and parks were founded.

Moscow baroque: In the 17th century, Moscow churches were traditionally decorated with glazed ceramic tiles. A wonderful specimen survives in First Krutitsky Lane (No. 4) – the Krutitsky *teremok*, which is part of the partially surviving estate. In the last quarter of the 17th century, old Russian architecture was dominated by the style known today as Moscow Baroque or the Naryshkin Style (named after one of the wealthiest aristocratic families between the 16th and the 20th centuries).

The best examples are the Pokrov Church in Fili (1693–94), and the Archangel Gavriil

The classic architecture of the 18th century is connected with the names of two famous Russian architects: Vassili Bazhenov (1737–99) and Matvey Kazakov (1738–1812). Bazhenov's best creation in Moscow is, without doubt, the Pashkov House – the former Rumiantsev Museum and now a part of the Lenin Library.

His second masterpiece is the Tsaritsyno Estate – an ensemble of the palace and several pavilions picturesquely scattered on the banks of a pond as befits a typical sample of romantic pseudo-gothic. Left unfinished owing to the wrath of Catherine II (she did not like the symbols of the Freemasons secretly introduced into the architecture) and partially redesigned by Kazakov, the ensemble stood in ruins for almost 200 years. It is currently being restored.

Matvei Kazakov was by right celebrated as a great architect. Since he built so many houses, people even speak about "Kazakov's Moscow". He built the Senate in the Kremlin (the Supreme Soviet Building), the Petrovsky Palace (today the Zhukovsky Academy), the University, which incurred a lot of damage during the 1812 fire and was rebuilt by Gilardi, and the Golitsyn Hospital (today the First Municipal Hospital).

construction boom, there appeared, instead of the Zemlyanoi Val, the Sadovoye Ring; the Neglinka River was channelled into a conduit, and Aleksandrovsky Gardens was founded on the site of the river.

It was a time for new talents to appear, of whom the foremost was Osip Bove who redesigned Red Square and participated in the construction of the Bolshoi Theatre and the planning of Teatralnaya Ploshchad.

In the second half of the 19th century, Russian architecture was gripped by crisis. From the artistic point of view, the period was dominated by eclectics. New compositions and layouts were mechanically deco-

It should be mentioned that the two architects engaged in open competition which never seemed to end. Both were willing to rebuild the Kremlin as a fairy-tale garden. Perhaps it is just as well that the Kremlin remained practically intact.

Reconstruction after the fire: The fire in 1812 put an end to the beauty of 18th-century Moscow architecture: 6,496 houses, 122 churches and over 8,000 trading facilities were burned to the ground. In the ensuing

Left, baroque facades. **Above**, the Old University in Manege Ploshchad, restored in 1817–19.

rated with old forms and details borrowed from 17th-century Moscow churches. Witness the buildings of the Historical Museum, the Large Kremlin Palace and the Upper Market Rows (GUM).

The beginning of the 20th century was dominated by the Modern style. Its typical and most successful examples are the Riabushinsky Townhouse – now the Maxim Gorky Museum, and the Yaroslavl Railway Station.

Budding capitalism brought utterly novel architecture: profit houses for different social groups, workers' and soldiers' barracks, large department stores, factories, banks, stock exchanges and railway stations.

After the October Revolution (the new broom sweeps clean), there came several plans for new "socialist" construction in the city, called "New Moscow" and "General Plan for the Development of Moscow".

A time of "isms": The first decades of Soviet power turned out to be rather prolific architecturally, ranging from traditionalism (affinity for classical forms) and constructivism to avant-gardism and rationalism (laconic and economical). In the end, they all degenerated into gigantomania, self-congratulation in stone, and catering to mass

tastes. The buildings typical of that time can be found in Myasnitskaya Ulitsa (No. 39), Neglinnaya Ulitsa (No. 12), and in Red Square (Lenin Mausoleum). Another such project – the gigantic Palace of Soviets which was to have been topped by a huge Lenin statue – never materialised. This era also gave us the first metro stations, Kropotkinskaya and Mayakovskaya, which synthesise traditional architecture and the innovations of "proletarian culture".

In the 1950s and the 1960s, Moscow architecture was dominated by technologism – innumerable listless, faceless boxes of con-

crete and glass (mainly of concrete), designed for the maximal possible number of consumers at minimal cost. These include the Palace of Congresses in the Kremlin, the Pioneer Palace on the Lenin Hills, Domodedovo Airport Terminal and Vozdrizhenka Street and Novy Arbat.

The 1970s saw little change, other than the fact that the boxes got a little higher. New residential areas designed for "self-sufficiency" appeared – micro-cities with populations sometimes exceeding 250,000.

The 1980s brought hope. It seems that Russian architects are now acquiring a taste for architecture. Some go in for complicated associations with ancient art, while others lean towards modernism.

There's a great deal of restoration going on, frequently carried out by foreign contractors. Contemporary architectural experiments include Northern Chertanovo with its duplex apartments and underground garages, Krylatskoye and Strogino, and fledgling Solntsevo and Butovo. In a way, this also concerns the reborn Old Arbat, the redecorated Savoy and Metropol Hotels, and the newly built Slavianskaya Hotel. Not all the restorations may be aesthetically pleasing.

The face of the city is made up of the houses in which people live and work. Moscow was historically a city of active silhouettes; its skyline is made up of church cupolas, spires of the skyscrapers built in the 1950s, and towering modern hotels.

The main orientation point is the Kremlin with the golden Ivan Velikii; it is easy to make out the Sadovoye Ring by the highrises in Smolenskaya Ploshchad, Kudrinskaya Ploshchad, Komsomolskaya and Lermontovskaya squares. The Moskva meets the Yauza at the spot where there is another skyscraper (Kotelnicheskaya Embankment).

Another highrise – Ukraine Hotel – stands at the bend of the Moskva river. There is a kind of creative paraphrase in the Moscow skyline, which combines Gothic with those Russian tent compositions that so amaze newcomers with their "sharp tops", colours and gold.

Left, bulky Stalinist architecture: the foreign trade ministry.

THE CATHEDRAL OF CHRIST THE SAVIOUR

As Moscow contemplated the dawn of a new millennium, the city government, led by its aggressive, populist mayor, Yury Luzhkov, seemed to be fixated on reviving the past. Nowhere was this more apparent than in the fad for reconstructing monuments destroyed during the Stalin era. The Red Staircase in the Kremlin and the Kazan Cathedral and Resurrection Gate on Red Square are high-profile examples, but the most controversial project was the rebuilding of the Cathedral of Christ the Saviour on the banks of the Moskva River.

As early as December 1812, before the last remnants of Napoleon's Grande Armée had even left Russian soil, Alexander I was considering the idea of a patriotic monument which would celebrate Moscow's role as the symbol of resistance.

The scheme was dogged by problems. Construction of the first church on Sparrow Hills came to a halt in 1835 when the architect Alexander Vitberg was charged with embezzlement. Four years later the new tsar, Nicholas I, instructed Konstantin Ton to design a grander, even more ambitious cathedral closer to the Kremlin. This entailed the demolition of the Alekseevsky Convent, an act of vandalism which aroused the wrath of the abbess who warned Ton of an ancient curse on the site, traditionally known as Devil's Creek.

The dimensions of the cathedral, which was finally completed in 1883, were impressive – the dome rose to a height of 103 metres (338 ft) and was 30 metres (100 ft) in diameter. The walls were 4 metres (13 ft) thick and there was room for 10,000 worshippers. No expense was spared on the interior which was lavishly decorated with frescoes, expensive marbles, bronze and gold.

None of this splendour cut any ice with the Communists. The cathedral, all too visible from their Kremlin offices, was a provocation. Stalin had it blown up in 1931, provoking (necessarily muted) protests at this "act of barbarism". Anxious to impress on the world the grandeur of Soviet achievements, he announced a competition for a Palace of Soviets, the stipulation being that the new building should dwarf the cathedral in scale.

Some of the most brilliant European architects, including Le Corbusier and Walter Gropius, submitted designs but, not surprisingly, it was the home-grown team of Iofan, Gelfreykh and Shchuko who were awarded the contract for this megalomaniac scheme. A soaring, eight-tiered skyscraper was to have served as a pedestal for a 100-metre (330-ft) titanium statue of Lenin, the total height exceeding that of the Empire State Building.

The stupendous costs involved and the inter-

Right, the rebuilding nears completion in 1996.

vention of World War II put paid to the scheme and the site remained empty until 1958 when it was decided to build a heated open air swimming pool here – naturally the world's largest. But this project too was ill-fated: cracks soon began to appear in the lining, while the vast quantities of steam caused severe structural damage to the surrounding buildings. The pool finally closed in 1994.

The clerk of works in charge of the new cathedral project, Vassily Shakhovsky, combed Moscow for the original furnishings and decor. Most of these were looted for use in the metro and the Moskva Hotel, but he did find the original chandelier and the 20-metre (70-ft) high gilded iconostasis. All aspects of the building have come in for criticism. The cost, more than $150 million, was seen by many Muscovites as positively indecent at a time

when thousands of their fellow citizens had been forced onto the streets by poverty. Architectural purists, meanwhile, were appalled at the haste and lack of sensitivity with which the cathedral was constructed and were offended by such innovations as underground car parks, conference halls and the elevator which will take visitors to the top of the dome for spectacular views of the city.

The choice of the artist, Ilya Glazunov, to decorate the interior also proved contentious as critics have condemned his work for its superficiality and vulgar chauvinism. Even impartial observers see the controversy around the cathedral as a symptom of a deeper malaise, stemming from the failure to discover a new post-Communist identity for Russia that will unite rather than divide the nation. ∎

A characteristic of Moscow, just as of many other old Russian cities, is its radial layout. The **Kremlin**, or citadel, which had the form of an irregular ring, was surrounded, in stages, with new fortification walls, moats and ramparts. The gates in the wall were the starting points for highways which radiated out, linking the city with other cities. As the rings expanded, the defensive outposts on the approaches to Moscow were incorporated into the city, walls that hampered its growth were pulled down, the moats were filled in and the ramparts were replaced by extensive blossom-filled boulevards and streets. Monasteries that doubled as fortresses were built on remote approaches to the city.

Five rings circle the city: The historic radial layout of the city has survived to this day. The Kremlin wall still forms the nucleus of the city. Next comes the first ring, which is actually a semi-circle of streets, situated on the site of the former **Kitay-Gorod** walls. The second ring, also a semi-circle, is the **Bulvarnoye Koltso** (Boulevard Ring), which is formed by wide boulevards that replaced the walls of the *Bely Gorod* (White City) in the 18th century. Next is the **Sadovoye Koltso** (Garden Ring), laid on the site of the former *Zemlyanoi Val* (Earthen Rampart). The name "Garden" is a misnomer and is based on tradition. This is the city's most important transport artery, along which traffic flows from early morning until late evening.

Further out is a circular railway built in place of the **Kamer-Kollezhsky Val** (Rampart) – named after the Kammer Kollegium, the name of the Ministry of Finance during the reign of Peter the Great – which was Moscow's customs border in the 18th century.

Finally, the fifth ring is formed by the **Moscow Circular Road** and marks the city's present boundary. Beyond this boundary stretches a "green belt" of forests and meadows, where many Muscovites like to spend their weekends. It covers 1,800 sq. km (700 sq. miles).

Radiating roads and highways: A series of thoroughfares radiate from the centre, cutting across the rings on all sides of the city. **Bolshaya Lubyanka Ulitsa** leads north to become **Prospekt Mira** and then the **Yaroslavl Highway**. Myasnitskaya Street leads northeast towards the **Shchelkovo Highway**. **Solyanka Ulitsa** goes east towards the **Entuziastov Highway** and **Ryazansky Prospekt**. **Bolshaya Polyanka Ulitsa** leads south towards the **Kashira** and **Warsaw Highways**. Leading southwest, to the **Kiev Highway**, is **Bolshaya Yakimanka Ulitsa** and **Leninsky Prospekt**.

Vozdvizhenka Ulitsa and the **Ulitsa Novy Arbat** lead west towards the **Minsk Highway**. Finally, **Tverskaya Ulitsa** runs northwest towards the **Leningrad (St Petersburg)** and **Volokolamsk Highways**.

Each historical period left its own inimitable imprint on the architecture of the city. Today, however, it would hardly be proper to

Preceding pages: onion domes atop the Kremlin; golden lads and lasses on the International Freedom Fountain at the Exhibition of Economic Achievements; entrance to the Exhibition. **Left**, the Kazan church in Kolmenskoye.

speak about the Moscow of the days of Ivan the Terrible, Peter the Great or Catherine the Great. The past has merged with the present so closely that, with rare exceptions, it is difficult to single out any untouched architectural composition. Many structures have been pulled down or rebuilt, and every architect has proposed his own project for the development of the city.

Demolition and reconstruction: Much of the rebuilding occurred in the 1930s when the then still young Soviet government decided to make the city into a showpiece symbol of its triumphal advancement. The master plan for the reconstruction of the capital, adopted in 1935, envisaged the gradual redevelopment of the entire city on the basis of its historical radial layout. As a result, the central avenues were expanded, the embankments were overhauled and the built-up areas round the Kremlin were cleared.

The architects, eager to please the leadership, did not give a moment's thought to the historic value of the structures they demolished. Thus, the majestic **Cathedral of Christ the Saviour**, the **Sukharev Tower**, the triumphal **Red Gate**, the **Monastery of the Ascension**, the **Monastery of St Michael's Miracle at Chonae**, the **Convent of the Passion of Our Lord** on whose site the Rossiya Cinema was built, dozens of churches, the fortress walls of the Kitay-Gorod, and quite a few other structures disappeared without trace.

Today, much is being said about the need to preserve and to restore old historical and cultural monuments. Practically the entire centre of Moscow has been proclaimed a protected zone. An "architectural legacy" programme has designated nearly 10,000 architectural monuments to be placed under state protection, and calls for the restoration of more than 1,500 buildings of historical or cultural value. In the future it is proposed that new housing projects should be built outside the city limits.

Orientation: Our tour will follow the natural layout of the city. We will start with the **Kremlin**, the heart not only of Moscow but of the whole of Russia. From there we will visit **Red Square**, **Kitay-Gorod** and the inner city circle that surrounds the Kremlin walls. We will then visit four sections that surround the city centre.

Starting at **Prechistenskaya Naberezhnaya** we will stroll through the Arbat quarter as far as **Tverskaya Ulitsa**, following the radiating routes that leave the city and its side-streets. The next section then covers the area between **Tverskaya Ulitsa** and **Myasnitskaya Ulitsa**, followed by the stretch between Myasnitskaya Ulitsa and **Zayauze**. Finally we visit the part of the city on the other side of the Moskva River, **Zamoskvorechye**.

Street names: To find your way around Moscow today isn't that easy. Leaving aside the Cyrillic lettering, many street, square and metro names were changed in the early 1990s, giving back the historical names to squares and streets.

Some metro stations, however, still carry the Soviet name, even though the streets or squares they were named after have changed. Most street signs carry the new names and, while many Muscovites are getting used to them, others still use the names they grew up with.

Right, the staircase of the Pushkin Museum of Fine Arts.

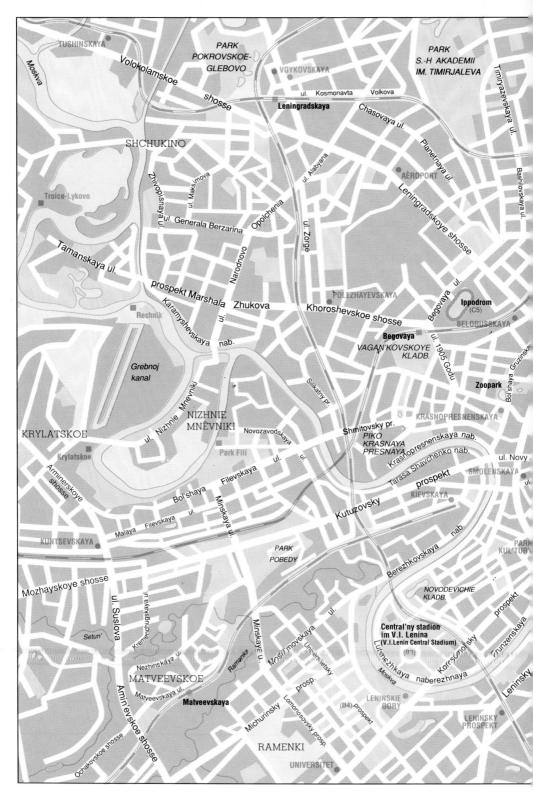

TUSHINSKAYA

Moskva

Volokolamskoe shosse

PARK POKROVSKOE-GLEBOVO

VOYKOVSKAYA

ul. Kosmonavta   Volkova

Leningradskaya

PARK S.-H AKADEMII IM. TIMIRJALEVA

Chasovaya ul.

Timirjazevskaya ul.

SHCHUKINO

Troice-Lykovo

Zhivopisnaya ul.

ul. Maksimova

ul. Alabyana

Planetnaya ul.

AÈROPORT

Bashilovskaya ul.

ul. Generala Berzarina

Opolchenia

ul. Zorge

Leningradskoe shosse

Tamanskaya ul.

Narodnovo

prospekt Marshala Zhukova

Karamyshevskaya

Rechnik

ul.

nab.

Khoroshevskoe shosse

POLEZHAYEVSKAYA

Begovaya ul.

Ippodrom (C5)

BELORUSSKAYA

Begovaya

VAGAN'KOVSKOYE KLADB.

ul. 1905 Godu

Grebnoj kanal

ul. Nizhnie Mnevniki

NIZHNIE MNÈVNIKI

Novozavodskaya

Slikatny pr.

Shmitovsky pr.

PIKO KRASNAYA PRESNAYA

Krasnopresnenskaya nab.

Tarasa Shavchenko nab.

Bol'shaya Gruzinska

Gruzinska

Zoopark

KRASNOPRESNENSKAYA

KRYLATSKOE

Krylatskoe

Arminerskoye shosse

Park Fili

Filevskaya

Bol'shaya Filevskaya

Minskaya ul.

ul.

ul.

ul.

ul. Novy

SMOLENSKAYA

prospekt

KIEVSKAYA

KUNTSEVSKAYA

Malaya Filevskaya

Kutuzovsky

Berezhkovskaya   nab.

PARK KUL'TUR

Mozhayskoye shosse

ul. Suslova

Kremenchugskaya ul.

PARK POBEDY

Minskaya ul.

Universitetsky

ul.

NOVODEVICHIE KLADB.

prospekt

Frunzenskaya

Setun'

Nezhinskaya ul.

Ramenka

Nosihi'movskaya

Luzhnechkaya

Central'ny stadion im V.I. Lenina
(V.I.Lenin Central Stadium)
(B3)

Komsomolsky

Moskva naberezhnaya

LENINSKY PROSPEKT

MATVEEVSKOE

Matveevskaya ul.

Matveevskaya

Michurinsky

prosp.

Lomonosovsky prosp.

LENINSKIE GORY

(B4) Prospekt

Leninsky

Amin'evskoe shosse

Ochakovskoye shosse

RAMENKI

UNIVERSITET

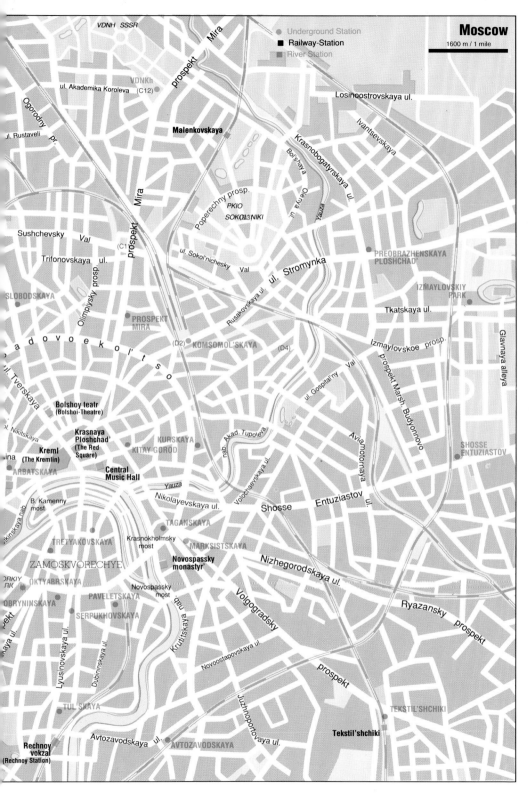

Moscow

1600 m / 1 mile

Underground Station
Railway-Station
River Station

VDNH SSSR

VDNKh

ul. Akademika Koroleva (C12)

Losinoostrovskaya ul.

Ogorodny pr.

ul. Rustaveli

Malenkovskaya

Ivantsevskaya

Krasnobogatyrskaya ul.

Bol'shaya Olena ul.

Yauza

Mira prospekt

Mira prospekt

Sushchevsky Val

(C1)

Trifonovskaya ul.

Poperechny prosp.

PKIO SOKOL'NIKI

PREOBRAZHENSKAYA PLOSHCHAD'

IZMAYLOVSKIY PARK

SLOBODSKAYA

ul. Sokol'nichesky Val

ul. Stromynka

Tkatskaya ul.

a d o v o e k o l't s o

PROSPEKT MIRA

Rusakovskaya ul.

Izmaylovskoe prosp.

prospekt Marsh. Budonnovo

Glavnaya alleya

ul. Tverskaya

(D2) KOMSOMOL'SKAYA (D4)

ul. Gospital'ny Val

Bolshoy teatr
(Bolshoi-Theatre)

ol. Nikitskaya

Krasnaya Ploshchad'
(The Red Square)

KURSKAYA

KITAY GOROD

nab. Akad. Tupoleva

Aviamotornaya

SHOSSE ENTUZIASTOV

Kreml
(The Kremlin)

ina

ARBATSKAYA

Central Music Hall

Volochaevskaya ul.

Yauza

B. Kamenny most

Nikolayevskaya ul.

Shosse Entuziastov ul.

nikinskaya nab.

TRETYAKOVSKAYA

TAGANSKAYA

Krasnokholmsky most

MARKSISTSKAYA

ZAMOSKVORECHYE

Novospassky monastyr'

Nizhegorodskaya ul.

ORKIY ПK

OKTYABRSKAYA

Novospassky most

Volgogradsky prospekt

Ryazansky prospekt

OBRYNINSKAYA

PAVELETSKAYA

ekt

SERPUKHOVSKAYA

Lyusinovskaya ul.

Dubininskaya ul.

Krutitskaya nab.

Novoostapovskaya ul.

Juzhnoportovaya ul.

TEKSTIL'SHCHIKI

TUL'SKAYA

Avtozavodskaya ul.

AVTOZAVODSKAYA

Tekstil'shchiki

Rechnoy vokzal
(Rechnoy Station)

115

Moscow Central

1000 m / 1100 yards

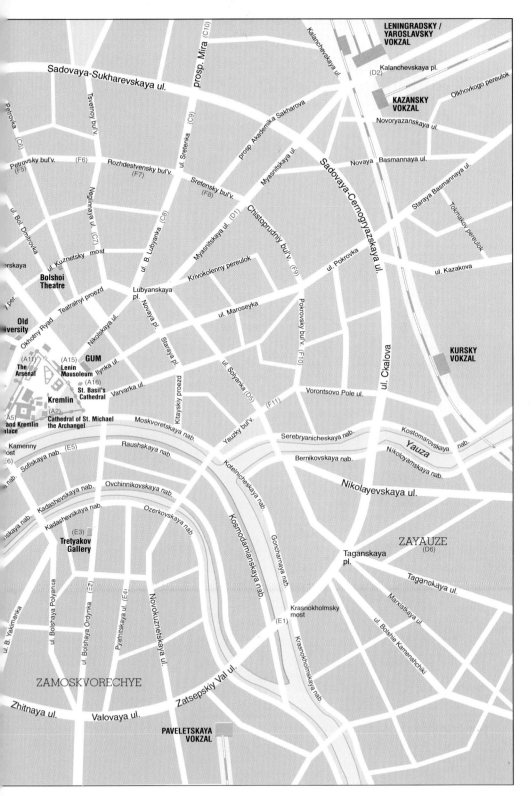

GETTING YOUR BEARINGS

Making your acquaintance with a new city is always both exciting and difficult – even more so when that city is the centre of a multinational country and one that encloses an incredible wealth of history within its walls but which is also torn by contradictions.

The desire to learn about all the joys and delights of the unknown is tempered by the strangeness of the city and the absence of habitual associations. Some people prefer to plunge headlong into the sea of novel experiences. Others, by contrast, take it gradually, step by step, prolonging the pleasure.

At first sight everything in this capital of the first workers' and peasants' state will probably strike you as strange and even, perhaps, frustrating.

Splendour in the muddle: Alongside the architectural splendour which makes Moscow a hub for fans of baroque architecture and 19th-century town planning, there are untidy roads; hotels still lack the comforts you would expect for your money; and there are not many cafés and restaurants offering the choice of dishes, the quality of food and the standard of service to which most foreigners are accustomed. Add to this a picture of residents who are perpetually worried about something and who rush single-mindedly about their various businesses.

And yet, you should not jump to conclusions. If you look at the city from a different angle, it will probably appear less unfamiliar, just as the apparent mess in your neighbour's home does not necessarily mean that your neighbour regards it as any kind of disorder.

The reappearance of old values: For fairness' sake you have to see that sorting out today's chaos is no easy task for the leaders of this multinational country. One day the problems that had been piling up for many years suddenly made themselves felt and swept through every sphere of economic and political life. The numerous opinions and many recipes for salvation are as contradictory as they are varied. There is only one thing about which everyone agrees: namely, that this is no way to continue, not any longer.

Moscow, with its democratically elected local government, is undergoing profound change. While concentrating on making life easier for its inhabitants the city authorities are also helping to unveil the hidden splendours of the ancient city. The old street names have reappeared and churches are being restored and reconsecrated. Slowly, the wonderful atmosphere, that was so unforgettably described by the great poets and writers, and that once made Moscow not only a centre of power but also a centre of western culture, is re-emerging.

For the time being, however, problems are in store for the capital of this once-powerful empire. The demise of Communism and the introduction of market forces have brought a number of chronic problems in their wake. Although food shortages are a thing of the

past, prices now far outstrip the wages of the average Muscovite. Spiralling inflation, unemployment, rising crime levels and a catastrophic collapse of the welfare system (including the health service) will probably trouble the city for many years to come.

Today, you often hear people saying that life in Moscow is not hard at all if you have enough money in your pocket. A foreigner coming to Moscow on a tourist visit will not be confronted with all the problems of this transitional period. They cannot, however, be avoided altogether, and you might even find yourself confronting them on arrival at Sheremetyevo-II, Moscow's International Airport.

Arriving: What awaits the traveller during his or her first meeting with the capital of Russia? Sensational reports in the newspapers and on television may lead you to expect a squad of trigger-happy militia men armed with sub-machine-guns. Alternatively an ocean of charming Moscow brides eager to fall in love with every foreigner who comes along. The truth is much more prosaic. Having received your luggage and experienced your first long queue at passport and customs control, you will at last get an opportunity to take a deep breath of the not very clean, yet highly distinctive, Moscow air. They say that every city has its own smell. This is certainly true of Moscow.

When Sheremetyevo-II Airport was built back in 1979, it was regarded as a showcase for the country. Even those few Muscovites who had had the opportunity to see a good deal of the world considered it to be a wonder of modern architecture. Today, however, when it is not only the select few who fly abroad, it is evident that the airport is much too small and that it is already congested, although only 15,000 passengers pass through it each day.

Located not far away is another terminal, Sheremetyevo-I, a typical Russian domestic airport. You will have to pass through it if you fly to St Petersburg or to

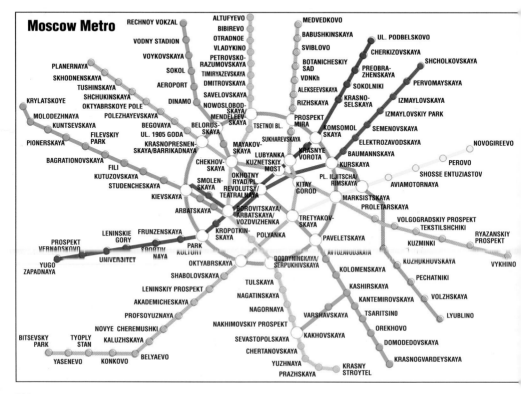

one of the cities in the Baltic republics. (Sheremetyevo is named after the former estate of the Counts Sheremetev.)

The transfer from the airport to one of the Moscow hotels in an Intourist car or bus will take about 30 to 50 minutes.

Your first tour: The first thing that strikes you when you join the main artery, the **Leningrad (St Petersburg) Highway** is a memorial in the form of a group of enormous anti-tank "hedgehogs" on your right-hand side. It was here that the Soviet counter-offensive that repulsed the Nazis from the Moscow environs began in the winter of 1941. What was then open fields is now covered by apartment blocks.

Lying ahead is a small suburban town, **Khimki**, conspicuous for nothing in particular, that stretches as far as **Moscow's Circular Road**. This is the first, and the longest, of five rings circling the city centre and running for 109 km (68 miles) around the city. Built in 1962, it was a kind of city boundary until quite recently. Today, several new districts situated beyond the road have been incorporated into the city.

The Leningrad Highway, as its name suggests, is the main thoroughfare linking Moscow with St Petersburg. Built in 1713 and having undergone a couple of name changes since, it remains the straightest and shortest road connecting the two capitals of the Russian state.

A port of five seas: On the right-hand side you can see the **Khimki Reservoir** with its own rowing canal, where the water sports facilities of a number of sports clubs and societies are located. From a distance, a tall spire glittering in the sun and topped with a gilt star can be seen towering over the greenery of a public garden. It marks the **Northern River Port**. Before 1937 the star adorned the Spasskaya Tower of the Moscow Kremlin. The facade of the port building spans 350 metres/1,150 feet. The central building resembles a three-decked ship with a captain's bridge, a mast, and anchors.

From here, modern ships and barges

The roads have become congested, creating problems for traffic cops.

go to Astrakhan, Rostov-on-Don, St Petersburg, Volgograd, Nizhny Novgorod, Ufa, and many other Russian cities. The building commands a fine view of a unique water development, the **Moscow Canal**. Built in 1937, it links the city with the waters of the Volga River, and since 1953, with the Don, thus making Moscow a port for five seas – the White Sea, the Baltic, the Caspian, the Sea of Azov, and the Black Sea.

When entering the flyover near the Voikovskaya Metro Station, you will see a curious sight. On either side of the flyover are hundreds of trolleybuses – one of the main means of public transport – in an open-air trolleybus yard. In Moscow there are about 70 trolleybus routes whose total length is in excess of 1,000 km(630 miles).

Next on the left-hand side of the Highway are the buildings of the Moscow Aviation Institute where the various types of Russian aircraft are designed. However strange this may seem, this highly popular college has also turned out quite a few talented writers, journalists, artists, actors and even diplomats.

The building with a colonnade houses an industrial art school, training students in various genres from folk to applied art. Ahead is a square where the road forks: it is the starting point of the Volokolamsk Highway. In the centre of the square is the 27-storey tower of the **Gidroproyekt Institute**, responsible for all water engineering in the country. It was here that Promethean programmes like the project to divert the rivers of Siberia to the arid regions of Central Asia was conceived (fortunately the plan was thrown out).

A village in the city: The high-rise buildings on your right-hand side hide from view a rather unusual residential district consisting of one and two-storey houses. They were built to look like traditional Russian peasant log cabins, each with a large plot of land but provided with every modern amenity. These are the houses of the **Sokol experimental housing co-operative**, built in the 1930s.

Moscow is still a city of readers.

The very idea of providing people with individual houses in the era of collectivisation comes as a surprise.

The streets in the settlement are named after celebrated artists such as Surikov, Polenov, Kiprensky, Shishkin, and Venetsianov. From the late 1940s to the early 1950s, the entire area round the Sokol Metro Station was a kind of proving ground for new construction methods.

On the same side of the thoroughfare, at 71 Leningradsky Prospekt, is the highly popular **Prokrovsky Chamber Music Theatre**.

The building at 37 Leningradsky Prospekt, also to your right, is the **Moscow City Air Terminal**, built in 1960. From here passengers are transported by express coaches to the various airports round Moscow – to Vnukovo, Sheremetyevo I and II, Domodedovo, and Bykovo. Many of the streets in this area, which was formerly known as Khodynskoye Field, are named after noted airmen and cosmonauts. On 18 May 1896, celebrations were organised here on the occasion of the coronation of Nicholas II. A great crowd gathered to enjoy themselves but during the distribution of royal gifts some 1,400 people were crushed to death in the frantic throng.

On the other side of the avenue stands the building of the **Zhukovsky Military Aviation Engineering Academy** with a semi-circular red brick wall and graceful turrets. The Academy occupies the former Petrovsky (Peter the Great's) Palace built by the architect Matvey Kazakov in 1775–82. Here, the imperial family would rest before entering Moscow on their way from St Petersburg.

Sports Avenue: Located along Leningradsky Prospekt are three large stadiums and numerous sports complexes. To your right you can see the sports complex of the **Russian Army Central Sports Club** and then, on the opposite side near Dynamo Metro Station, the **Dynamo sports complex** built in 1928. The Dynamo Sports Society, the oldest in this country, was established in 1923

Spring's first sun on Red Square.

on the initiative of the head of the Russian secret police, Felix Dzerzhinsky. Farther along on your right is yet another sports complex, the **Krylya Sovetov (Soviet's Wings) Sports Palace**.

On the same side of Leningradsky Prospekt, at the crossing with Begovaya Ulitsa, is the **Young Pioneers' Stadium**, opened in 1920. It is the country's biggest training ground for young athletes.

Beyond Begovaya Ulitsa, in Khodynskoye Field, is the **Hippodrome**. It is adorned with bronze figures of horses by the sculptor Pyotr Klodt and was built at the end of the 19th century with funds provided by the Racing Society. The Hippodrome is a venue for both national and international horse and trotting races. On weekends both Muscovites and visitors who are fond of equestrian sports and those not averse to some betting come here to root for their favourites.

At the intersection with Raskovoy Ulitsa stood one of the most popular turn-of-the-century Moscow restaurants, the **Yar**. Famous for its Gypsy choir, it was a favourite haunt of the city's gilded youth at the time.

The building, completed in 1910, was subsequently rebuilt on more than one occasion and finally, in 1950, became part of the **Sovetskaya Hotel**. In the 1960s, the Sovremennik (Contemporary) Studio Theatre gave performances in the hotel's concert hall. Today, it houses the **Roman Gypsy Theatre**, founded in 1931. Thus, the Sovetskaya Hotel continues the tradition of the Yar restaurant.

Where the "truth" is printed: A little further to your left you will see Pravdy (Truth) Ulitsa branching off from the thoroughfare. It is named after the **Pravda Publishing House** and Printing Works. *Pravda*, the bankrupt mouthpiece of the Soviet Communist Party, now appears in more liberal form and, together with *Izvestia*, it remains an important national daily newspaper.

After Ploshchad Tverskoy Zastavy, the Leningradsky Prospekt becomes Tverskaya Ulitsa and continues to the city centre.

A day out in Revolution Square.

FOOD

Moscow's restaurants, having been transformed by the market economy and the power of foreign currency, are daring to experiment. They use mushrooms (*gribi*) and Siberian cranberries (*klukvi*), for example, to make interesting sauces. Others specialise in the tastier foods of the former Soviet republics, such as spicy Georgian cuisine. Former client states are well represented too – restaurants feature the food of North Korea, Vietnam and China. Foreign firms have opened joint-venture restaurants offering Western cleanliness, comfort, food and service – at a price.

The one truly gourmet food is genuine black caviar (*ikra* in Russian). With traders now selling openly on the streets, a 4-oz. (113-gram) glass jar of Beluga sturgeon eggs is affordable. (Be sure it's viscous, wet and black, not brown or dried up.) In rouble restaurants, caviar is also inexpensive, and especially delicious served on thin pancakes known as *blini*. Red caviar (*krasnaya ikra* instead of *chornaya ikra* or black caviar) is also good. Restaurants occasionally offer canned crab (*krabi*) or shrimp (*krevetki*) from the Soviet Far East.

Russians also do wonderful things with their immense variety of mushrooms. Families go mushrooming in the woods for weekend outings. One popular dish is *julienne* (in Russian, *zhulienn*), a tiny casserole of mushrooms and sour cream served in individual metal dishes.

All of these are found on the *zakuski* or *hors d'oeuvre* section of the menu, and the most expensive private restaurants will have them waiting on the table when clients arrive. Other *zakuski* include slices of sturgeon or fatty sausage. *Salat* might be a dish of tomatoes or cucumbers, but for greens there's *travi* (literally, "grass") and in reality fresh basil, dill and green onions. Lettuce is unknown.

Main courses are likely to be *kotlcti* (ground meat patties) or *bif-shtek* (beef), *svinina* (pork), or just plain *myaso* (meat of indeterminate origin). Chicken can be *tsiplyonok* or *kuritsa* but beware: foreigners joke that the Russian method of slaughtering poultry is starvation.

One reason Muscovites traditionally put up with poor food in a restaurant is because the main point of going there in the first place was to get drunk. Among Russians, drinking is a major form of social bonding, especially among men. A good restaurant, therefore, is one where the white table-cloths are covered in bottles in preparation. Top-quality Stolichnaya vodka is widely available (locals always check to make sure the cap is still factory-sealed in case they end up with an expensive bottle of rubbing alcohol). Russian champagne (*shampanskoye*) is also excellent, as long as the drinker is not expecting the subtlety of the French variety. *Konyak* is the Russian word for brandy, and the ones from the former Soviet republics of Armenia or Georgia which have been aged for 10 years or more have a fine smooth flavour.

For a good and authentic meal, there's little to beat getting invited to someone's home. Despite food shortages and high prices, Russian generosity blossoms when there is a guest for dinner. Be prepared to stuff yourself, and then discover that there are three or more courses yet to come. The names of the dishes may be the same as on a restaurant menu – ravioli-like *pelmeni* (stuffed cabbage leaves), *pirozhki* (deep-fried parcels of meat, rice or potato) and pots of meat-and-potato stew – but there's no comparison. Russian housewives know all the tricks for plucking a feast out of a bare pantry, and they always have something set aside for a special occasion.

Be sure you bring flowers for the hostess, but never an even number of blooms – an omen for a death in the family. Hosts also appreciate a gift of Western food or drink – these items are still exotic in spite of their increased availability. Try whisky, Swiss chocolates or something really practical like a canned ham. ∎

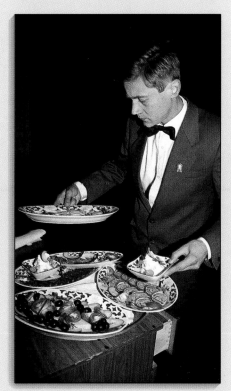

An Uzbekistan restaurant on Neglinnaya Ulitsa.

THE KREMLIN

"The Kremlin sits high on a hill like the crown of sovereignty on the brow of an awesome ruler", wrote Russia's great poet Lermontov back in 1833. His impression is as valid today as it was then.

The Kremlin rises 25 metres (82 ft) on **Borovitsky Hill** and is traditionally regarded as the inviolate nucleus of Moscow. Muscovites sometimes dub their city the Third Rome, for Moscow, just as the great city of Rome, was also built on seven hills, though the grand dukes of Moscow didn't think of Rome – they considered themselves to be the inheritors of Byzantium's glory.

The ensemble of the Moscow Kremlin developed over many centuries. In the days of Dimitry Donskoy, in the 14th century, the original oak walls and towers were replaced by white-stone. In the 15th century, during the reign of Ivan III, the present walls of red brick were built under the supervision of the Italian architects Marco Ruffo and Pietro Antonio Solari.

The Kremlin wall, which forms an irregular triangle when seen from above, is 2,235 metres (7,300 ft) long, from 3.5 metres (11½ ft) to 6.5 metres (21 ft) thick and from 5 metres (16.5 ft) to 19 metres (62 ft) high. Above the crenelated walls with bifurcated merlons are 19 elegant towers – 18 battle towers and the graceful tent-shaped **Tsarskaya Bashnya (Tsar's Tower)** – four of which have entrances.

Opposite the **Troitskaya (Trinity) Tower** is another, smaller one, the **Kutafya Tower**, built in the early 1500s as a bridgehead watch-tower. Connected with the Troitskaya Tower by the **Troitsky Bridge**, it has long been one of the official entrances to the Kremlin, used by Moscow tsars and by Napoleon.

Kremlin, meaning "citadel" in Old Russian, supposedly derives from an Old Slavonic word denoting a fortified place. The principal stone structures, such as the **Palace of Facets**, the central cathedrals and a number of service buildings, were erected over a brief period from the late 15th to the early 16th centuries.

Stars replaced the eagles: Until 1935, five of the Kremlin towers were topped with double-headed eagles – symbols of tsarist autocracy. Eventually they were taken down and gilt stars were put up in their place. In 1937 they were replaced by stars faced in three-layer ruby glass. They are mounted on swivels so as to turn sideways into the wind.

The round corner tower on the far left (looking from across the Moskva River) is called the **Vodovzvodnaya (Water) Tower**. The name dates back to 1633, when devices for raising water were installed and the first pressure water supply in Russia was used to carry water to the royal palaces and gardens.

Standing in the middle of the south wall is the **Taynitskaya Tower (Tower of Secrets)**. The name of the tower comes from the secret well that was

Preceding pages: the Saviours Tower.

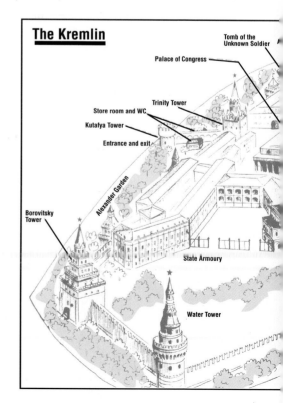

The Kremlin

Tomb of the Unknown Soldier

Palace of Congress

Trinity Tower

Store room and WC

Kutafya Tower

Entrance and exit

Alexander Garden

Borovitsky Tower

State Armoury

Water Tower

hidden inside it. At one time the Tower of Secrets had great strategic significance and a supplementary fortification was attached to it with entrance gates and an underground passage to the river.

Immediately beyond the **Moscow River Tower**, which stands at the southeast corner, is the **Konstantino-Yeleninskaya (St Constantine and Helena) Tower**. It was popularly known in the days of old as the **Torture Tower**, because of the torture chamber inside.

Not far from it is the **Tsarskaya Tower**, the youngest in the Kremlin. To be precise, it is not really a tower but a stone turret placed on the wall. In olden times a wooden tower stood here, from which, as legend has it, the young Ivan the Terrible watched executions in Red Square; hence its name, the Little Tsar's Tower.

The corner **Borovitskaya Tower** stands at the foot of Borovitsky Hill, where the Kremlin arose. The name comes from a pinewood (*bor*), which once covered the whole hill upon which

Yury Dolgorukiy founded his fortress. This tower differs from the others by its gradational form.

Cathedral Square: In the days of old, the central streets of Moscow such as Borovitskaya, Troitskaya and Nikolskaya streets converged in Cathedral Square. It is here that the oldest Kremlin structures are located.

The imposing building in the center of the square is the white-stone **Cathedral of the Assumption**, (*Uspensky Sobor*, also called Cathedral of the Dormition). It was built on the site of a 14th-century church of that name. In 1474 the unfinished walls and vaults of a new cathedral collapsed, apparently because the weakness of the mortar was aggravated by an earthquake.

The following year, the Italian architect Aristotile Fioravanti was commissioned to build a new cathedral which was completed in 1479. This was no easy task; it involved the skilful combination of the traditions of Old Russian architecture with Italian building tech-

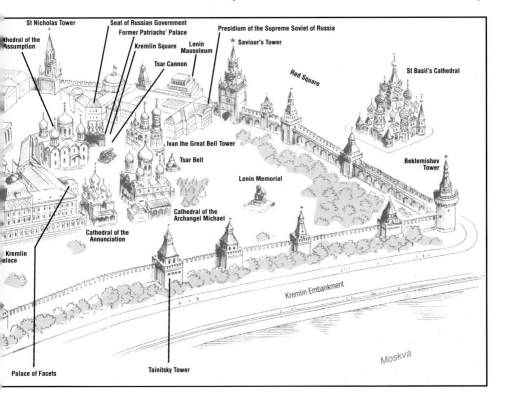

St Nicholas Tower

Cathedral of the Assumption

Seat of Russian Government
Former Patriachs' Palace

Kremlin Square

Lenin Mausoleum

Tsar Cannon

Presidium of the Supreme Soviet of Russia

Saviour's Tower

Red Square

St Basil's Cathedral

Ivan the Great Bell Tower

Tsar Bell

Lenin Memorial

Beklemishev Tower

Cathedral of the Archangel Michael

Cathedral of the Annunciation

Kremlin Palace

Palace of Facets

Tainitsky Tower

Kremlin Embankment

Moskva

niques. Before starting work, Fioravanti visited Vladimir and Novgorod and thoroughly studied the architecture of Old Russian cathedrals. He decided to build the vaults and drums of the cathedral from brick made to his own formula, which he believed to be stronger than stone. Five years of careful and steady effort resulted in the emergence of a majestic cathedral crowned with five gilt domes.

The throne of Monomakh: The cathedral contains many fine examples of Old Russian applied art. Among them is the southern door, known as the **Korsun Door**, which was made in 1405 for the Dormition Cathedral in Suzdal. This oak door is covered with copper sheets on which you can see 20 Biblical scenes and inscriptions in Old Slavonic made in gold on black lacquer.

Next to it is the **Throne of Monomakh**. Twelve carvings depict the Grand Prince Vladimir Manomakh (1113–25) receiving the "Crown of Monomakh" from the Byzantine Emperor Constantine IX Manomachus. This throne, made for Ivan IV (the Terrible) in 1551, supports the claim that Moscow is the heir to Byzantium.

The amazingly spacious interior is decorated with beautiful frescoes. Most of these were executed by the famous Russian artist Dionysius in 1514 but some date from a later period. There is also a collection of unique icons including a copy of the **Vladimir Icon of the Mother of God** (11th/12th centuries – the original is in the Tretyakov Gallery) and the **Trinity** (14th century).

The Cathedral of St Michael the Archangel: Near the southern wall of the Kremlin, to the east of the Assumption Cathedral, is the Cathedral of St Michael the Archangel (*Arkhangelsky Sobor*), which was built between 1505 and 1508 under the direction of another Italian architect, Alevisio Novy. This cathedral was the burial place of Moscow's grand dukes and tsars. Here again you can see the result of combining the techniques characteristic of Old Russian

The Cathedral of the Assumption.

buildings with elements of the architecture of the Italian Renaissance. Of exceptional interest is the interior of the cathedral with its 18th-century carved gilt iconostasis and its frescoes painted by masters of the Armoury under the supervision of Simon Ushakov in the mid-17th century. The wall paintings include over 60 so-called *parsunas*, stylised portraits of historical personalities buried in the cathedral.

Under the cathedral vaults are 46 tombs, including those of grand dukes Ivan Kalita, Dimitry Donskoy and Ivan III, and of the Tsars Ivan the Terrible and Mikhail and Alexei Romanov. Among the portraits painted on the columns are those of grand dukes Yaroslav Vsevolodovich and Alexander Nevsky.

The Bell Tower of Ivan the Great: On the eastern side of Cathedral Square is an architectural complex which includes the Bell Tower of Ivan the Great, a campanile and the Filaret Annex. In 1329, Ivan Kalita built the Church of St John Climacus on the site of the present

bell tower. Two centuries later when the church fell into disrepair and was pulled down, a new two-storey church, which formed the basis of today's bell tower, was erected in its place. In the mid-16th century the Italian architect Petrok Maly built a five-storey campanile for the large bells on its northern side.

In the late 16th century Tsar Boris Godunov decided to build a new great church in Moscow. Still another tier crowned with a gilt dome was added to the bell tower. A quarter of a century later the master builder Bazhen Ogurtsov erected a four-storey belfry with a hipped roof, the **Filaret Annex**, on the northern side of the campanile. In the 19th century still another addition was made to the ensemble: the **Dormition Bell**, weighing more than 70 tons, was hung in the central opening of the campanile.

When completed, the bell tower reached a height of 81 metres/266 ft. The enormous structure rests on wooden piles, each no longer than 1.5 metres (5 ft) and 25 cm (10 in) in diameter. De-

<u>Below</u>, the Cathedral of St Michael the Archangel. <u>Right</u>, the Bell Tower of Ivan the Great.

spite their seeming fragility, they have been excellently coping with their task to this day.

According to historians, Boris Godunov prohibited, under pain of severe punishment, the building of any bell tower, higher than his creation in the Kremlin.

The Cathedral of the Annunciation: On the western side of Cathedral Square stands the **Cathedral of the Annunciation**, built of brick by master builders from Moscow and Pskov in 1484 to 1489. The cathedral served as the domestic chapel of Moscow's grand dukes and tsars. The floor of the cathedral is faced in jasper.

Its iconostasis, with icons painted by Theophanes the Greek, Prokhor of Gorodets and Andrei Rublev as early as 1405, is of exceptional artistic and historical value. The frescoes on its walls were executed by Feodosi, the son of Dionysius. In the 16th century, a high white-stone porch was added to the cathedral specially for Ivan the Terrible.

Initially the cathedral had three domes. During its reconstruction in the mid-17th century, another six domes were added.

The Grand Kremlin Palace: Immediately to the west of the Cathedral of the Annunciation stretches a great palace with a high wrought-iron fence along the southern wall of the Kremlin. This three-storey building with carved white-stone platbands round the windows is the Grand Kremlin Palace. It was built between 1838 and 1849 in neo-Russian style by the architect Konstantin Ton on the site of an older palace damaged by the great fire of 1812. This palace was the Moscow residence of the Russian emperors. The ensemble of the palace includes 15th to 16th-century chambers, royal private suites and a winter garden.

The largest hall in the palace has a seating capacity of approximately 2,500 and is used for large assemblies and political meetings. It was built in the 1930s by combining the former **Alexan-**

Left, construction of the Bell Tower. Below, the Cathedral of the Annunciation.

drovsky (**St Alexander**) and **Andrey-evsky (St Andrew) Halls**. The first congresses of the Communist International were held here.

The second largest hall in the Kremlin is the ceremonial **Georgievsky Hall**, named after St George the Victorious. The hall is richly ornamented with stucco moulding and 18 convoluted zinc columns, each supporting a statue of Victory crowned with a laurel wreath, sculpted by Giovanni Vitali.

In the tall niches along the walls are marble slabs engraved in gold with the names of units that distinguished themselves in battle, and of officers and men awarded the Order of St George. Today the Georgievsky Hall is used for state receptions and official ceremonies.

During the revolution and the Civil War, a priceless collection of paintings evacuated from the Hermitage was kept in the cellars of the Grand Kremlin Palace. In the 1920s the collection was returned to St Petersburg. The octagonal **Vladimirsky (St Vladimir) Hall**

In the Palace of Facets.

connects the Grand Kremlin Palace with a building dating to the 16th and 17th centuries.

The Palace of Facets: Next to the Cathedral of the Annunciation and adjoining the Grand Kremlin Palace is the Palace of Facets, one of the oldest buildings of the Moscow Kremlin. Its facade, finished in faceted white stone, overlooks Cathedral Square. The palace was built by the Italian architects Marco Ruffo and Pietro Antonio Solari between 1487 and 1491.

In days of old, the Palace of Facets was the place where the *Boyar Duma*, the main legislative body of Russia, held its sessions. It was also here that foreign ambassadors were received and victories celebrated. Today the palace is occasionally used for sessions of the country's supreme bodies of state power and, as before, for state receptions.

The interior of the palace is decorated in traditional Russian style. Its spacious square hall is 9 metres (30 ft) high, has an area of some 500 sq. metres (5,389

sq. ft) and is covered by four cruciform vaults supported by a central pillar. In the 1890s, the Belousov brothers, masters from Palekh (a village renowned for its distinctive paintings), reproduced on the walls and the vault subjects taken from the 16th-century murals that originally covered the walls of the palace. They followed an exact description left by the famous Russian icon painter Simon Ushakov. The ceremonial Red Staircase outside the palace was rebuilt in 1994.

The Terem Palace: Adjoining the Palace of Facets is the Terem Palace. This multi-storey structure incorporates part of a 16th-century palace. The palatial ensemble includes the **Church of the Nativity of the Virgin-over-the-Vestibule** whose side chapel is the **Church of the Resurrection of Lazarus** (late 14th century), the oldest building to have survived in the Kremlin. Very close to it is the **Upper Cathedral of the Saviour**; its frieze and the drums of its 11 domes are decorated with multi-

coloured tiles. In 1680 they were all united by a single roof. Adjoining the Upper Cathedral of the Saviour is the 16th-century **Lesser Golden Chamber**, thus named from the decor of its interior, featuring ornaments covered with gold leaf.

Standing next to the Terem Palace is the single domed **Church of the Deposition of the Robe**, built in the late 15th century by master builders from Pskov as a domestic chapel for Moscow metropolitans. The frescoes in this church were executed by Sidor Osipov and Ivan Borisov.

The Kremlin Palace of Congresses: Wedged in between the Patriarch's Chambers and the Armoury is a monolithic block of concrete and glass, the Kremlin Palace of Congresses. It was built in 1961 by a group of architects headed by Mikhail Posokhin. A feature of the Palace of Congresses is that it is sunk some 15 metres (50 ft) into the ground so as not to impede views of the surrounding buildings. It has about 800 rooms, including a huge auditorium that seats 6,000 people. During archaeological excavations, the white-stone chambers of Natalia Naryshkina, the mother of Peter the Great, and, even before that, in the 14th century, the palace of Sophia Paleologos, the wife of Ivan III, were found on this site.

The Armoury: Standing along the western wall of the Kremlin is the Armoury, the oldest museum in Moscow. The emergence of the Armoury as a depository for Moscow's grand dukes and tsars dates back to the 16th century. The Armoury owes its name to the fact that it was once the Kremlin workshops which manufactured, purchased and stored weapons, jewellery and articles used in the palace.

The Armoury was transformed into a public museum at the start of the 19th century. Today's Armoury was constructed in 1844–51 by Konstantin Ton and Nikolai Chichagov.

The Collection: The celebrated Armoury collection is arranged chrono-

Iconostasis in the Cathedral of St Michael the Archangel.

logically and is spread over two floors.

Pride of place among the jewellery in room 1 belongs to the Ryazan treasure, an enormous hoard of golden bracelets, earrings and rings, all from the 12th century.

The second room has a stunning exhibition of Russian gold and silverwork from the 17th century – the icon covers in particular are magnificent. Room 2 is also famous for its jewellery from the house of Fabergé. It includes a tiny replica of the cruiser, *Pamyat Azova*, on which Nicholas II sailed to Japan just prior to becoming tsar.

Rooms 3 and 4 have a comprehensive display of Russian and European armour and cut-and-thrust weapons, dating mainly from the 16th and 17th centuries. The oldest exhibit here is the iron helmet of Yaroslav, the father of Alexander Nevsky, which was discovered on the site of a medieval battlefield in 1808.

By the 17th century, Russia was a fully integrated member of the network of European trading nations. Merchants and diplomats from as far afield as England and Persia came to Moscow where they presented the tsar with tokens of their governments' good faith. These presents (exhibited in room 5) included beautifully crafted gold and silver plate, the most outstanding examples of which were manufactured in Augsburg.

Room 6 has a priceless collection of religious vestments and other sacred objects. The silk robe, embroidered for the Patriarch Nikon in 1654, weighs more than 24 kilograms (53 pounds) owing to the precious gems and pearls with which it is studded. There is also a remarkable collection of royal wedding and coronation dresses here, among them the robes worn by the Empress Alexandra at the last imperial coronation in 1896.

Thrones and imperial regalia are on show in room 7. More than 2,000 precious gems adorn the throne presented to Tsar Boris Godunov by the Shah of Persia in 1604 – the arms and back are covered with turquoises and gold leaf.

The 13th-century Monomakh crown in the Armoury.

From a historical perspective, however, the most important item is the sable-trimmed Crown of Monomakh, dating from the late 13th century and used in all coronations until 1682.

The tsars' stables are the basis for the collection in room 8 of saddles and richly decorated harnesses used on ceremonial occasions.

The parade of carriages in room 9 is one of the finest in the world. The oldest was presented by King James I of England to Boris Godunov in 1603.

Also housed in the Armoury is a remarkable exhibition: the Russian Diamond Fund, which contains some of the finest diamonds in the world.

The Diamond Fund Exhibition: Seven legendary gems are the pride of the Russian Diamond Fund, which was brought to Moscow from St Petersburg soon after the outbreak of World War I.

The largest of the seven, the **Orlov** diamond, was brought to Russia from India. Count Orlov presented it to Catherine the Great on her name day in 1773 and, to show her gratitude, the empress named it after him. In 1914 the gem fell out of the mounting on Nicholas II's sceptre. This accident made it possible to measure the weight of the diamond: it was 189.62 carats.

Ivan the Great's Square: To the east of Cathedral Square is Ivan the Great's Square. In days of old it was a place where the tsar's *ukases* (orders) were announced and it was always crowded with people. Because of the incredible noise, the criers often had to shout at the top of their voice. This gave rise to the Russian phrase "to cry for all of Ivan Square to hear".

A gun that never fired, a bell that never rang: The famous **Tsar Bell**, cast from bronze in 1733–35 by Ivan Motorin and his son Mikhail here in the Kremlin, is displayed in the square. The bell was intended for the Bell Tower of Ivan the Great. During the Great Fire of 1737 the bell was still lying in its casting pit and attempts to extinguish the fire led to water falling on the red-hot bronze. The

Left, the Tsar's Cannon. **Below**, the Tsar's Bell.

result was that an 11-ton chunk fell off the bell. In 1836 the bell was raised from the pit and put on a special pedestal. It weighs over 200 tons.

Not far from the Tsar Bell, also on a special pedestal, stands the no less famous **Tsar Cannon**, the largest artillery piece of the period. It was cast by Andrei Chokov in 1586. This formidable gun has a bore of 890 mm (35 in) and weighs 40 tons. The gun was never fired, just as the bell was never rung.

Behind the cannon is a five-domed building, the **Cathedral of the Twelve Apostles** (*Sobor Dvenadtsati Apostolov*). It forms a long structure with the **Patriarch's Palace** (*Patriarshiye Palaty*) which houses the **Museum of 17th-Century Life and Applied Art**.

To the southeast of Ivan the Great's Square at the foot of the hill stretches the **Tainitsky Garden**. Situated here were the Monasteries of St Michael's Miracle at Chonae and the Monastery of the Resurrection. They were badly damaged during the artillery bombardment of the Kremlin by revolutionary troops in October 1917. Later on, they were pulled down.

The Arsenal: The Arsenal occupies the northern corner of the Kremlin. It was built on the order of Peter the Great in 1701 for the storage of weapons and as a museum of military trophies. After the fire of 1737, the Arsenal had to be rebuilt. In 1812, Napoleon's retreating troops blew the building up and it was only in the 1830s that it was restored. Playing a significant role in its restoration was the celebrated architect Osip Bove. Along the southern facade of the Arsenal are cannons captured by the Russian troops from Napoleon's Grand Army.

The Senate: South of the Arsenal is the former Senate, built in 1776–87 by Matvey Kazakov. It was intended to house two departments of the Senate, the Judicial Department and the Department of the Nobility, which was transferred from St Petersburg to Moscow. After the Soviet government headed by

The Arsenal.

Lenin moved to Moscow in March 1918, the government and Bolshevik Party leaders took up residence in this building. In the spring of 1919 the red flag of the Soviet Republic was raised above its huge dome. Lenin was given a flat in the Senate building and it was here that he lived and worked from March 1918 to May 1923. **Lenin's flat-museum** was dismantled on the orders of President Yeltsin in 1995.

Standing next to this building, close to the Kremlin wall, is the **Amusements Palace** built for the Boyar Miloslavsky in 1651. It was named thus because entertainments for the court members were staged in it.

The Presidential Residence: Near the Senate is another building, the former Presidium of the Supreme Soviet, which with its yellowy-white walls, green roof, portico and facade looks as though it dates from the reign of Catherine the Great. Yet it was in fact built between 1932–34 by von Röhrberg on the site of the Small Nicholas Palace and the Mon-

astery of the Miracles. It is now the official residence of the State President.

The Alexandrovsky Gardens: On leaving the Kremlin by way of the Trinity Gate, you will find yourself in the Alexandrovsky Gardens laid out in the early 1820s above the covered channel of the Neglinka river. In the early 18th century Peter the Great ordered earthen bastions to be put up around the Kremlin. The Neglinka river was thus channelled into a special moat. Later, during the reign of Catherine the Great, the scheme was extended and practically the whole of the Neglinka river was piped underground.

Near the **Middle Arsenal Tower** at the foot of the Kremlin wall is a somewhat unusual structure reminiscent of the ruins of an ancient Greek temple. This is a grotto named **Ruins**, a typical example of 19th-century park and garden architecture, built by Osip Bove in 1821.

Opposite the grotto, beside the central alley, stands a light grey obelisk. Originally set up in 1913 to commemorate the 300th anniversary of the House of Romanov, the obelisk was crowned with a double-headed eagle. After the revolution, the eagle was removed and the names of the tsars were erased from the obelisk and replaced with the names of Marx, Engels, Plekhanov and other Communist theoreticians. This, the first monument of revolutionary Russia, was unveiled in 1918.

Behind the fence, at the foot of the Kremlin wall, is a low structure of red granite and black marble with an eternal flame burning in its centre. This is the **Tomb of the Unknown Soldier**. In 1966 the remains of an unknown soldier, who died during the battle with the Nazis on the approaches to Moscow, were brought here from the common grave at the 41st kilometre on the St Petersburg Highway and ceremonially buried by the Kremlin wall. It has become a custom for newly married couples to lay a bouquet of flowers on the tomb after their wedding ceremony.

Left, newlyweds often lay flowers on the Tomb of the Unknown Soldier. **Right**, Ivan the Great's Bell Tower and the Cathedral of the Annunciation.

RED SQUARE

Having passed the gently sloping cobblestone **Istorichesky Passazh**, you will reach the main square of the capital, **Red Square** (*Krasnaya Ploshchad*). It did not always bear this name. Before the 15th century, it was a market centre called *Veliky Torg* (Great Marketplace). After the fire of 1403, which destroyed more than half the wooden structures in the square, it was called *Pozhar* (Fire Site).

Only in the mid-17th century, when official ceremonies began to be held here and the *ukases* (decrees) of the tsar were announced at the southern end, was it given its present name. At that time, the square was adorned with new stone structures while tall, hipped roofs were added to the Kremlin towers. People began to call the square *Krasnaya*, which then meant beautiful as well as red.

Facing the square is one of the most beautiful Kremlin towers, the **Spasskaya (Saviour) Tower**. Its gate is the main one in the Kremlin. The tower was built in 1491 to the design of Pietro Antonio Solari. The first clock was installed in it in the late 15th and early 16th centuries. The clock that adorns the tower today was made in the mid-19th century by the Vutenop brothers. During the October 1917 uprising, the clock was damaged by a shell and, on Lenin's instructions, was repaired by the clockmaker N. Behrens. The Spasskaya Tower was once regarded as holy, and everyone, even the tsar, had to remove their hat when passing through.

Where Napoleon lost his hat: According to the chronicles, in 1812 Napoleon, elated by his victory, decided to enter the Kremlin on his white horse through the Spasskaya Gate. He did not bother to take off his general's hat. As he was riding under the arch his horse, suddenly startled, reared; Napoleon lost his hat and very nearly fell off his horse. After that the belief that the tower really was holy became even more firmly established in peoples' minds.

Along the Kremlin wall to the right

and left of the **Senatskaya (Senate) Tower** is the burial place of prominent statesmen and public figures of the Soviet period. The proletarian writer **Maxim Gorky**, Lenin's wife **Nadezhda Krupskaya**, the first Soviet cosmonaut **Yuri Gagarin**, and the inventor of the Soviet atomic bomb, **Igor Kurchatov**, lie buried here. A number of noted military commanders and the "father of all peoples", **Josef Stalin**, are also buried here. Stalin's embalmed body was transferred here from the Mausoleum, having lain for several years alongside Lenin.

Lenin's uncertain future: The body of **Lenin** was placed in the **Mausoleum** on his death in 1924. The original wooden mausoleum was replaced by the present granite structure, built in the style of a pre-Columbian temple, in 1930. Inside the **Funeral Hall** (*Traurny Zal*) constant air temperature and humidity are maintained. Since August 1924, except for a brief sojourn in the Urals during World War II, Lenin's body has been exposed to public view in a sarcophagus.

Will the mausoleum be Lenin's final resting place? Many Russians feel that his body should receive a proper burial, possibly with his family in St Petersburg. Meanwhile, the number of locals and tourists queueing up to pay their respects had drastically declined.

Above the Mausoleum are stands from where the leaders of the Soviet state used to greet Muscovites during parades on national holidays. The changing of the guard ceremony at the mausoleum's entrance was discontinued in 1993.

St Basil's, the epitome of Russia: Nearby, on the southern side of the square, stands the festive-looking **Cathedral of the Protecting Veil**. It is also known as the **Cathedral of St Basil the Blessed** after the saint who was well-known in Moscow when it was built and whose grave is next to it. For many people around the world, the picture of this cathedral has become a potent symbol of Russia.

The cathedral was built between 1555 and 1560 on the order of Ivan the Terrible to commemorate the victory over the

Kazan Khanate. It is believed to have been erected by a Russian master builder by the name of Postnik Barma. Having created this complex composition of nine tower-like churches built on a common foundation, the great master builder lost his sight. Tradition has it that the cruel tsar ordered the master to be deliberately blinded so that he could not create anything else that would be as beautiful.

Incidentally, contrary to Russian tradition the cathedral was built in a market square, apparently still another manifestation of the wilful tsar's capricious character. Each of the nine domes of the cathedral forms the top of a separate church, each dedicated to a saint on whose feast day the Russian army achieved a victory. The inner walls are decorated with patterns featuring Russian folk motifs. After decades of use as a branch of the Historical Museum, St Basil's was finally returned to the Orthodox Church for the Easter festivities of 1991.

In front of the cathedral is a monument to two popular heroes, **Kuzma Minin** and **Prince Dmitry Pozharsky**, who saved the city from an invasion by Polish troops led by the impostor False Dmitry II in 1612. The Monument, executed by the famous sculptor Ivan Martos, was erected by public subscription in 1818.

Near the cathedral is a small stone mound, the so-called **Lobnoye Mesto**, or Place of Execution. This round platform of white stone was built in the 16th century in front of the main gate of the Kremlin on the crest of the hill where it starts sloping downward. The tsar's decrees were proclaimed here and public executions were carried out.

Red Square has witnessed many historical dramas. In 1698 it saw the execution of the *streltsi*, royal musketeers, who, incited by Sophia, Peter the Great's sister, rose in revolt against the tsar. In 1671 Stepan Razin, the leader of a peasant uprising, was executed in Red Square and a century later it saw the end of still another rebel, Yemelyan Pugachev.

Once the shoppers' dream: Along the entire length of the square stretches the

The Lenin Mausoleum on Red Square.

144

building of the former Upper Trading Arcade, which subsequently became the State Department Store better known as **GUM**. Built in 1888–93, it contains three passages running throughout the length of the building. It is covered with a glass roof, so the interior is always relatively light no matter what the weather is like outside. Before the revolution this huge building contained several hundred small private shops where you could buy just about anything. Today, many western firms have outlets here and GUM is experiencing a revival.

On the corner of Red Square between GUM and the Historical Museum, the old **Kazan Cathedral** has been rebuilt and dedicated on its original site. It was here, on a visit to Russia, that US President Bill Clinton lit a candle for his mother.

On the northern side of the square stands the building of the **Historical Museum**, erected in 1878. The architect Vladimir Sherwood tried to combine in this building the styles of different architectural periods. It became the main museum of the former USSR, documenting the history of the Soviet people from prehistoric times. Further exhibits have been acquired from the old Lenin Museum, closed since 1986, and the refurbishment has been extensive.

Next to the Historical Museum is another red brick building, the former City Duma (City Hall) of Moscow, built in 1890. In the 17th century the small structure in the courtyard housed the **Mint** where silver and gold coins were made; and one of the annexes was used as a prison known as the **Yama** (Pit). In 1775, Yemelyan Pugachev, the leader of a peasant war, was kept here before his execution in Red Square.

Between the Historical Museum and the former City Duma is the **Resurrection Gate** (Voskresenskiye Vorota). Rebuilt in 1995 after being demolished by Stalin in the 1930s, the gateway was originally part of the Kitay-Gorod fortifications. Just outside is the Chapel of the Iverian Virgin, originally built in 1791 to house a precious icon of that name.

he Historical
Iuseum.

KITAY-GOROD

Beyond Red Square, bordered by the **Moskva River** to the south and by **Okhotny Ryad Ulitsa** to the north, is the oldest residential district of Moscow, Kitay-Gorod. The name of the area, however, has nothing to do with *Kitay*, which is the Russian name for China. It is derived from the Old Slavonic *kita*, which meant a bundle of stakes, for these bundles formed the basis of the earthworks which surrounded the original area.

The *posad* (trading quarter) emerged outside the Kremlin wall back in the hoary past. It was connected with the Kremlin by way of Velikaya (Great) Street. In the 14th century it was known as *Veliky Posad* (Great Trading Quarter). At that time it was surrounded by a rampart to which a moat and wooden fortifications were added in the early 16th century.

In the mid-16th century a stone wall in the form of a horseshoe was built round the *posad*. The wall began near the Beklemishev Tower, passed along the bank of the Moskva River and then went round the *posad* on the east and north to join the Kremlin Wall near the Arsenal Tower. The wall had 14 towers altogether, including six with gates. This was Moscow's second ring. Today only two small fragments of the fortress wall, one not far from the northern entrance of the Rossiya Hotel and the other near the Revolution Square Metro Station, have survived.

A 16th-century ground plan: At the end of the 16th century the *posad* area began to be built over with boyars' and clergymen's mansions. At the same time, monasteries, foreign embassies and trade missions began to emerge here. Finally, in the late 19th and the early 20th centuries Kitay-Gorod became the financial and commercial district of Moscow.

The basic layout of Kitay-Gorod comprises three streets which radiate from the Kremlin gate towers. (To reach them take the Metro to Ploshchad Revolyutsii or Kitay-Gorod stations.)

Varvarka Ulitsa: Vasilyevsky Ulitsa Slope, which begins immediately behind St Basil's Cathedral, affords a splendid view of the district on the opposite side of the Moskva river, known as the Zamoskvorechye. Walking down the slope you will reach one of the busiest streets in Moscow, **Varvarka Ulitsa**. Varvarka was the ancient road from the Kremlin to Ryazan and Kolomna. In the 14th century Prince Dimitry Donskoy returned by this road after victory at the Battle of Kulikovo. The first thing that strikes the eye here is the remarkable mixture of architectural styles: old churches stand next to monumental neo-classical structures which, in turn, contrast with the modern building of the huge Rossiya Hotel.

The street was named after an earlier Church of St Barbara (*Ts Vavara*) built by the architect Alevisio Novy in the early 16th century. Considered to be

Preceding pages: a city of pet lovers. Left, staircase in the GUM. Right, an antiquarian bookshop.

one of the finest examples of Russian Classical architecture, the present church was built to the design of the architect Matvey Kazakov in the 18th century.

Further along is a striking structure with narrow asymmetrical window apertures and a steep wooden roof which dates from the 15th and early 16th centuries. This is the **Old English Court**, which was set up after the establishment of diplomatic and trade relations between England and Russia. It is called the "Old" Court because in 1636 the English were offered a new building in Moscow outside the Ilyinskiye Gate and this one was sold to Boyar Ivan Miloslavsky.

The building was reconstructed more than once and by the turn of the century was no longer considered of any value as an architectural monument. In the 1950s there were even plans to pull it down. Restorers, however, have succeeded in reconstructing its original facades and interiors and it is now open as a museum.

Nearby is the austere single-domed **Church of St Maxim the Blessed**, built in 1699 with a bell tower added two centuries later. On the same side of the street is the former **Monastery of the Sign**, including the five-domed Cathedral of the Icon of the Mother of God. The Monastery of the Sign was built by stonemasons Fyodor Grigoryev and Grigory Anisimov in 1679–84 on the grounds of the Old State Court. Its Brethren's Building with monastic cells and a two-tier cathedral have survived to this day. The cathedral, resting upon oak piles, was built in 1864 and then rebuilt so often that, by the beginning of the 20th century, it had virtually lost its original appearance. The cathedral is sometimes used for concerts.

No. 10 Varvarka Street was the **Palace of the Romanov Boyars** and dates back to the 16th and 17th centuries. The old building was rebuilt several times and its appearance was changed considerably. In the 19th century the architect Richter carefully restored the mansion in old Russian style. Today, it houses a

Left, renovation in progress. **Below,** Saint Varvarka gave her name to the quarter.

museum devoted to everyday life and applied art in old Moscow.

The left side of the street was mostly built up in the 18th to early 20th centuries. The structures seen here include a former shopping arcade, the **Old Merchant's Court** (Gostiny Dvor). Further on are the early 20th-century offices of commercial and industrial companies.

The last side street running off to the left of Varvarka Ulitsa, **Ipatyevsky Pereulok**, contains a mid-17th century mansion known as the **Borovskoye Podvorye**, which housed the workshop of Simon Ushakov, the noted Russian iconpainter who painted quite a number of churches throughout the country.

In neighbouring **Nikitnikov Pereulok** is the **Church of the Trinity in Nikitniki**, built in the 1630s. Its oldest part is the side chapel of **St Nikita the Martyr**, the burial place of the merchant Nikitnikov with whose money the church was built. The beautiful murals and iconstasis were executed by Yakov Kazanets and Simon Ushakov, masters

from the Armoury. Today the church has become a branch of the State History Museum.

Zaryadye: The district on the right side of Varvarka Ulitsa was formerly known as the **Zaryadye** (Beyond the Stalls). In the 15th and 16th centuries a main street linking the Kremlin with wharves on the Moskva River passed through here. At that time the district was inhabited by merchants and artisans and, later on, by boyars and clergymen. By the turn of the century the structures in this district had fallen into utter disrepair and it had become a hotbed of disease and crime.

In 1960 most of the houses were pulled down to make way for the construction of the **Rossiya Hotel**, the biggest in the country. It took seven years to build. Its four 12-storey wings form an enormous cube with an inner courtyard. The central part of its northern wing is surmounted by a 23-storey tower in the shape of a ship's bridge. The hotel can accommodate 5,300 guests. Its facilities include several restaurants, numer-

treet selling
ecame a
ay of life
or many.

ous bars, a 2,600-seat **Concert Hall**, and the **Zaryadye Cinema**.

To the southeast of the Rossiya is one of the oldest structures in the Zaryadye, the late 15th-century **Church of the Conception of St Anne in the Corner**, called thus because at one time the church stood in the corner formed by the eastern and southern walls of the Kitay-Gorod (demolished in the 1930s).

Beyond the church, along the river bank, is a building erected in the mid-18th century, which today houses a **military academy**. Before the revolution it was the Imperial Home for Orphans and Illegitimate Children. Some of them trained in dance here and formed the basis of the Bolshoi Corps de Ballet.

At the spot where Kitaysky Proezd meets Varvarka Ulitsa, the Varvarskiye Gate of Kitay-Gorod once stood. The square has now been renamed Ploshchad Varvarskikh Vorot.

In Soviet times the square was almost entirely rebuilt. Of its old structures only the 16th/17th-century **Church of**

All Saints in Kulishki (Kulishki was the area's ancient name) has survived.

On the right is the massive grey building of the former Business House with a porch in the form of a classical portico, built in 1913.

In the centre of the square are the **Ilyinsky Gardens**, which were laid out in 1882 and named after the former *Ilyinskiye Gate* of Kitay-Gorod. In the upper part of the gardens stands a **Monument to the Russian Grenadiers** who fell in the siege of Plevna in 1878. The monument was erected by the architect and sculptor Vladimir Sherwood from subscriptions collected by the men and officers of the Grenadier Corps. Inscribed on the monument are the names of those grenadiers who gave their lives for the liberation of Bulgaria from the Ottoman yoke.

On the left side of the gardens is **Starya (Old) Ploshchad**, which emerged back in the 17th and 18th centuries. At one time it was one of the busiest market squares in Moscow where, ac-

The Polytechnical Museum.

cording to historians, one could buy practically anything. At the turn of the century tenement houses were built here in place of the market. In 1923 the Central Committee of the Communist Party occupied the building at No. 4 and No. 6. On the right side of the Ilyinsky Gardens is **Lubyinsky Proezd**.

In the centre of the square, near the former Ilyinskiye Gate, is the **Polytechnical Museum**. It was built in phases over a period of 30 years and was completed in 1907. The central part of the building (1877) and its right wing (1896) were built in traditional 17th-century Russian style while its left wing, added in 1903–07, is an example of art nouveau.

The museum was opened in 1872 to popularise natural science. Today its displays, occupying about 80 halls, explain recent developments in science and technology. The museum is also noted for its wide range of historical displays, from antique mining lamps to models of spacecraft. The lower floors of the building house the *Znaniye*

(Knowledge) Society, the principal non-governmental body engaged in promoting knowledge of science, technology and politics.

On the left side of **Novaya (New) Ploshchad**, at No. 12, is the building of the former **Church of St John the Divine**, built between 1825 and 1837. Since 1934 the building has housed the **Museum of the History and Reconstruction of Moscow**. The museum was founded in 1896. At that time, it occupied the Sukhareva Tower, which has not survived.

Lubyanka Ploshchad: The facade of the left wing of the Polytechnical Museum overlooks a circular precinct which once carried the name of Felix Dzerzhinsky, one of Lenin's closest associates and the first head of the Cheka (All-Russian Extraordinary Commission for Combating Counter-revolution, Sabotage and Speculation) the predecessor of the KGB. Today the square has been given back its historical name, Lubyanka Ploshchad, originally conferred by the inhabitants

Inside the Polytechnical Museum.

of Novgorod, who settled here in the 15th century, in memory of Lubyanitsa Street in their native city.

It was in this square in August 1991, after the failed coup against Mikhail Gorbachev, that cranes hauled down the monument to Dzerzhinsky, erected in 1958 in place of a fountain. Opposite the Polytechnical Museum is the huge building of the **Detsky Mir (Children's World) Department Store**, built in 1957 on the site of the former Lubyansky Shopping Arcade. In the 15th to 18th centuries this was the Gun Foundry. Master founder Andrei Chokov, who was responsible for casting the Tsar Cannon in the Kremlin, worked here.

Frightful cellars: The massive yellow building to the right, at the spot where **Myasnitskaya Ulitsa** and **Bolshaya Lubyanskaya Ulitsa** radiate from the square is the former headquarters of the KGB. This building, formerly the offices of the Rossiya Insurance Agency, was erected in 1899 on the site of the former Royal Secret Dispatch Office.

Its deep cellars were once a dreadful prison. The dispatch office was liquidated on the orders of Emperor Pavel I after the death of Catherine the Great. The cellars remained and, in the days of Stalin's regime, they were once again used for their terrible purpose.

Okhotny Ryad Ulitsa: Descending from Lubyanka Ulitsa is the former Marx Prospekt (*Prospekt Marksa*), again divided, as in olden times, into three sections: **Okhotny Ryad (Hunters' Row)**, **Teatralny Proezd** and **Mokhovaya (Moss-Grown) Ulitsa**.

The solid grey buildings on the right side were constructed in the late 19th century. At present they house various ministries and departments. In a small passageway between some of these buildings you will find **Moscow's Central Bath-House**, once known as the Khludov Public Baths, which are still the most popular in the capital, along with the **Sandunov Public Baths**, not far away, in l-ya Neglinnaya Pereulok.

There is a small public garden imme-

Bath-houses have a social function.

diately opposite the bath-house entrance. Here you will see the monument to Russia's printing pioneer, **Ivan Fedorov**, who printed the first Russian book in 1563.

Next to it stands a tower with a decorative roof in neo-Russian style. Through an arched gateway, you pass into the **Tretyakovsky Proezd** linking Okhotny Ryad Ulitsa with **Nikolskaya Ulitsa**.

The tower and gateway, designed by the architect Alexander Kaminsky, were erected in 1870 and funded by the Tretyakov brothers, well-known collectors and art patrons. Adjacent to the gateway is a surviving fragment of the ancient **Kitay-Gorod wall** and the **Metropol Hotel**.

The Metropol is one of Moscow's finest and best-known hotels. It was built between 1899 and 1905, a typical specimen of Russian art nouveau. In the early 1990s the building was almost entirely reconstructed by Finnish and Swedish construction companies. The only piece of exterior decoration reminding you of its former appearance is the inlaid mosaics made after drawings by Mikhail Vrubel. The Metropol is not only magnificent, it is also one of the most expensive hotels in Moscow.

Returning to the heart of Kitay-Gorod, we will now walk along **Nikolskaya Ulitsa,** named after the Nikolskaya (St Nicholas) Gatetower of the Kremlin. The latter took its name from the 14th-century Greek St Nicholas Monastery.

If you turn right, you will see the side of **GUM**, the State Department Store, mentioned earlier on. In the courtyard of 9 Sapunovsky Proezd is the surviving ensemble of the **Icon of Our Saviour Monastery**, founded back in 1600. The many-tiered cathedral was reconstructed in the early 18th century, using a variety of decorative baroque elements.

Next to the monastery, on the left-hand side of Nikolskaya Ulitsa, are the surviving remnants of the former **Slav-Greek-Latin-Academy** – the first institution of higher learning to have appeared in Moscow. The Academy was

The Metropol Hotel.

founded by Silvestre Medvedev in 1687, converted from a former monastery school. Mikhail Lomonosov, the great Russian scholar, studied here.

In the early 18th century there were over 600 students from all over Russia. In 1814 the Academy was reorganised into a theological academy and transferred to the Trinity-St Sergius Monastery in the town of Sergiyev Posad (*Zagorsk*). Today, the building houses the **Moscow Institute of Historical Records**.

Another building, with two high spires, stands out among the structures in this street: the former **Synodal press** was built in 1810–14. Over its entrance is a sundial topped by a lion and a unicorn – the coat-of-arms of the Royal Print Yard of 1553. It was here that Ivan Fedorov produced the first printed Russian book, *The Acts of the Apostles*. In the courtyard of the former printing plant is one of Moscow's oldest civilian structures – the **Chambers**. Fedorov lived here in his day.

One of Moscow's best-known and most popular restaurants, the **Slavyansky Bazaar**, was located at No. 17 Nikolskaya Ulitsa (on your left coming from Red Square). The building was reconstructed late in the 19th century to house a hotel and a restaurant. In 1930 it was used to accommodate a puppet theatre then, in 1966, the restaurant was reopened. The rich decor of the interior, the distinctive layout and a wide choice of Russian dishes earned it the love of many residents and visitors.

The forgotten Russian cuisine: You should beware that the finer points of Russian cuisine have been all but forgotten, to be supplanted by more diversified West European food. Until recently it was difficult to name any typically Russian drink or dish except *vodka*, *kvass* (Russian rye-beer), *borscht* (highly seasoned Russian soup of various ingredients including beetroot), and, perhaps, *pelmeni* (a kind of ravioli from Siberia). Today, this modest menu has been appreciably diversified by the efforts of

Typical starters in a restaurant.

historians and cookery experts. They have rediscovered what seemed to have been irretrievably lost – recipes for preparing *rasstegais* (open-topped pastry), chitterlings, Poltava cutlets, Moscow pancakes and a whole host of other tempting dishes.

In the adjacent house, at No. 21 Nikolskaya Ulitsa, is still one of Moscow's first chemist's, once known as the **Ferein Drugstore**, after its owner's name. The right side of the street was occupied by the so-called **Sheremetev Coaching Inn**. Today it houses all kinds of offices, stores and workshops.

But, to the delight of Muscovites, the new city authorities have already drafted an ordinance requiring most of the present occupants of Moscow's historical downtown area to leave their premises. Under the latest Moscow reconstruction plan, the entire area within the limits of the former Kitay-Gorod will become a pedestrian zone. New shops and numerous cafés and restaurants are due to open.

Ilyinka Ulitsa : This street runs parallel to Nikolskaya Ulitsa. Before the revolution, this was Moscow's central street. Most of the buildings date from the late 19th century and the early 20th century, designed in what was considered to be a modern style, typical of those prosperous times. They housed banks and trade offices, as well as institutions like the central stock exchange.

A small square, **Birzhevaya Ploshchad**, stands at the intersection of this street and Bogoyavlensky Pereulok. On the opposite side of the street is a building with a semi-circular facade built in 1873–75. At one time it accommodated the Stock Exchange. At present it is the offices of the Russian Chamber of Commerce and Industry.

In Bogoyavlensky Pereulok, branching off to the left, is the ensemble of the former **Monastery of the Epiphany**, founded by Prince Daniil of Moscow back in the 13th century. The monastery has been reconstructed more than once. At present it incorporates the Cathedral of the Monastery of the Epiphany, monks

Gathering the apples.

cells, built in 1693–96, and the belfry built next to them in the 18th century.

Restoration work in the monastery that took place in 1986 led to the discovery of the base of the walls of a whitestone church, the **Epiphany of Stone**, that stood here in the mid-14th century. It is the oldest stone structure in Moscow's trading quarter.

On the left of Birzhevaya Ploshchad is the solid building of the **Ministry of Finance**, amalgamating the premises of the former Petersburg and Azov-Don Banks.

Almost the entire right side of the street is built up with lavish premises of the former banks of the late 19th and early 20th centuries. An entire block between Ilyinka Ulitsa and Varvarka Ulitsa is occupied by the mammoth building of the former **Arcade (Gostiny Dvor)**, built in 1791–1805 by the architect Giacomo Quarenghi. You can easily recognise it by the massive Corinthian columns along the facade. The building was restored after the 1812 fire.

The building of the former **Church of Ilya the Prophet**, constructed in the 16th century, has survived at the very end of the street, nearly abutting onto Red Square.

Crossing the Square and passing the Historical Museum we leave Kitay-Gorod proper to arrive at **Ploshchad Revolyutsii** with the **Monument to Karl Marx** in its centre. Until 1961 a sculpture of French revolutionary Georges Danton's "guillotined" head rested on a solid granite base here – an object-lesson for all revolutionaries. Then, apparently considering that the implication was much too obvious, the head of one unfortunate revolutionary was replaced by that of a more fortunate one.

Moscow's centre of the arts: The square between the two facades of the Metropol and Moskva hotels is called **Teatralnaya (Theatre) Ploshchad**. Theatre Square got its name in the late 18th century from the Petrovsky Theatre which stood here at the time. It burnt down in 1805, and the new building, designed by Osip Bove, appeared as late as 1825. It served the **Bolshoi Imperial Theatre Company**, founded in 1776.

The Bolshoi Theatre burned down again and was reconstructed by architect Albert Kavos in 1856. The reopening of the Bolshoi Theatre was rushed to coincide with the coronation of Alexander II. In consequence, a huge crack appeared in the theatre's wall in 1890. The Neglinnaya river, flowing virtually beneath the building, had eroded the foundation and the building subsided. You can see the crack when you have a side view of the Bolshoi Theatre's portico.

The base was underpinned at the end of the 19th century. During a matinée in 1906, however, the wall of the auditorium bowed unexpectedly. The audience panicked. Many exit doors jammed and horror-stricken spectators had to try to push their way through. Only in 1921 was the nearly destroyed wall underpinned again. Incidentally, the theatre never closed during these repairs.

Monument to Karl Marx on Revolution Square.

The Bolshoi Theatre has often been the venue for important social and political gatherings, such as the Congresses of Soviets and sessions of the Comintern. Lenin frequently spoke there. In 1988 the stage was placed, for the first time, at the disposal of the Orthodox Church for its celebration of the *Millennium of the Baptism of Rus*.

When the Bolshoi Theatre company is on tour, the stage is taken over by foreign troupes such as the French Grand Opera, the Swedish Royal Theatre and Britain's Royal Shakespeare Company.

From the Bolshoi you can see on your right the **Maly Theatre** (Little Theatre), for many decades Russia's leading classical drama theatre. The Maly Theatre Company performed here before the building became its permanent home. In 1938–40, after it became the company's property, the building was substantially reconstructed.

Immediately opposite the Maly is the **Children's Theatre**, built in 1821. The Children's Theatre was formed on Len-in's initiative in 1921 and has performed in this building since 1936.

Manezhnaya Ploshchad: Walking along **Teatralny Proezd** you reach Manezhnaya Ploshchad. The square is dominated by two huge buildings – the **Moskva Hotel**, built in the 1930s on the site of the former Okhotny Ryad (the local market), and the premises of the **Imperial Manege**, built in 1817. It was used for parades of the Moscow military garrison and for cavalry unit exercises.

Since 1831 this building has served as host to various exhibitions, including an international exhibition of automobiles and bicycles. It has also been used to stage musical recitals. After reconstruction in 1951, it housed the **Central Exhibition Hall** hosting major national and republican art displays.

The building is of a unique design – it is 166 metres (545 ft) long and 45 metres (148 ft) wide and is covered with a roof resting on wooden beams that lack any central supports.

The white-columned, bright-green

The Bolshoi Theatre.

building opposite the Moskva Hotel, near the **Teatralny Proezd**, is the **House of Trade Unions**. It was built in 1770 for Prince Dolgorukiy of the Crimea. Later the building was bought by the Moscow nobility as a convenient home for their club – the **Assembly of Nobility** – which was frequented by Moscow's high society and intellectuals.

The **Hall of Columns** and the **October Hall** of the House of Trade Unions are often used to host festivities and social functions. In 1931 the playwright George Bernard Shaw was honoured here on the occasion of his 75th birthday. The building was also the scene, in the 1930s, of the notoriously repressive show trials. It was also where the bodies of former statesmen lay in state including Leonid Brezhnev, Yuri Andropov, Lenin and Stalin.

Next to the House of Trade Unions is the 11-storey building of the former **State Planning Committee of the USSR**, now the Russian Duma (Parliament). This colossal building of granite, built in 1932–35, embodies the heavy burden of decision-making that the nation's top planning agency had to bear.

Moscow's main street, **Tverskaya Ulitsa**, starts immediately opposite the Historical Museum.

On the corner of Tverskaya Ulitsa is the six-storey **National Hotel**, built in 1902 in a rather unusual eclectic style. In 1918 Vladimir Lenin lived here in Room 107. The National Hotel – one of the capital's most popular and fashionable hotels – has been restored to its former splendour.

The house nearby is the headquarters of **Intourist** – the National Tourist Organisation. The United States Military Mission had its headquarters here during the years of World War II.

A little further on along the **Mokhovaya Ulitsa** you will find the old buildings of the Lomonosov Moscow State University, founded in 1755. Originally, the university was housed in a chemist's shop that stood on what is today the site of the **Historical Mu-**

The old State Planning Committee building.

seum. Today's University buildings were erected in 1786–93 and were designed by Matvey Kazakov. The building caught fire and was restored in 1817–19. At present it houses an exhibition of rare books and manuscripts.

The University's second building, close by, was taken over in 1833–36 and was reconstructed in 1904. Adjacent to the lecture halls is the University's **St Tatyana's Church**. In 1953 most faculties moved to a new complex on the Lenin (now Sparrow) Hills. Only the Department of Journalism, the Institute of the Countries of Asia and Africa, the editorial offices of several magazines and the University Museum remained.

A library of 36 million books: A long block on the right-hand side of **Mokhovaya Ulitsa** houses the premises of the **Russian State Library**, formerly known as the Lenin Library.

The present building was erected in 1928–40. The facades are adorned with medallions and sculptural portraits of famous writers and scientists. Adjacent

to the building is a nine-storey repository containing close to 36 million books, representing practically all of the world's languages. When the Metro was being constructed, the building subsided and a huge crack appeared across its wall.

The books in this repository, especially those in the basement premises, are kept in appalling conditions, and many priceless manuscripts have been damaged beyond repair. But the Library lacks the means for major repairs, and public funds are scarce.

Opposite the library building is the former mansion of Prince Shakhovsky, built in 1821. In the Soviet era it was a memorial museum to Mikhail Kalinin, President of the Presidium of the Supreme Soviet of the USSR throughout the Stalin era.

Mokhovaya Ulitsa ends at **Borovitskaya Ploshchad** onto which the Kremlin gate of the same name opens. Several old streets – Volkhonka, Znamenka and Bolshaya Polyanka – converge here.

The Russian State Library.

THE ARBAT AND BEYOND

This chapter covers the quarter of Moscow between Prechistenskaya Naberezhnaya (Embankment) of the Moskva river and Tverskaya Ulitsa, an area once inhabited by the Moscow nobility.

Volkhonka Ulitsa starts at the Borovitskaya Gate outside the Kremlin. This is another of Moscow's old streets and one that has been uncommonly lucky, having been neither renamed nor reconstructed. The entire right side of the street is made up of small mansions, typical of the noblemen's Moscow of the 18th and 19th centuries. In the courtyard of No. 8 Volkhonka Ulitsa are the surviving 17th-century chambers of the Volkonsky princes. This street, which once led to Smolensk, may well have been named in their honour.

Moscow's finest museum: Beyond the facade of the Volkonsky chambers stands a building of dark-grey stone, with a massive colonnade and a glass roof: the **Pushkin Fine Arts Museum**. The museum was opened in 1912 on the initiative of Professor Ivan Tsvetayev of Moscow University. Originally, the museum was conceived as an extensive visual aid for art students. It had a collection of casts and copies of works of art from the ancient world and Western Europe. The annexe next door, which opened in 1994, is known as the museum of private collections and contains an excellent exhibit of Russian paintings of the 19th and 20th centuries. (*For fuller details, see pages 184–85.*)

As mentioned earlier, Volkhonka was the noblemen's suburb of Moscow. The seat of the Golitsyn princes was at No. 14 Volkhonka Street. The neighbouring house, which was the seat of the Dolgorukiy princes, is now home to the Institute of Philosophy of the Russian Academy of Sciences.

Beyond **Ploshchad Prechistenskie Vorota** (Metro Kropotinskaya), Volkhonka Ulitsa splits into **Ostozhenka Ulitsa** and **Prechistenka Ulitsa**. The former took its name, in the 17th century, from the local *ostozhie*, or meadow. Both sides of the street are lined by former guesthouses. Today the **Ostozhenka Café** occupies the ground floor of the corner-house on the left: a welcome retreat in the bustling city. On the right are some 17th-century chambers which once belonged to the Golitsyns.

The **Conception (Zachatievsky) Monastery**, in Zachatievsky Pereulok, is considered to be the oldest structure in the whole district. It was founded in 1584. Unfortunately, little has survived – only a few fragments of the rampart and the gate church can still be seen. Despite restoration work, daily services are still held here.

No. 38 Ostozhenka Ulitsa – a large house with a massive portico – belonged to Pyotr Yeropkin, Governor-General of Moscow. Alexander Pushkin, while a boy, attended balls here. From the early 19th century it housed a commercial college and, on the 30th anniversary of the Soviet regime, the house was turned over to the Moscow Institute of Foreign Languages.

Yet another green-coloured building on the left side is the former **Kadkovsky Lycée**. Immediately after the Revolution it housed the offices of the People's Commissariat for Education and has now become the Diplomatic Academy.

Beyond the Garden Ring: Ostozhenka Ulitsa continues as **Komsomolsky Prospekt** which was laid out in the late 1950s. It leads to the Luzhniki Sports Stadium and, beyond the bridge, to Moscow University (MGU).

The avenue cuts through what was the 17th-century Khamovniki weavers' settlement. On the right side is the five-domed brightly coloured **Church of St Nicholas the Weaver**, dating from the late 17th century. The church was fortunate in having been permitted to function as a church in Soviet times.

Turn right behind the church to arrive in **Lev Tolstovo Ulitsa**, where the urban estate of the writer Leo Tolstoy still stands. Today, it is a superbly evocative memorial museum. The left side of Komsomolsky Prospekt is occupied principally by blocks of flats and a variety of shops. Prominent is the former **Patronage House**, an early 19th-century building with a tall four-columned portico. Now the house is occupied by the Board of the Union of Russian Writers.

Across the street are three early 19-century buildings of the Khamovniki Barracks. Here, Alexander Griboyedov, the Russian poet and playwright who so pointedly ridiculed Moscow high society, joined the Hussar Regiment. Today, the former barracks houses the Faculty of Military Conductors of the Moscow Conservatory of Music.

Near Frunzenskaya Metro Station is the massive cube-shaped building of the **Youth Palace**. This is said to have been built with the money earned by teams of young workers on *subbotniks* – unpaid working days, named after *Subbota* (Saturday). Possibly that is why it took nearly 20 years before young people were able to gain admission. Now it is used for exhibitions and festivals.

In a small public garden, awash with greenery, not far from the Frunzenskaya Naberezhnaya, is the **Moscow Choreographic College**, the main training ground for Russian ballet dancers. Founded as far back as 1773, it boasts such famous graduates as Maya Plisetskaya, Marius Liepa and Yekaterina Maximova. The General Staff of the Soviet Armed Forces had its headquarters nearby on the Embankment.

Home of the 1980 Olympics: Komsomolsky Prospekt ends at the Central Lenin Stadium in Luzhninki. The **Stadium** (Metro Sportivnaya) was built in the 1950s on what was the site of Luzhnikovo Village and a small sports stadium. More than 140 different sports-installations were built on an area of 180 hectares (445 acres), comprising a swimming pool, tennis court, various sports grounds, a covered Palace of Sports and the Grand Sports Arena with a football pitch and stands to seat almost 100,000.

Peace-Rock Festival in Luzhniki Park.

This was the venue of the 1980 Moscow Olympics.

The sports complex incorporates a splendid public garden with numerous cafés and restaurants. Not far from the Grand Arena, on the Moskva River Embankment, are two of the most popular restaurants – **Olimp** and **Olimpiada**.

Cross the river by the two-tier Metro Bridge, which was built in the late 1950s and which was then considered to be just about the peak of engineering science, and you will be in **Vernadskovo Prospekt**. At this point, the Moskva river curves to form a kind of peninsula.

On the right side of the avenue are the **Vorobïevskye Gory** (Sparrow Hills), as they have been known since the 15th century. Here Peter the Great and Catherine II both had country palaces in the 17th and 18th centuries. In the 19th century there were many *dachas* (cottages) here.

A city within the city: In the late 1940s, Stalin ruled that the new **Moscow University** (Metro Universitet) be built on the heights of the Sparrow Hills. A 35-storey building was erected in the space of four years. The central section stands about 240 metres (790 ft) high. The top floor houses the university museum. The main building has 18-storey towers adjoining it on four sides. These contain student dormitories and are adjoined by four more nine-storey wings providing accommodation for post-graduate students. Finally there are four 12-storey buildings with apartments for the teaching staff.

The entire university complex incorporates about 60 academic faculties providing instruction for a total of more than 30,000 students from all over Russia and from various foreign countries. The university has its own research institutes, observatories, libraries, botanical gardens, sports complexes and camps.

Spread around the university area is a small student township complete with shopping centres, laundries, cafés and cinemas. Moscow University is like a

Trees protected from the cold at the Moscow University.

small city, with the same unwieldy administrative machinery as any typical Russian city. The university recently became independent from the Ministry of Education and is now sole proprietor of all its property.

At the fork of Vernadskovo Prospekt and Lomonosovsky Prospekt are the new premises of the **Moscow Circus**, built in 1971. Nearby is a children's music theatre. Vernadsky Prospekt ends at the junction with Leninsky Prospekt in Troparevo, a district known for the late 17th-century **Archangel Michael's Church**.

The road to the convent: Returning to Ploshchad Prechistenskie Vorota (by Metro to Kropotkinskaya) we will now walk along **Prechistenka Ulitsa**. This street was named after the icon of the Novodevichy (New Maiden) Convent. In the 16th century it served as the main road from the Kremlin. It is easy to see, by observing the architectural development of the street, how the tastes of the Moscow nobility changed over the years.

Many of the mansions still standing belonged to the families of famous Decembrists. The **Leo Tolstoy Memorial Museum**, at No. 2 Prechistenka Ulitsa, once belonged to the poet Lopukhin. The Tolstoy Museum, which was founded before the revolution, is one of the few museums in Moscow whose basic function remained the same after the revolution.

The building across the street has been known as the **House of Scholars and Scientists** since 1922. At one time the house belonged to the Military Governor of Moscow, Arkharov, whose name has passed into common parlance as a symbol of vulgarity and cruelty.

From 1921 to 1923, No. 20 Prechistenka Ulitsa was the home of the famous American ballet dancer Isadora Duncan and her lover, the poet Sergei Yesenin.

The large two-storey house, with a six-column portico and a huge loggia, belonged to Prince Dolgorukiy at the end of the 18th century. The neighbouring house, No. 21, which belonged to

At the Moscow Circus.

the millionaire and patron of the arts, Savva Morozov, in the early 20th century, now accommodates the offices of the Institute for Art History, where painting exhibitions are sometimes held.

The first Moscow co-operative restaurant opened in 1987 at No. 36 Prechistenka Street. It has a pleasing interior and background chamber music.

Moscow's Latin Quarter: We will start our walk through the Arbat quarter at **Znamenka Ulitsa**, a small street running from Borovitskaya Ploshchad, just outside the Kremlin, to the Arbat. As early as the 14th century, this was the road to Novgorod the Great. At the beginning of the street is a small house with caryatids, built by the architect Tyurin for his own occupation in the early 19th century.

Further along, No.12 was Count Vorontsov's house in the mid-18th century and later accommodated Prince Urusov's opera-house at the end of that century. This was the forerunner of the Bolshoi Theatre.

Across the street, at No. 19 Znamenka Ulitsa, is **Apraxin's palace**, a late 18th-century structure designed by the Italian architect Camporesi. Performances in the central hall of the palace were staged by the Moscow Imperial Theatre which subsequently split into the Bolshoi and the Maly Theatres. Late in the 19th century it was the seat of the Alexander Military College. Today, this building, along with most of the surrounding monumental structures, belongs to the Russian Ministry of Defence.

In Starovagankovsky Pereulok, which crosses Znamenka Ulitsa, are the chambers of the 17th-century **Royal Pharmacy Yard**. It once belonged to German chemists who laid out a medicinal herb garden on Vagankovo Hill.

A Bohemian nest (Metro Kropotkinskaya or Arbatskaya): **Sivtsev Vrazhek Pereulok** is a reminder of the days when a gully (that's what *vrazhek* means) was cut through here, with the River Sivets running at the bottom. After the river was "imprisoned" in a conduit, the street

The Leo Tolstoy Memorial Museum.

above became the Bohemian nest of writers, poets, artists and actors. No. 9 was the home of Vuchetich, the famous sculptor. The 19th century radical Alexander Herzen preferred No. 27, a house built in Moscow's classical style. Today, it houses a **literary museum**.

On the right side of this street is a mansion behind an iron grille. Sergey Aksakov, the writer, lived here in the late 1840s. Opposite, at No. 31, were the homes of celebrated World War II marshals – Bagramyan and Bagritsky. Mikhail Sholokhov, author of *And Quiet Flows the Don*, lived at No. 33.

Changing times? Sivtsev Vrazhek Pereulok is also famous for a massive edifice of red-black granite. This relic of Stalin's day was, for many years, an outpatients' clinic for top party and government bureaucrats. Cafés, restaurants, photographic studios and small shops continue to spring up in **Old Arbat** like mushrooms after rain.

In **Plotnikov Pereulok**, which forms a cross-roads with Sivtsev Vrazhek

Pereulok, is the old **Oktiabrskaya Hotel** – now the **Arbat Hotel**. Nearby are several multi-storeyed brick buildings, which are architecturally out of place. In **Maly Vlasievsky Pereulok** is the recently restored 17th-century **Vlasii Church**, with its ancient frescoes. It is now a concert hall.

Running parallel to Sivtsev Vrazhek Pereulok from Plotnikov Pereulok to Gogolevsky Bulvar is **Gagarinsky Pereulok**, which has a large Empire-style mansion (built in the 1830s) where Alexander Pushkin stayed when in Moscow. Today, it is occupied by the Council of the All-Russia Society for Protection of Historical and Cultural Monuments. No. 15 with the wooden mezzanine is where Ivan Turgenev, the writer, lived in the 1830s.

No. 35 **Starokoniushenny Pereulok** was the former residence of millionaire Maecenas Sergey Shchukin and the home of his famous collection of old European paintings. When Shchukin gave them to the city in 1918 the paint-

Left and **below**, House of Economic Friendship, Vozdvizhenka Ulitsa.

ings were moved to the Pushkin Museum of Fine Arts. At the very end of the street is a wooden tower decorated with lace-like carvings, which was built in 1871 for demonstration at international exhibitions.

Cosy Moscow: The entire block to the right of Prechistenka Ulitsa all the way to Arbat Ulitsa is criss-crossed by very narrow intertwining streets, always quiet and serene. All are bracketed under one name: *Stary Arbat* (Old Arbat).

This has long been considered one of Moscow's most privileged districts. The tenants may have changed since the 1917 revolution, but not the principle.

In this quarter, **Denezhny Pereulok** (*Money Lane*) branches off from Bolshoy Levshinsky Pereulok towards Arbat. Here, at No. 5, where the German Embassy was located in the first few years after the revolution, the terrorist, Blumkin, assassinated the German Ambassador, Mirbach, on July 6, 1918. It is now the Italian Embassy.

Today many houses in the Old Arbat are occupied by foreign embassies and trade missions. There are several monuments of early 19th-century wooden architecture surviving on Denezhny Pereulok, such as No. 9 and No. 11 – houses which belonged to officers who participated in the 1812 war against Napoleon. The street ends at the high-rise building of the Russian Ministry of Foreign Affairs.

The church on Devil's Creek: "A kopeck candle in Arbat burned down Moscow", says a 15th-century chronicle. The fire of 1365 was the worst in the history of the city. A small candle was left burning in the wooden "All-Saints Church" that stood on a stream with the peculiar name of Chertory (*chyort yego ryl* means "the Devil dug it"). The resultant fire, which started where Volkhonka Ulitsa meets Prechistenka Ulitsa, razed the city to the ground.

Muscovites claim that the place was no site for a church: it was damp, boggy, cursed. The Devil's Creek meandered (or, as they said in days of yore, "hunch-

A delegation arrives at the foreign trade ministry.

backed") throughout the length of Arbat Ulitsa. In consequence, the Arbat wall was anything but arrow-straight – a tricky place to negotiate in a coach.

The Alekseevsky Convent was built on the site of the ill-starred church, but did not survive for long. Nicholas I, wishing to glorify Russia's military might, built the enormous Cathedral of Christ the Saviour in its place. Under Stalin the church was razed to the ground and the site used for the huge, circular Moskva open-air swimming pool. The cathedral has now been rebuilt.

A name with many meanings: There is still no consensus as to the origin of the word "Arbat". Some believe that it comes from Arabia, from the ancient settlements of Arab merchants who found their way into Rus in the 7th century; others say it derives from the Mongol word *arba* – a "sack for collecting tribute". Still others claim it stems from the Latin *arbutum* – "cherry", because there were once cherry orchards on the high Vagankovsky Hill, planted

by German apothecaries. Most probably, however, the name comes from the Russian *gorbaty*, meaning "hunchbacked place", which, owing to the Moscow tradition of omitting the initial consonant and pronouncing "o" as "a", reduced "gorbat" to "arbat".

One way or another, Arbat has always been one of the best-known streets in Moscow, although it is no longer the only pedestrian precinct. The facades of its historical mansions were restored several years ago and the street was paved with cobblestones. After pretty lamp posts and ornate flowerbeds were added the street assumed the old Moscow look – or so its restorers claim. But judge for yourself.

Arbat Ulitsa is a short street, only a kilometre (half a mile) long, yet it is famous worldwide. In the 16th and 17th centuries this was a district of artisans. Hence the names of the side-streets – **Plotnikov (Carpenter's)**, **Serebryany (Silversmith's)**, **Kolashny (Baker's)**, **Starokoniushenny (Equerry's)**.

Early in the 18th century, Arbat became the aristocratic district of Moscow. In the 19th century it was populated by lawyers, artists and top-level state officials. The early 20th century added the homes of industrial magnates and bankers.

Arbat Ulitsa starts in **Arbatskaya Ploshchad** (Metro Arbatskaya) where Gogolevsky Bulvar meets Vozdvizhenka Ulitsa. Here, on the boulevard, is the **Praga Restaurant**, a late 18th-century coaching inn that was revamped in 1955 by a team of architects from Czechoslovakia.

Arbat is full of fun. There are amateur street-bands and young poets out to conquer the world; there are artists and artisans out to air their creations; and there are Moscow's first video-rental shops which opened a few years ago and caused a small revolution in culture and technology. One immediately feels the unique atmosphere of the area. You can have your portrait sketched here in a few minutes, listen to a favourite tune,

Staircase in the Georgian Trade and Culture Centre, Arbat Street.

buy a painting or a souvenir. Chekhov's words still ring true: "the Arbat and its adjoining side-streets may be the most pleasant on earth."

Arbat has always attracted celebrities. The **Literary Café**, formerly at No. 7, was a haunt for the poets Mayakovsky and Yesenin in the 1920s. Leo Tolstoy was a frequent guest at No. 9, where his niece, Obolenskaya, lived. On both sides of the street are houses built by speculators, rebuilt in the 1930s. Their ground floors contain small shops and cafés.

No. 35, which dates to the turn of the century, is a huge house whose facade is decorated with statues of knights. The first floor is occupied by the **Samotsvety (Precious stones) Shop**.

On the opposite side of the street is another large building – the **Vakhtangov Theatre**. It was founded in 1921 by the director, Yevgeny Vakhtangov. The theatre has been losing points with its patrons, probably because of its lacklustre productions. The street bearing to the right also bears Vakhtangov's name.

Here, at No. 11, the composer Skriabin lived and worked in the early 20th century. Today there is a museum in the house. No. 12 across the street houses the **Shchukin Higher School of Theatre** and the **Opera Studio of the Moscow Conservatory**. Among the graduates of the school are numerous stars of Russian stage and screen.

A block ahead is **Spasopeskovsky Pereulok**, which runs parallel to **Vakhtangova Ulitsa**. It owes its name to the former church of **Spasa-na-peskah (Saviour-on-Sand)**, which was built in the 17th century. An idea of what the square used to look like can be gleaned from Vasily Polenov's painting *Moscow Courtyard*, now in the Tretyakov Gallery. This side-street ends in a spacious square with a garden. Here you will also find a modern statue of the poet Pushkin by Nikolay Lvov. Nokolay Vtorov, the banker, chose the square as the site for his townhouse which was built in neo-Empire style (1913–14). In 1933 it was turned over to the US Em-

Arbat buskers.

bassy and was promptly renamed **Spaso House**.

There are also some modern structures in Arbat Ulitsa. No. 42, built in 1987 by a team of Georgian architects, houses the **Georgian Centre of Commerce and Culture** – *Mziuri*. On the ground floor you can buy souvenirs from Georgia and in the basement you can try national Georgian dishes.

Pushkin's happiest moments: Before we leave Arbat Ulitsa, let us stop at No. 53, which is the pride of the street. The small, azure two-storey mansion with an open-work balcony and metal grille is the only apartment Pushkin rented in Moscow. On 18 February 1831, the young poet brought his wife here after their wedding in the Church of the Great Ascension. Here he spent the happiest three months of his life before moving to St Petersburg and it was from here that he attended with wife and friends at the Assembly of the Nobility. In 1875, Pyotr Tchaikovsky lived in the house. After the place was restored in 1986, it reopened as the **Pushkin Museum**. Arbat Ulitsa ends in Smolenskaya Ploshchad (Metro Smolenskaya). On the right is the central **Smolensky Supermarket**.

Vozdvizhenka Ulitsa owes its name to the 16th-century Krestovovozdvizhensky (Exaltation of the Cross) Monastery that unfortunately no longer exists. The region beyond Arbatskaya Ploshchad is now called Novy Arbat. It became a fashionable avenue when aristocrats started to build their residences here in the 19th century.

Facing the Manege Building is the former **residence of Prince Gagarin** (early 19th century).

How to get a ticket: Today there are several theatre-ticket offices in its vicinity. It isn't easy for Muscovites to buy tickets for performances in Moscow theatres.

The corner building on the right of Vozdvizhenka Ulitsa was the **Peterhof Hotel** in the late 19th century.

The adjacent mansion was built for Count Razumovsky in the late 18th cen-

Pushkin Museum.

tury, and then sold to Prince Sheremetev. Late in the 19th century, the **Moscow Duma** (municipal council) met here until it moved to new quarters on Kremlevsky Proezd. The premises were later occupied by the prestigious Hunting Club. At one time the Moscow Arts Theatre, under its director Konstantin Stanislavsky, rehearsed here.

Romanov Pereulok goes off to the right. It was the home of many famous Soviet scientists and statesmen and dates to the late 19th century. After the revolution, it was invaded by military top brass and party bureaucrats. Frunze, Kosygin, Voroshilov, and, for a time, even Khrushchev, lived here.

The opposite side is occupied by the imposing grey-black building of the **Russian State Library**, which was built after the end of World War II. The next building is the former Talyzin estate (late 18th-century). Today, you will find the **Shchuser Museum of Architecture** here. No. 9 once belonged to Leo Tolstoy's grandfather, Count Volkon-sky, and now belongs to the Russian Committee for UNESCO Affairs.

The home of Anarchists: On the opposite side, beyond the small garden to the right, is a rather unusual mansion, which was built in 1894–98 in picturesque pseudo-Moorish style for the millionaire Alexy Morozov. The building belonged to the **Union of Anarchists** in the first years after the revolution. Sergei Yesenin lived here for a short time in 1918 (he wrote the script for the film *Beckoning Dawns*, dedicated to the October Revolution here).

Before World War II, the building housed the Proletkult (Proletarian Culture Movement). Since 1959, it has belonged to the Society of Friendship with Foreign Countries.

At the crossroads with Kalashny Pereulok, which leads to the right just before the Boulevard Ring, is an eight-storey building with a turret, built in the 1920s in the constructivist style. The house was the first Soviet skyscraper. Here, in **Arbatskaya Ploshchad**, the

Signs of the times.

old part of the avenue comes to an end.

New Arbat: Novy Arbat Ulitsa was designed in the 1960s by architect Mikhail Posokhin, who served for a long time as Moscow's chief architect and city planner. The high-rises on both sides of the avenue create the impression of airiness and distance, even though the street is barely a kilometre long. Until recently, the avenue bore the name of Mikhail Kalinin, President of the Soviet Union from 1919 to 1946. But Muscovites always referred to the area as New Arbat.

Novy Arbat is the main western route out of the capital. It connects the Trinity Gate of the Kremlin with the Kalinin Bridge over the Moskva River and consists of two parts: the first, from the Kremlin to Arbatskay Ploshchad (now called Vozdvizhenka Ulitsa), is lined with houses built mostly in the 18th and 19th centuries; the second, from Arbatskaya Ploshchad to Kalinin Bridge, was built in the early 1960s.

The left-hand side of the New Arbat is lined with 26-storey twin towers, looking like open books. The upper floors are occupied by offices. The ground floor has supermarkets and department stores, with numerous service agencies.

The wide pavements make Novy Arbat a favourite promenade. But life here is different from that on Tverskaya Ulitsa or on Old Arbat. The tempo is more subdued and controlled.

Novy Arbat ends near Kalinin Bridge, which was built in 1957. A wonderful panorama of the river bend and the high-rise **Ukraine Hotel** can be enjoyed from this spot. In the distance is the concrete-and-glass **International Trade Center**, consisting of an administrative building with offices of foreign firms and banks, the international Mezhdunarodnaya hotel and several restaurants.

Close to the quay is the mayor's office, completed in the late 1960s.

On the right, high on the bank of the Moskva river, is Moscow's "White House", Russia's former Parliament building. At the centre of the action **Arbat crowds.**

during the 1991 coup and then finding itself besieged by Yeltsin's troops in October 1993, this building has had an eventful, high-profile recent history.

Beyond the New Arbat: Crossing Kalinin Bridge, the continuation of Novy Arbat is called **Kutuzovsky Prospekt**, (Metro Kutuzovskaya) named after Mikhail Kutuzov, the Russian general. The avenue was built in the late 1930s in place of the Old Dorogomilov Quarter. At the beginning of the avenue, on the right, is one of Moscow's seven skyscrapers – the Hotel Ukraine, built in 1957. The 170-metre (560-ft) tall hotel can accommodate more than 1,600 people.

Most buildings on Kutuzovsky Prospekt date from the mid-1950s. From the start it was a privileged area. Foreign diplomats, famous scientists, actors and artists, political and state figures live here. Leonid Brezhnev occupied two floors at No. 26. Another former party boss, Yury Andropov, also lived in the right-hand wing of that house.

At the junction with **Bolshaya Doro-gomilovskaya Ulitsa** (at the site of the former Dorogomilovskaya Zastava Gates) stands an obelisk erected in honour of the Hero City Moscow. Behind the stele, in a glass building, is a branch of Pizza Hut.

Even though the avenue is by far the widest in Moscow, traffic jams are not uncommon, because the normal traffic flow is often blocked to make way for some VIP escort. Kutuzovsky Prospekt is the road that leads to the *dachas* of the *nomenklatura* (old Soviet elite).

Stalin's orderly: It all goes back to Stalin. The "father of all peoples" built an out-of-town residence beyond **Poklonnaya Hill** in Kuntsevo where he lived from the beginning of the war until his death. From here his body was brought to the House of Unions for a final farewell.

Stalin, who was subject to assorted phobias and manias, tried to spend as much time alone as he could. There was only one person he trusted: his manservant. Yet even he suffered the fate of

tourist from isneyland.

hundreds of thousands of slandered "enemies of the people".

Stalin's orderly, who had been with him since the days of the revolution, showed his zeal by stalking the house at night in his coarse woollen socks to collect the scraps of paper that his "teacher" discarded. After examining every suspicious paragraph, he tore these papers into confetti for fear that even a passing thought of the Great Leader should fall into the hands of "the uninitiated". The orderly's activities were detected by equally zealous servants and reported to Stalin. Without even bothering to hear the man out, Stalin gave the order to get rid of him.

Legends about Stalin abound. Some say that his *dacha* was even connected to the Kremlin by a tunnel, along which ran a special train.

The avenue passes through the **Triumphal Arch**, built in 1829 to 1834 by Osip Bove in commemoration of Russia's victory in the 1812 war against Napoleon. The arch was initially situated near the Belo Russian Station. During the reconstruction of the 1930s, it was removed and later rebuilt in its present location. Over 150 sculptures and 12-metre (40-ft) high iron columns were cast in the process. The arch is decorated with the coats of arms of Russia's 48 provinces.

To the right of the arch is the **Borodino Panorama**. This museum was built in 1962 on the 150th anniversary of the battle at Borodino. Inside is a 150-metre (500-ft) long canvas depicting a key moment in the battle. The huge painting is the work of Franz Roubeaud (1912).

The left side of the avenue embraces the remains of Poklonnaya Gora (Hill of Greeting). Here, Napoleon, enthused by his easy victory, awaited (in vain, of course) for the Governor of Moscow to bow and present him with the keys of the city. In the 1980s the hill was landscaped to create space for a gigantic monument commemorating the heroism of the Soviet people in World War II. The decision unleashed a wave of

Mural outsid the Borodino Panorama.

178

indignation and protests against the thoughtless destruction of historically valuable terrain. Construction was stopped and a contest for a better project was announced. The present monuments include a museum, memorial and the first new Orthodox Church to appear in Moscow since the revolution.

The village of Fili: Beyond Poklonnaya Gora, Kutuzovsky Prospekt becomes **Mozhaisk Highway** and then **Minsk Highway** – the main road to the West (Minsk, Brest and Western Europe). The highway passes through the former villages of Kuntsevo, Troekurovo, Fili and Mazilovo, which were engulfed by Moscow in the 1950s. In Fili, at No. 6 **Novozavodskaya Ulitsa**, is one of the best specimens of 17th-century Naryshkin baroque – the **Church of the Intercession**, which is included in the list of outstanding architectural monuments drawn up by the UNESCO Committee for the Protection of Cultural Heritage.

Return to Arbatskaya Ploshchad (by Metro to Arbatskaya) to continue our walk inside the Garden Ring on **Povarskaya Ulitsa**. Lost among the modern giants is a miniature church, which generates a change of mood and makes one want to escape the imposing heaviness of the concrete structures. It is the only surviving church in the area – the 17th-century **Church of Simeon Stolpnik**. Here, in days of yore, Count Sheremetev secretly married the serf actress Parasha Kovaleva-Zhemchugova.

Nikolai Gogol was a member of the church's community in the 19th century. Povarskaya Ulitsa's name stems from Povarskaya, or Cook's Village. Together with Arbat Street, it was once one of the most fashionable streets in Moscow. In the final years of the 19th century, the street was lined with lime trees and grandiose mansions, many of which are now occupied by foreign embassies.

The huge building on the left houses the **Supreme Court**, the country's highest judicial body. The court examines most important cases connected with crimes against the state. Beria was tried here and, in the final years of the USSR, the court building saw a host of Brezhnev's corrupt cronies.

No. 25 Povarskaya Ulitsa belonged to Prince Gagarin in the 19th century and in 1937 was turned over to the **Gorky Institute of World Literature**. This institute, which numbered many prominent Soviet writers among its graduates, was famous throughout the land.

The next block is almost entirely taken up by the **State Musical Institute** named after the Gnessin sisters. The institute was opened in 1944 on the basis of a network of music schools founded by the sisters in 1895.

A club of former political prisoners: No. 33 Povarskaya Ulitsa is the **Studio Theatre of Cinema Actors**, a kind of a stage school for movie actors. The house was built in the 1930s in the constructivist style as a club for "former political prisoners and exiles".

On the opposite side of the street is the sprawling townhouse of the Dolgorukiy family, which dates from the late 18th

century. In 1920, the **House of Arts** was opened here. Blok, Yesenin and Pasternak read their poems here; in 1930, Vladimir Mayakovsky arranged his exhibition entitled *"Twenty Years of Work"*. Today, the building belongs to the Writers' Union. Next door, in the former Alsufiev residence, is the **Literary Union**. Writers come here for professional conferences, and to meet with their readers and foreign guests.

One hundred metres from **Sadovoye Koltso**, at **Trubnikov Pereulok**, is an interesting high-rise building decorated with eagles and lion heads. The basement of this house is where Count Golitsyn, the famous winemaker, stored his collection of wines. After restoration, the cellars were turned over to the Museum of Industrial Architecture. Povarskaya Ulitsa ends near the Sadovoye Koltso in **Kudrinskaya Ploshchad**.

Bolshaya Nikitskaya Ulitsa: This narrow street appeared in place of the former highway to Novgorod, which existed in the 15th and 16th centuries. Its name comes from the Nikitskiye Gates of the White City. The street is cut in two parts by the Boulevard Ring. The first part is lined with 18th to 19th century mansions. The quarter which contains Malaya Nikitskaya Ulitsa, Granatny Pereulok and Spiridonovka Ulitsa has the garish, late 19th-century townhouses of industrial magnates and bankers.

At the very beginning of the street, on the Okhotny Ryad side (Metro Okhotny Ryad), are the old University buildings. They form a kind of gate, situated as they are on either side of the street. Practically the entire block beyond is filled with buildings which are connected with the university in one way or another.

Geniuses of music: At the crossing with Nikitskiy Pereulok (which leads to the right) is the Zoological Museum of the University. No. 13 in Bolshaya Nikitskaya Ulitsa belongs to the foremost school of music in the country – the **Moscow Conservatory**. The house was built late in the 18th century and belonged to Princess Dashkova, who was **Pets for sale.**

President of the Russian Academy. In the 19th century it was purchased by Count Vorontsov and then, in 1871, by the Moscow Conservatory, founded by professor Nikolay Rubinstein. In 1898, the Bolshoi Zal (Great Hall) of the conservatory opened its doors. Tchaikovsky, Rachmaninov, Skriabin and many other famous composers worked here. Since 1958, international contests for violinists, cellists, pianists and vocalists have taken place here every four years.

Several houses on Bolshaya Nikitskaya Ulitsa are connected with the names of prominent composers, actors, directors and writers. Shostakovich, Kabalevsky and Khachaturyan lived on the corner at No. 8. Today, it houses the board of the Composers' Union.

On the corner with Malaya Kislovsky Pereulok is a three-storey brick house dating to the mid-18th century. This was the Paradise Theatre which produced Chekhov's first plays. After the revolution, the theatre was renamed Theatre of Revolutionary Satire. Today its stage belongs to the **Moscow Mayakovsky Theatre**. Next-door, at No. 23, is the **Helicon Opera Theatre**. Nearby is a pleasant restaurant, **U Nikitskikh Vorot** (Near Nikitskiye Gates), specialising in Russian and European cuisine.

The Gate to the White City: The crossroads of Bolshaya Nikitsky Ulitsa and Suvorovsky Bulvar form the square, **Ploshchad Nikitskikh Vorot**, the former gates of the White City. On the right is the central entrance to the **ITAR–TASS** building. ITAR–TASS is Russia's largest telegraph agency, with correspondents in more than 300 countries. Until recently, it was practically the only supplier of information from within the Soviet Union for Soviet and foreign mass media. It now faces considerable competition from several new independent news agencies.

Kachalova Ulitsa: Bolshaya Nikitskaya Ulitsa divides near the Nikitskiye Gates. The right branch is Malaya Nikitskaya Ulitsa. In the centre of the square, where the two streets meet, stands the **Church**

alm reader t work.

of the Great Ascension (late 18th to mid-19th century). Two famous Russian architects – Matvey Kazakov and Osip Bove – worked on this church. In 1831, before the church was complete, Alexander Pushkin and Natalia Goncharova were married here. Behind the church is the 17th-century **Fyodor Studit Church**.

At the very start of Malaya Nikitskaya Ulitsa, opposite the Church of the Great Ascension, is one of Moscow's most curious mansions, built in modern style in 1901. The facade is decorated with ornate stained-glass windows and wood carvings and the building has a glass roof. Maxim Gorky lived here between 1931 and 1936. Like many houses of the famous, it is now a museum.

Spiridonovka Ulitsa used to be named after the writer Alexei Tolstoy, who lived on the adjacent Spiridonievskaya Ulitsa at No. 2. Here he wrote his novels *Peter the Great, Ivan the Terrible*, and many other works. It is also a museum.

On the opposite side of the street, at No. 17, was the **Bukhara House of Enlightenment** – a boarding school for children from Bukhara. That was in 1923. Now, in its place, is the Reception House of the Ministry of Foreign Affairs. The Africa Institute of the Academy of Sciences occupies No. 30.

The surrounding area was occupied in former times by artisan settlements – *Bronnaya* (Armorers), *Kozia* (Wool-Spinners), and, in the 16th and 17th centuries, *Patriarshaya* (the Patriarch's fishponds and grazing pastures).

Granatny Pereulok used to be named after Shchusev, a famous Soviet architect. This street runs to the left of Spiridonovka Ulitsa. Here, at No. 3, is where the architect lived. The house is now occupied by the Board of the Architects' Union.

The Patriarch's Pond: If you turn right at the end of Granatny Pereulok, walk up Vspolny Pereulok and enter a small square formed by the intersection of three streets – Zholtovskogo Ulitsa, Mitskevich Ulitsa and Malaya Bronnaya Ulitsa – you will reach the place known as Goat's Marsh in the 16th century. Three ponds were dug here to supply the Patriarch's household with fish. Only one of them survived – Patriarch's Pond.

Closer to the centre of the square is a **monument to Ivan Krylov** the fable-writer, surrounded by bronze characters from his fables. Muscovites associate the place with another writer: Mikhail Bulgakov. He chose the site for *Master and Margarita*, to which the café *At Margarita's* pays tribute.

Malaya Bronnaya Ulitsa: This street owes its origins to the ancient road from the Kremlin to Tver. Most of its surviving buildings date to the late 19th and early 20th centuries. It starts at the **Moscow Theatre** on Malaya Bronnaya Ulitsa. Before World War II, there was a Jewish theatre here. Its star actor, Mikhoels, was killed by Stalin's henchmen. Before the revolution the entire area was Moscow's Latin Quarter. The group of houses on the left side offered lodgings for students at moderate prices.

Left, fruit seller. Right, handrail in the Gorky House.

THE PUSHKIN MUSEUM OF FINE ARTS

Moscow has many repositories of masterpieces such as the State Museum of Art of Oriental Peoples, the Museum of Decorative and Applied Arts, the Andrei Rublev Museum and others. But there is only one where the visitor can marvel at classical sculptures from ancient Greece and Rome and at renowned ancient and modern paintings.

The Pushkin Museum of Fine Arts, on Volkhonka Ulitsa (daily 10am–8pm except Monday, Tuesday 10am–9pm), is relatively young. It was opened on 31 May 1912 when, in the presence of Tsar Nicholas II, the doors swung open to the accompaniment of a cantata, written especially for the occasion and sung by a choir of 700. Roman Klein was the author of this architectural isle from Ancient Greece under the Moscow sky. Moscow owns this museum of world art that is second only to the Hermitage.

Intended to display a collection of copies, the museum gradually acquired a collection of originals. Antiques now occupy an area of 400 sq. metres (4,300 sq. ft). There are thousands of items, including the marble sarcophagus *Drunken Hercules*, a torso of Aphrodite, Corinthian vases, terracotta statuettes, beads, bracelets, rings.

The picture gallery began with a small collection of Italian paintings of the 18th and 19th centuries (a gift of the Russian diplomat M. Schekin). Muscovites will proudly tell you that the Museum now has six Rembrandts, five Poussins and Rubens, Jordans and Teniers canvasses. And the French collection! It is among the best in the world. Even the French will tell you that it's better to get acquainted with the Barbizon School in Moscow.

Gauguin's tropical pastorals represent the artist's vision of an integrated disposition, which fell victim to the civilisation of machines. *Bathing on the Seine* and *Nude on a Couch*, both world-

Left, detail from Botticelli's *Annunciation*. **Below, Renoir's portrait of the actress Jeanne Samary.**

famous, reassert Renoir's reputation as "the painter of happiness". Some visitors will be burned by the red-hot disc of the sun in van Gogh's *Red Vineyards*, some will surrender to the colours and naiveté of Henry Rousseau, the French primitive. Every collection, every name fuels admiration and pride.

Muscovites have grown accustomed, thanks to this museum, to seeing on occasions, "all the flags" of art from different times, peoples and continents as "our guests". They have included Leonardo's inspired *Mona Lisa*, the treasures of the tomb of Tutankhamun, the redeemed glories of the Dresden Picture Gallery and the joys of the Prado.

The museum never stops making Muscovites happy with new exhibits of painting and sculpture from throughout the world. Of course, like all other museums, there is the problem of funds for such basic necessities as the restoration of rooms and the acquisition of new works of art. The city fathers are determined to remedy this situation.

Where to find the exhibits: Art from ancient civilisations is displayed on the **ground floor**, with the exhibits originating from Urartu in Armenia, the Nile valley, the Scythia region around the Black Sea, Babylon and Greek and Roman settlements. Another downstairs room is devoted to the Italian Renaissance with a fine selection of paintings by Botticelli, Perugino, Canaletto, Tiepolo and Veronese. The work of many French rococo painters such as Boucher, Watteau, Poussin and Fragonard, plus Impressionists such as Cézanne, Ingres, Renoir, Monet, Degas and Gauguin, is displayed. Spanish artists represented include El Greco, Murillo, Ribera and Zurbaran. Other European artists include van Dyck, Jordaens, Brueghel, Rembrandt and Cranach.

On the **first floor** can be found ancient Greek art of the 5th to 1st centuries BC, medieval art, collections of European paintings of the 19th and early 20th centuries, and copies of some of the world's best-known sculpture.

Pushkin Museum

1	The art of ancient Egypt	**17**	European art of the first half of the 20th century
2	The art of ancient civilizations	**18**	Post-Impressionist art - Cézanne and Gauguin
3	Hellenistic, Coptic & Byzantine art	**19,20**	Temporary exhibition halls
4	Italian art of the 13th-15th centuries	**21**	European art of the last third of the 19th century
5,6	The art of Italy, Germany and the Netherlands in the 15th-16th centuries	**22**	The art of the French Impressionists
7	The art of ancient Greece, Rome and the Northern Black Sea region	**23**	European art of the first half of the 19th century
10	Dutch art of the 17th century	**24**	Greek art of the late Classical and Hellenistic period
11	Flemish and Spanish art of the 17th century	**25**	The art of ancient Italy
12	Italian art of the 17th – 18th centuries	**26,27**	European art of the Middle Ages, Dutch and German sculpture
13	French art of the 17th – 18th centuries		of the 15th – 16th centuries
14	The Greek courtyard	**28**	The sculpture of the Italian Renaissance
15	The Italian courtyard	**29**	The sculptures of Michelangelo
16a,16	The art of the Aegean world and ancient Greece	**30**	Concert hall

Ground Floor

First Floor

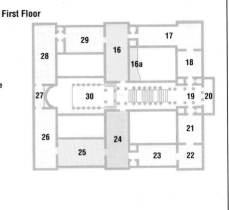

MOSCOW PROPER

Our tour around the centre of Moscow now brings us into the quarter between **Tverskaya Ulitsa** and **Myasnitskaya Ulitsa**. We will start by walking along Tverskaya Ulitsa from Okhotny Ryad towards the Garden Ring.

The old and the new: Tverskaya Ulitsa is special not only because it is Moscow's main street but also because it blends different epochs, different styles, different moods and different impressions. Architecturally it tells the story of Moscow. Like many other main streets in the world, it lacks cohesiveness, being a conglomeration of separate microcosms, each quite different in terms of rhythm and atmosphere. In a subtle way, they convey the mood of the past, the present and even the future.

Its history starts in the 14th century, when a road to Tver was built here. In the 17th century, the *Tverskaya-Yamskaya Sloboda* (Quarter) appeared outside the earthen city ramparts.

Early in the 18th century Tverskaya Ulitsa assumed a festive air – it was by that time the processional entrance to the city, and the wealthiest and best-known Moscow aristocrats lived there. By the end of the 19th century the street was filled with shops. In 1901 it was illuminated with electric lights – the only one in Moscow to be so privileged.

The original street was not as long as it is now – it ended near Sadovoye Ring, where the Triumphal Arch once stood.

The street starts with houses built in this century (Metro Okhotny Ryad. It is the widest part of the otherwise narrow Tverskaya Ulitsa. On the left, are two hotels: the **National**, which dates to the turn of the century, and the **Intourist**. Each has its fans and its character. Since its complete refurbishment in 1995, the National has become one of the most sought-after hotels for business men and wealthy tourists.

Nearby is a small building with an arched entrance – the **Yermolova Theatre**. At the end of the 19th century, a hotel and a shop stood here and, after the revolution, Meyerhold's Theatre was located at this spot.

At the crossing with Gazetniy Pereulok is the huge building of the central telegraph authority and the Ministry of Communications. It was built in 1927 as the central studio of Soviet radio. Today, Moscow telegraph offers myriad services, including personal telex and telefax numbers for those who don't own their own machines.

On the corner of Kamergersky Pereulok stands the theatre that Konstantin Stanislavsky and Vladimir Nemirovich-Danchenko founded in 1898. Anton Chekhov's play, *The Seagull*, was premiered here to great acclaim in 1901. Since then the seagull has been the theatre's emblem. Today, **Khudozhestvenny (Moscow Arts) Teatr (MKHAT)** has two companies and two stages – the original one here and a new one in Tverskoy Bulvar.

At the corner of Tverskaya Ulitsa and Gazetniy Pereulok is a monumental building with a ground-floor gift shop. Its outer wall is lined with granite captured by the Russian troops during the battle of Moscow in 1941. The granite was brought by the Nazis from Finland. They planned to use it for a monument commemorating the victory of Germany over the Soviet Union.

Stoleshnikov Pereulok is a side-street which branches off to the right of Tverskaya Ulitsa. It's one of the busiest places in Moscow and designated to become the city's second pedestrian area. The name comes from the village of Stoleshniki (tablecloth weavers), which existed here in the 16th and 17th centuries.

In the second half of the 19th century the area became the shopping centre of Moscow. No. 9 was the home of probably the best-known reporter in Moscow: Vladimir Gilyarovsky, the author of *Moscow and Muscovites*.

The other attraction of the area is the **Literary Café Stoleshniki**. The basement of this old building, which dates to the 17th century, has recently seen the ceremonial opening of two halls – **Reporter's Hall** and **Moscow and Muscovites**, where Giliarovsky Medals are awarded every year to the writers of the best articles about Moscow.

The dark red building with white columns in **Tverskaya Ploshchad** is the headquarters of the **Moscow City Council** – the city's legislature. Built in 1782 by Matvey Kazakov, the house belonged to the Governor General of Moscow, Count Chernyshov, the general whose troops took Berlin in 1760. When the street was rearranged in 1939, the building was moved back 14 metres (46 ft) and two floors were added. Until the 1990s it was traditional in the Moscow Soviet to register Vladimir Lenin as deputy No.1 before the first session of the newly-elected deputy corps. But times change, and so do traditions.

The square in front of the building was once the site of the ceremonial changing of the guard. Today Yury Dol-gorukiy, the founder of Moscow, sits high above the square on his mighty steed on a pedestal. The building on the right side of the monument stands on the site of the Dresden Hotel (favoured by such literary lights as Turgenev, Nekrasov and Chekhov). The composer Robert Schumann also stayed here. Today the ground floor is occupied by the Georgian **Aragvi Restaurant**. Representatives of this fun-loving nation laud the foresight of Prince Yury, who went out of his way to build a city around the Georgian restaurant.

No. 10 Tverskaya Ulitsa is the **Tsentralnaya Hotel** (built in 1911 as the Liuks Hotel). In the first years after the revolution, the poet Sergei Yesenin lived here; between the 1920s and the 1940s most of the people who stayed here worked for the Communist International.

Moscow's shopping paradise: No. 14, a late 18th-century house, is well-known to Moscow shoppers as **Yeliseev's**. In the 1820s, it belonged to Zinaida Volkhonskaya, the "queen of Muses and

The world's most successful McDonald's branch.

beauty", whose celebrated salon was attended by Pushkin, Vyazemsky and Baratynsky. At the end of the 19th century the ground floor became a shop where the rich merchant from St Petersburg, Yeliseev, decided to open a branch of his Petersburg grocery store.

As you've probably guessed by now, the entire right-hand side of the street is filled with shops: each caters to its own distinct clientele. It is, after all, difficult to mistake the sybaritic sense which attracts buyers to the **Gift Shop**, to the intimate perfume of **Estée Lauder** cosmetics, or to the products of the **Dieta foodstore** and the hustle and bustle amid the glittering bronze and crystal at **Yeliseev's**. For those who seek food for the soul, there are two bookstores, **Akademkniga** (on the left-hand side) and **Moscow Books**, which stock volumes in many foreign languages.

Pushkinskaya Ploshchad is one of the liveliest squares in Moscow. Bordered by a large movie theatre, the editorial offices of newspapers and magazines and, best of all for many locals, by Russia's first **McDonald's** restaurant, the plaza attracts tens of thousands of young people every day. In the last few years it has also been the site of political rallies and angry demonstrations.

The square first appeared in the late 18th century and, until 1931, was known as *Strastnaya Ploshchad* because of the Strastnoy Monastery, which was built near the Tverskiye Gates of the White City in 1640 and which was torn down in the reconstruction of the 1930s. Its place was taken by the **Izvestia Building** and the **Rossiya Movie Theatre**.

In front of the Rossiya, a small garden with fountains was built around the **Monument to Alexander Pushkin**, erected in 1880 with money voluntarily donated by the public.

Under the square are three metro stations – Tverskaya, Pushkinskaya and Chekhovskaya – connected by long underpasses. Here the first part of Tverskaya comes to an end. The next section stretches to Triumfalnaya Ploshchad.

All dressed up – but not, perhaps, for McDonald's.

On the left side of the street, in the red mansion behind the antique grille, are the mighty lions described by Pushkin in *Eugene Onegin*. After its reconstruction by Gilardi in 1831, the house was purchased by the English Club – one of the cultural nests of Moscow's aristocracy. Leo Tolstoy and Alexander Pushkin attended its famous balls. The house was turned over to the Museum of the Revolution in 1924. The exposition reflects the history of the revolutions from 1905 to 1917 and their consequences. Next door, at No. 23, is the **Stanislavsky Drama Theatre**, founded in 1935.

Malaya Dmitrovka Ulitsa starts at Pushkinskaya Ploshchad. Chekhov lived here in the 1890s. On the right-hand side of the street is the **Church of the Birth of the Virgin in Putinki** (*Putinki* means crossroads), which dates to the 17th century. The delicate miniature church is one of the best tent-roofed structures in town. It still has its 17th-century frescoes – a souvenir of when the Polish House stood behind the church where foreign ambassadors were received.

The next house was built in neoclassical style early this century. In the first years after the revolution, it was home to a Communist University. In 1933, the house was turned over to the Theatre of Working Youth, later renamed Leninskiy Komsomol Theatre.

Beyond the Garden Ring: The junction of Tverskaya Ulitsa and the Garden Ring forms **Triumfalnaya Ploshchad** (Metro Mayakovskaya). In the 15th century, ceremonial greetings were extended here to foreign ambassadors; in the 18th century the place was the entrance to Moscow from the new capital of St Petersburg. Today, the **Monument to Mayakovsky**, erected in 1958, stands in the centre of the square.

The character of the square is determined by several key buildings. On the left side, down Bolshaya Sadovaya Ulitsa, is the **Tchaikovsky Concert Hall** with its massive colonnade. The house was built for Meyerhold's Theatre in the 1930s. Opposite is a white edifice

At the Mayakovskaya Metro Station.

with picturesque turrets, which was built in 1946 for the **Pekin (Beijing) Hotel**. The hotel has a recently restored restaurant, with a wide selection of Chinese dishes prepared by chefs from China.

Near the Tchaikovsky Hall is the modern building of the **Satire Theatre**, one of the most popular in Moscow. On the right, the square is completed by the **Sofia Restaurant**. Below the square is the Mayakovskaya Metro station. The city block to the left of Tverskaya Ulitsa, formed by Perviy/Vtory (1st/2nd) Tverskoy-Yamskoy Ulitsa, holds the office of Moscow's chief architect.

The **Central Cinema House** at the corner of Vtory (2nd) Tverskoy-Yamskoy Ulitsa shows new films. The board of the Union of Cinematographers, which meets in this house, organises international film festivals and meetings with film makers.

The gateway to Western Europe: Tverskaya Ulitsa ends in **Ploshchad Tverskoy Zastavy**, which was the site of the gates in the Kamer-Kollezhsky Wall on the

road to Tver. In 1870 a railway station was built near here. Known first as Smolensky and then as Aleksandrovsky Station, it was rebuilt in 1909 and renamed **Byelorussia Station** after the revolution. It is Moscow's main gateway to Western Europe and is where most foreign visitors who do not come by plane first set foot on Moscow soil.

A number of statues on Tverskaya Ulitsa add character to the area. Yury Dolgorukiy is proud and unbending as, with his outstretched arm, he orders the construction of a great city. Pushkin is pensive, proudly alone, oblivious of the hustling crowd below. The gigantic Mayakovsky on Triumfalnaya Ploshchad is full of dynamism and energy. Gorky, on the other hand, looks tired, as if just off the train. The street reflects this pattern, changing from arrogant pride to pensive melancholy to chaotic rambling.

Petrovka Ulitsa: (Metro Ploshchad Teatralnaya). This runs parallel to Bolshaya Dmitrovka Ulitsa. In the old days a road here along the Neglinka river led

Byelorussia Station.

to the village of Vysokoye, which stood on a hill in the White City. Petrovka Ulitsa starts in **Teatralnaya Ploshchad** with the old building of the Muir and Merrilees Department Store. Today, the building belongs to TsUM (Central Department Store).

In the old days, Petrovka Ulitsa, Kuznetsky Most (Blacksmith Bridge) Ulitsa and Neglinnaya Ulitsa were Moscow's shopping streets. In the 18th century they were lined with small shops and stores owned by various trade companies. These offered the latest in Paris fashions, cheeses from Holland and Switzerland, guns from Germany and America – in a word, anything that a person could wish.

Early this century the street was filled with high-rise administrative and residential houses. The next building is Petrovsky Passage, once one of the largest shops in town. The mall, built in 1906, resembles the GUM building in miniature. The monumental white edifice with the colonnade is the former seat of the Raevsky family. Today, the building houses the *Russkiye Uzory* (Russian Lace) shop and a salon of art.

A short distance from the Boulevard Ring is the tall spire of the **Vysokopetrovsky Monastery**. This institution was founded in the 14th century on the bank of the Neglinnaya river in honour of the victory over the Mongols at Kulikovo Field. In 1612, the monastery was an invaluable stronghold in the war against Poland. The monastery has a collection of monuments, most of which were built by the Naryshkin family in the late 17th and 18th centuries.

In the middle of the complex is the main church standing above the Naryshkin family crypt. The **Sergiy of Radonezh Church** and **Peter the Metropolitan Church** are next to it.

The last section of the street is called **Karietny Ryad** (Carriage Row). The name refers to the time when, in the late 18th century, carriages were sold here. Some of the shops which sold the carriages have survived.

On the right side is a structure with high arches. The vast area behind this was rented by Sergey Shchukin, the industrialist and art patron, in 1894. He founded the Hermitage Garden here. Today the park is home to the **Theatre of Miniatures**, the **Sphere Theatre**, and an outdoor concert stage.

The street above the water: The next street that leads from the city centre towards the Garden Ring is **Neglinnaya Ulitsa**. The name comes from the Neglinnaya river, channeled through an underground conduit at the order of Catherine the Great. The conduit, however, was too narrow and caused flooding, particularly during the spring thaw. In 1975 a larger pipe was installed. Opposite the Kremlin's Water-Raising Tower, the Neglinnaya falls into the Moskva.

Contemporaries say that the Neglinnaya River was the sewer of Moscow. Although dumping waste into the river was prohibited by law, the rich aristocrats who lived in the street built drainage systems running directly into it. The

Western luxury goods draw a crowd.

"services" of the underground river were also used by criminals who used it to dispose of bodies and "hot" loot. These bodies and corpses of dead animals frequently jammed the pipe and caused flooding, which affected even the Bolshoi Theatre.

A club, a casino and an old Moscow bathhouse: No. 9 **Pushechnaya Ulitsa** housed the German Schuster Club – an aristocratic establishment for Moscow gentry. Today, there is another club here – the **Club of Art Workers**.

On the corner of Pushechnaya Ulitsa and Rozhdestvenka Ulitsa is one of the most expensive and fashionable hotels in Moscow – the **Savoy** – built in 1913 by the architect Velichkin. After the war it was renamed the Berlin and neglected. Recently, the hotel opened its doors after restoration under its original name. It offers all the amenities of hotels in the west, including a casino.

On the right of Neglinnaya Ulitsa is the old building of Sandunov's Baths, originally dating from 1808. The owner of the best bath-house of the time was the actor Sandunov. The baths have been restored, and seem to be regaining their former glory. On the left side is **Uzbekistan**, an Uzbek restaurant.

Bolshaya Lubyanka Ulitsa (Metro Lubyanka) leads into Sretenka Ulitsa and then becomes Prospekt Mira.

A little further on, the palatial mansion at No. 14 Bolshaya Lubyanka was built by Rastrelli and figures in Tolstoy's *War and Peace* in a scene during the fire of Moscow. At the end of the street is the **Cathedral of the Sretensky Monastery** that goes back to 1395 and contains restored frescoes from the 18th century.

Where the icon was met: Beyond the Boulevard Ring is **Sretenka Street**. The name derived apparently from the word *Vstreteniye*, meaning "meeting". In 1395 the Vladimir Icon of the Mother of God was brought from Vladimir to Moscow to be placed in the Cathedral of the Dormition and was solemnly met at the gate of the White City. In the 17th century all the surrounding area was

On parade at a nightclub.

occupied by artisans' quarters, where printers, founders and gunsmiths had their shops. In the 19th and early 20th centuries the street was built over with tenement houses and shops.

At the very beginning of the street, on the left side at the junction with the Boulevard Ring, is the small **Church of the Dormition at Pechatniki**, built in the late 17th century. Most of the houses lining the street are now being restored and its historical appearance reconstructed. The architectural make-up of the street at its further end, near the Sukharevskaya Metro Station, was spoiled in the 1930s after the Sukharev Tower was pulled down and the square was cleared for the construction of the metro. At its junction with Sadovo-Sukharevskaya Ulitsa, stands the **Church of the Trinity at Listy**, which was built in the 17th century.

On the other side of the Garden Ring, Sretenka Ulitsa becomes **Prospekt (Peace) Mira** (Metro Prospekt Mira). The street emerged on the site of an old road that led to the Trinity–St Sergius Monastery, Yaroslavl, and then on to the north of Russia.

In the 17th century the *Meshchanskaya Sloboda* (Tradesmen's Quarter), inhabited by immigrants from Byelorussian and Ukrainian towns, sprang up here. The street was named after this quarter. During the 19th century bankers' and industrialists' mansions and tenement houses began to be built here. In the Soviet period, in the 1930s and 1940s, most of the houses were rebuilt and the street was widened and extended.

A wedding palace: On the left side of Prospekt Mira is No. 5, the house of Perlov, the well-known tea merchants. It was built in the late 19th century in renaissance style. On the opposite side of the avenue is the early 18th-century mansion in which Jacob Bruce, Peter the Great's comrade-in-arms, lived. No. 18 on the same side of the avenue, built by the architect Bazhenov in the late 18th century, has been converted into a

Wedding Palace where young couples are married.

Moscow fashion and Russian rock: Practically opposite the palace is the centre of **Vyacheslav Zaitsev**, the leading Moscow fashion designer. His designs have been highly successful in West Europe and in Japan.

On the right side of the avenue, near No. 26, are the grounds of the country's oldest **Botanical Gardens**. Founded in 1706 by Peter the Great for growing medicinal herbs, it was known as the "apothecary's garden". For more than 250 years the gardens have been managed by Moscow University.

In the late 1970s the **Olimpiisky (Olympic) Sports Complex** was built opposite the Prospekt Mira Metro Station. Russian and foreign rock and pop music concerts are periodically held in the complex's central arena.

In front of the monolithic sports palace is the miniature **Church of St Filipp the Metropolitan of Moscow**. It was built in the late 18th century and, like so

The Vostok rocket catapulted Russia into the space age.

many other buildings of that time, was designed by Matvey Kazakov.

Further along, on the same side, is **Rizhskaya Ploshchad**. It emerged on the site of the Krestovskaya Gate of the Kamer-Kollezhsky Rampart in the early 19th century. On its left is the building of the **Riga Railway Station**, built at the end of the 19th century. From here trains run to the Baltic republics.

One casualty of the end of Communism has been the disappearance of the famous Rizhsky Market and the even more famous flea and thieves' market. This used to be the only place in Moscow where trade in all types of home-made goods produced in the old USSR was officially permitted. Here you could buy a fur hat, a national costume, a military uniform and many other items. Not infrequently, stolen goods were sold here.

Immediately ahead is the Krestovsky Flyover under which the Oktyabrskaya Railway passes. Branching off from Prospekt Mira, near the VDNKh Metro Station, is **Ulitsa Akademika Korol-**

Gagarin, the first man in space.

yova, named after the chief designer of Soviet spacecraft. The street leads to yet another historical district, **Ostankino**. In fair weather the tall spire of the **Ostankino TV Tower** can be seen practically from anywhere in the city. The 540-metre (1,770-ft) TV tower was built in 1967.

On the right side of the avenue opposite the VDNKh Metro Station is the colossal **Cosmos Hotel**, built in the late 1970s by a joint team of Soviet, French and Yugoslavian builders.

Facing the hotel is the entrance to the **All-Russian Exhibition Centre** (VVT's), the biggest permanent exhibition in Russia. The tradition of arranging exhibitions of this type, demonstrating Soviet achievements, originated in 1939. At that time each of the 15 Union Republics had its own pavilion built by Moscow architects in pseudo-national styles. Everything was designed to demonstrate the indestructibility of the multinational union and the might of the world's first socialist state.

In the course of time, the pavilions were shuffled and then divided by industries. This was a kind of first warning bell, indicating that the republics, being completely dependent on the central government, had nothing to demonstrate individually. Now, more than 70 pavilions situated on an area of 234 hectares (578 acres) are used by businesses and private commerical organisations to advertise their products.

In front of the central entrance to the exhibition stands the sculptural composition, *Worker and Woman Collective Farmer* by the sculptor **Vera Mukhina**. The original idea was to place a frontier guard with a dog on the pedestal, thus personifying the inviolability of the country's borders. However, since the idea of "inviolability" had also the connotation "no one will be let out", the frontier guard was replaced by the neutral figure of a worker.

Beyond the Severyanin Railway Station, Prospekt Mira becomes **Yaroslavl Highway** and leads to Archangelsk far in the north of Russia.

IN THE FORMER FOREIGN QUARTER

In this chapter we will follow Myasnitskaya Ulitsa to Nemetskaya Sloboda, the ancient foreigners' settlement, and then cross the Yauza River to Zayauze.

Myasnitskaya Ulitsa emerged in the late 15th century on the site of a road leading to the Moscow grand dukes' estates in the environs of Moscow. Its name, meaning Butchers' Street, goes back to the 17th and 18th centuries when the quarter was full of butchers' shops. In the late 18th century aristocratic mansions began to be built here. Subsequently, it became one of the fashionable business streets in Moscow.

The first part of the street up to the Boulevard Ring is occupied by monumental pre-revolutionary structures, which formerly belonged to banks and various trading firms, and by apartment houses. At the crossing with Bolshoy Zlatoustinsky Pereulok stands one of the most interesting buildings in art nouveau style built at the end of the 19th century by the famous architect Shekhtel. At one time it was the headquarters of the trading house of Kuznetsov, the noted manufacturer of porcelain and the owner of the Dulyovo Porcelain Factory.

Home of Armenians and Poles: In nearby **Armyanskaya Pereulok**, named after the *Armyanskaya Sloboda* (Armenian Quarter) which was here in the 17th and 18th centuries, stands a mansion with stone lions guarding the entrance gate. At one time it housed an Armenian school, set up in 1814 with funds provided by the merchants Lazarev. Later, it was converted into an Institute of Oriental Languages, also known as the Lazarev Institute. Today, the building houses the **Armenian Embassy**.

Branching off from Myasnitskaya Ulitsa to the left is **Milyutinsky Pereulok**. At the beginning of the street, near the former Polish Quarter, is the Roman Catholic Church of **St Peter and Paul**, built in the mid-19th century. It survived the anti-religious attitudes of the last decades.

One unusual house in Myasnitskaya Ulitsa, designed in a Chinese style, was built in the late 19th century by Perlov to promote the selling of Chinese tea which his firm imported. Today the shop on its ground floor still sells tea which is, however, far below its former standard.

The next building, No. 21, was erected in the late 18th century by the architect Vassili Bazhenov for a rich nobleman, Yushkov. In the 19th century it was a school of painting, sculpture and architecture. Such noted artists as Shishkin, Levitan, Serov and Vasnetsov taught here. In 1872 an exhibition by the famous *Peredvizhniki* (Itinerants) was held at the school. In the early post-revolutionary years such painters as Petrov-Vodkin, Saryan and Malevich studied and taught here. The poet Vladimir Mayakovsky also appeared here before the public more than once. The school later became the **Surikov Moscow Arts Institute**.

The last building on the right near the Myasnitskaya Metro Station is the **Moscow General Post Office**. It was here, at No. 40 Myasnitskaya Ulitsa, that the first post office was opened in Moscow in 1700. The present building of the GPO, reminiscent of some romantic medieval edifice, was built in 1912.

Stalin's fallout shelter: Beyond **Turgenevskaya Ploshchad**, Myasnitskaya Ulitsa runs parallel to the wide Prospekt Akademika Sakarova. At No. 37 is a house built in the early 18th-century by the architect Osip Bove. It belonged to Soldatenkov, a merchant and patron of the arts, and was a favourite meeting place for Moscow writers. The house was also famous for its excellent library and splendid picture gallery. In the years of World War II, the Soviet Supreme Commander-in-Chief, Josef Stalin, took a fancy to this house. His choice was not entirely accidental, for the house stood near the Kirovskaya Metro Station, one of the deepest in Moscow, which was connected with the house by a special underground passage. In the event of an air attack he could take shelter deep underground in no time at all.

Further along, at No. 39, is a building of glass and concrete, the work of the French architect **Le Corbusier**, built in the early 1930s.

Where the trains converge: Myasnitskaya Ulitsa comes to an end at the Garden Ring not far from **Kalanchevskaya Ploshchad** – "Three Stations Square" (Metro Komsomolskaya). On the south-eastern side of the square you can see the central facade of the **Leningrad Hotel**, one of the famous Moscow wedding-cake skyscrapers. Russia's first casino opened here at the end of the 1980s.

This place was known since the 17th century as *Kalanchevskoye Field*. At one time a royal coaching palace with a high watchtower (*kalancha*) stood here, and the tsar would stay in this place overnight on his way from the Kremlin to the village of Krasnoye.

The **Leningrad** (formerly *Nikolay-evsky*) **Railway Station**, the oldest in town, was built in 1849 by the architect Konstantin Ton. Characteristic features of St Petersburg architecture can clearly be seen in its design. The railway, which linked the two capital cities, was one of the first to be built in Russia. It was laid practically as the crow flies across forests and marshes; its total length is 650 km (400 miles).

Starting point of the Trans-Siberian: The neighbouring **Yaroslavl Railway Station** was built in the early 20th century by the architect Shekhtel. Its design was strongly influenced by art nouveau. Under the arch over the entrance to the station building are the ancient coats of arms of Moscow, Yaroslavl and Ark-hangelsk. The sturdy pillars and fanciful turrets are reminiscent of the traditional image of northern Russia. The Yaroslavl Station is the starting point of the world's longest railroad, the **Trans-Siberian Railway**, which runs to the Pacific shore of Russia. Its total length is 9,300 km (5,770 miles); travelling time is 143 hours.

On the square's opposite side is the biggest and the busiest of all the Moscow

On Three Stations Square.

202

railway stations, the **Kazan Station**. This was built between 1913 and 1926 by the architect Shchusev. From here trains run to the Caucasus, Central Asia, Western Siberia and the Altai. Every day up to 150 long-distance trains arrive at this station.

Two million passengers daily: In all, the daily flow of passengers through the three stations exceeds two million. This does not mean that all these people have Moscow as their destination. Many people are travelling to other places. The structure of the Russian railway network is such that all the railways intersect in Moscow and you have to travel to the capital even if you wish to reach some other place. Tickets are often in short supply, since it is impossible to forecast the number of passengers travelling in any one direction. Because of this, many people are compelled to spend the night at the station, for, as is well known, hotels in Moscow are always overbooked.

To brighten up the cheerless stay of the unbidden visitors to the capital, the **Moskovsky Department Store**, the big-

gest in Russia, has been built on the right side of the square.

Beyond Kalanchevskaya Ploshchad the road goes northeast by way of the **Sokolniki Park** to the wooded tract of *Losiny Ostrov* – area 11,000 hectares (27,000 acres) – then to **Baumanskaya Ulitsa** and a district that was at one time known as *Nemetskaya Sloboda*, the Foreign Quarter.

In the former Foreign Quarter: The Foreign Quarter emerged in the 16th to 17th centuries. It was inhabited by immigrants from various European countries who came to serve the Russian government. The Foreign Quarter was distinguished by a clear cut layout, numerous Protestant churches and small taverns and by its inhabitants, who wore outlandish garments and spoke strange languages.

During the reign of Peter the Great the **Foreign Quarter** and the neighbouring village of **Preobrazhenskoye** (Metro Preobrazhenskaya) became the tsar's residence until the transfer of the capital to St Petersburg. From that time the names of

Waiting for the Trans-Siberian Railway.

a number of lanes such as Aptekarsky Pereulok, Poslannikov Pereulok, Starokirochny Pereulok, and Lefortovsky Pereulok (called after the Swiss-born general Franz Lefort, Peter the Great's comrade-in-arms) have survived.

The mansion in today's **Vtoroye Baumanskaya Ulitsa**, presented to Lefort by Peter the Great for the entertainment of foreign guests, has been preserved to this day. In the 18th century it was bought and rebuilt by Prince Alexander Menshikov. Today, it houses the **Central State Archives**. Alongside it stands a palace which belonged first to Bestuzhev-Ryumin, then to Count Orlov and finally to General Field Marshal Kutuzov. Upon its reconstruction by Gilardi and Grigoryev, the palace was turned over to the Moscow Higher Technical School, now the **Moscow State Technical University**.

Catherine's former Palace, rebuilt from the Petrovsky (Peter the Great's) Palace by a group of architects headed by Kazakov and Camporesi in 1774–96, has survived. Today, this huge building with a colonnade of 16 Corinthian columns houses the **Malinovsky Academy of Armoured Troops**. Adjoining the palace is Petrovsky Park, which now belongs to the headquarters of the Moscow Military District.

In this district is the old **Vedenskoye Cemetery**, also known as the **German Cemetery**, where Lefort and French pilots from the Normandy-Niemen Division who died fighting the Nazis during World War II lie buried.

The **Cathedral of the Epiphany at Yelokhovo** (1837–45) is one of the district's most beautiful structures. The first church on its present site was laid down by Peter the Great in commemoration of the annexation by Russia of the Caspian lands in the northern Caucasus. Later, it was rebuilt and consecrated in honour of the victory over Napoleon. Not long ago a record of the birth of Alexander Pushkin, who was born on May 26, 1799, in the house of Titular Counselor Skvortsov in Malaya Pochtovaya Ulitsa, was found in the parish register. Behind the cathedral **Green Moscow.**

is a small and cosy restaurant bearing a historical name, **Razgulyai** (roughly translated "have a good time"), that serves Russian cuisine.

In nearby **Preobrazhensky Val Ulitsa** the late 18th and early 19th-century ensembles of the **Preobrazhenskaya (Transfiguration) Old Believers' Community** and the **Old Believers' Monastery of St Nicholas** have partially survived. From 1918 this has been the centre of the *Bespopovtsi* (Priestless) branch of the Russian Old Believers. The Churches of the Exaltation of the Holy Cross and of St Nicholas, built with the participation of Vassili Bazhenov, have also survived.

We return now to the city centre (by Metro to Kitai Gorod) and to a quarter of Moscow on the opposite side of the Yauza River. But before crossing the river, we will walk along **Solyanka Ulitsa**. Its name is one of the oldest in Moscow. It led from the Varvarskiye Gate of Kitay-Gorod to the city of Vladimir and dates back to the 17th and 18th centuries. At the very beginning of the street, where it meets Podolokolny Pereulok, stands the former **Church of the Nativity of the Most Holy Virgin at the Spit** (1800), now a cosmetic institute.

Moscow's Jewish centre: In Bolshaya Spasoglinishchevsky Pereulok, branching off to the right, and uphill towards Maroseika Ulitsa, is the building of the **Moscow Choral Synagogue**, built in the late 19th century. It is the spiritual centre of Moscow's Jewish community.

In neighbouring Starosadsky (Old Gardens) Pereulok, named after the grand duke's gardens that used to be here, is the building of the **Historical Library**, the biggest library of historical literature in Russia; the stock, based generally on private collections, runs into more than 3 million books in various languages.

The next structure, the **Church of St Vladimir in the Old Gardens**, dates to the early 16th century. It was built by the architect Alevisio Novy, the same architect who built the Kremlin. Today the church is a book depository.

At the corner with Zabelina Ulitsa

Local resident.

stands a grim building with blind walls and towers. This is the former St John Convent founded in the 16th century. Here the mysterious Nun Dosifeya, better known as the Princess Tarakanova, the natural daughter of the Empress Elizabeth Petrovna, was confined on the orders of Catherine the Great. In the 18th century the convent was rebuilt and after the revolution its buildings were given to the Cheka, the KGB's predecessor .

Across the Yauza: We will now cross over the Yauza by way of the Astachov Bridge to **Zayauze**. At the spot where the Yauza flows into the Moskva river rises one of the seven Moscow skyscrapers. This 176-metre (586-ft) high building was built in 1952. One of the wings of the skyscraper houses the **Illusion Movie Theatre**, well-known and popular for showing masterpieces of cinematic art. It is the only movie theatre of its kind in Moscow and getting a ticket for a show is no easy matter. During the construction of this tall building, the remains of an old riverside quay, dating back to the 15th

century, were found. At the time the Yauza was still navigable.

The church on "lousy" hill: Beyond this monolithic building lies **Taganskaya Hill**. It was once known as **Shvivaya Hill**, which, perhaps, is a corruption of the word *vshivaya*, meaning "lousy". On its slope lies the former *Shvivaya Ulitsa*, now called **Goncharnaya Ulitsa** or Potter Street. In this street is the shining white **Church of St Nikita the Martyr Beyond the Yauza**, built in the early 16th century on the very crest of the hill.

At the very end of Goncharnaya Ulitsa is the **Church of the Dormition of the Mother of God in Gonchary**, whose name suggests the former presence of a *Goncharnaya Sloboda* (Potters' Quarter) in the area. The five-domed church is of a traditional shape and was built in the mid-17th century; it is decorated with coloured tiles showing full-size human figures. Nearby, near the entrance to the Taganskaya Metro Station in **Verkhovaya Radishchevskaya Ulitsa**, is the late 17th-century **Church of St Nicholas at the Taganskiye Gate in Bolvanovka**.

The street ends at Taganskaya Ploshchad which emerged at the Taganskiye Gate back in the 17th century. From the square, roads led to the Monastery of St Simeon the Stylite, the New Monastery of the Saviour, and to the Alexeyevskaya, Semyonovskaya and Vorontsovskaya Slobodas (Quarters).

A library of 132 languages: Another main thoroughfare in Zayauzye is **Nikoloyanskaya Ulitsa**. This emerged back in the late 17th century on the site of a coachmen's settlement. It was the ancient road to Vladimir. At the beginning of the street, on its left side, stands the modern-looking multi-storey **Library of Foreign Literature**, erected in 1967 by the architect Chechulin. Today the library, the biggest of its kind in the country, has a stock of some 5 million books and periodicals in 132 languages.

At the end of the street, on the right, is the **Church of St Simeon the Stylite**, built at the end of the 18th century by the architect Matvey Kazakov.

An area rich in icons.

THE MAFIA

For decades, generations of Russians were trained to believe that in the "society of developed socialism" there was no organised crime. Yet a mafia in Russia undoubtedly existed under Communism, feeding off the capital controlled by state authorities, and today it is flourishing as never before. Most reports in the foreign press concentrate on its high-profile activities in Moscow and St Petersburg, but it extends as far as the wild eastern borders of the country, where cities like Vladivostok and Khabarovsk are controlled by gangsters behaving like feudal lords.

The mafia operates in many spheres. Firstly, it is active in the fertile field of privatisation, a process governed by a narrow circle of state functionaries who can decide who, and at what price, is given property for businesses and housing. The volume of bribery has spiralled.

Secondly, through bribery and blackmail, the mafia tries to channel state money into the black economy. They are aided by corrupt government officials with purchasing duties.

Thirdly, the Russian mafia has become a key player in the international drug trade. Russian drug dealers are behind shipments to Scandinavia, Germany, France, Greece and Poland.

Fourthly, there are the huge sums of money that the Communist Party spirited into Western banks during the Soviet era. When privatisation began, they made their way back to the inner markets of Russia, usually through joint ventures, but not to the benefit of the State.

Lastly, there are the racketeering, prostitution and weapons trades. The mafia benefited from the national conflicts, and the withdrawal of Soviet troops from the former Soviet republics. Some sources even claim the conflicts were engineered by the mafia.

Mafiosi from all republics converge on Moscow, working out their multi-billion deals in the city's deluxe restaurants, and all too often the police are on their payroll. The city's mayor, Yury Luzhkov, despaired of breaking this connection. "We have given the police everything," he complained. "Enough money to equip them as well as New York City's police. Sixty-five new office buildings better than palaces, garden allotments, flats – and what results do we get? None!"

Different mafia groups are engaged in an armed struggle for control of key zones The Chechen mafia removed its competitors by planting a bomb at the Moscow railway station: one person was killed and a few people were wounded. But the real battles started when the law arrested Aleksandr Malyshev, a top member of the city's mafia, and one of the leaders of the Tambov city mafia operating in St Petersburg. In both cases the police seized weapons and valuables worth several million roubles. The mafia responded by killing Evgeny Oleinik, the former chief of the service charged with the struggle against economic crimes.

Big joint ventures with foreign participation have set up their own security services, not even hoping for help from the local police. Smaller firms hire local policemen or private security agents. After a number of Americans, Britons and Germans had been kidnapped, Lloyd's of London brought out a policy offering to reimburse ransom payments made to kidnappers and compensate companies for the wages paid to executives while held hostage. Another phenomenon are the "night butterflies" – prostitutes who rob their clients. Prostitutes in Russia work under strict mafia control.

"Crime has become a real threat to the national security of Russia," admitted President Yeltsin. "Not infrequently, it is the police themselves who are passing information to criminals." He had reason for concern. A *Moscow News* report listed the prices charged by contract killers. These started at $7,000 for hitting an average citizen without a bodyguard. The most expensive contract was for $180,000 – the price for rubbing out Boris Yeltsin. ∎

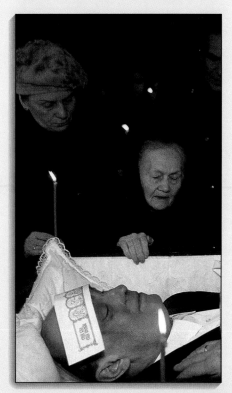

Mafia victim.

IN THE BEND OF THE RIVER

We continue our way through Moscow by crossing the Moskva river by way of the **Krasnokholmsky Most**, which leads from Zayauze to **Zamoskvorechye**, another historical district. In the north it is confined by the Moskva river and in the south it is surrounded by the arc of the Garden Ring.

The first settlements in this area are believed to have emerged in the 13th and 14th centuries. It is known from historical chronicles that Ivan IV, the Terrible, settled the *streltsi* (royal musketeers) in *Zarechye*, which is an older name for this area.

The artisans' district: The main thoroughfare in the district, crossing from north to south, **Ordynka Street**, emerged on the site of a historical road leading to the Golden Horde. During the 16th century, artisans quarters known as *Kadashevskaya* (weavers), *Khamovnaya* (barrel makers), *Kozhevennaya* (leather workers) and *Kazachya* (servants) suburbs came into being on both sides of the road. Today their names can still be traced in the names of some streets.

The emergence of these artisans' quarters resulted in the construction of separate churches in practically every district, because they are an integral part of every Russian settlement. One of the most beautiful 17th-century Moscow churches is the **Church of the Resurrection at Kadashi**, located in Vtory Kadashevsky Pereulok.

Most of the houses in **Bolshaya Ordynka Ulitsa** date from the 19th and early 20th centuries. The most prominent example of neo-classicism is the former house of the merchant Dolgov, built at the end of the 18th century to the design of the architect Vassili Bazhenov. Later on, after a fire, the house was rebuilt by Osip Bove. It now houses the **Institute of Latin America** of the Russian Academy of Sciences. Immedi-

ately opposite is the **Church of the Icon of the Mother of God, "Joy of All the Afflicted"**. Like the house, the church was erected by Bazhenov and then rebuilt by Bove. The **Church of St Nicholas** at Pyzhi, built in the mid-17th century with money donated by the *streltsi* regiment under the command of Colonel Pyzhov, is another adornment of this street.

Further on the right side, beyond wrought-iron gates, is the ensemble of the former **Convent of St Martha and Mary**, built in the early 20th century as a charitable institution for war invalids. The ensemble includes a **Church of the Protecting Veil** and hospital buildings.

At the very end of the street is still another church, the late 18th-century **Church of St Catherine**. In Shchetininsky Pereulok the museum of the artist Tropinin displays a collection of paintings by a number of early 19th-century Moscow artists.

The Tretyakov Gallery: In **Lavrushinsky Pereulok** are several attractions. The principal one, located nearer to the embankment, is the building of the universally famous **Tretyakov Gallery**, the outstanding museum of Russian and Soviet art. The facade of the building, erected in the early 20th century, was designed by the artist Viktor Vasnetsov. Next to it is the house in which Pavel Tretyakov, the celebrated founder of the gallery, lived.

Today the museum has 20 buildings, including the **New Tretyakov Gallery** at the central House of Artists in Krymsky Val Ulitsa (near **Gorky Park**) where there is a permanent display of modern paintings from the Tretyakov collection. (*For fuller details about the galleries, see pages 214–15.*)

Branching off to the right from Serpukovskaya Ploshchad and leading into the heart of Zamoskvorechye is another main thoroughfare, **Pyatnitskaya Ulitsa**, named after the **Church of St Parasceve** which has not survived.

The entire block at the beginning of the street, on the right side, is occupied by the 1st Model Printing House, built in 1876. Located in Chernigovsky Pereulok, which branches off to the right, is the 16th-century **Church of St John the Baptist at the Pinewood** (*pod borom*) and, next to it, the late 17th-century **Church of St Mikhail and Fyodor of Chernigov**.

In **Klimentovsky Pereulok**, across the street, are several old historical monuments. The building at No. 7, erected between 1762 and 1770, was once the Church of St Clement the Pope, after whom the lane is named. This huge building, whose walls and towers are decorated with Corinthian columns, is being converted into a concert hall.

Pyatnitskaya Ulitsa ends at the **Chugunny Most** (**Iron Bridge**) across the Bypass Canal. Having walked over the bridge to the other side of the canal, you will arrive at the **Balchug Kempinski Hotel**, built in 1898. It stands on Ogunny Balchug Ulitsa (*balchug* means "mud" in Tatar). It is not accidental that the street has a Tatar name: there were Tatar

settlements here in the days of the Tatar-Mongol yoke.

Along the **Sofiyskaya Naberezhnaya** are many old mansions. No. 34 was a hotel in which the American delegation stayed that was sent to Russia by US President Lincoln to express the American people's gratitude for Russia's support in preventing an Anglo-French intervention in Northern America in 1865. The next building, formerly Kharitonenko's Mansion, houses the **British Embassy**, the first embassy of any Western power to be opened in the Soviet Union following the revolution.

Proceed towards **Bolshoi Kamenny Most** and you will reach **Bolotnaya Ploshchad** (Boggy Square). This was the location before the revolution of the well-known Bolotny Market. It was here that Yemelyan Pugachev, the leader of the insurgents in the Peasant War, and his comrades-in-arms were executed in 1775. After World War II, at the time when the 800th anniversary of Moscow was celebrated, a public garden with fountains was laid out in the square.

Beyond Bolotnaya Ploshchad, stretching from the Bolshoi Kamenny Most, is the shortest street in town, **Serafimovicha Ulitsa** (known as *Vsekhsvyatskaya Ulitsa* or All Saints before 1933). Its length is 363 metres (1,200 ft).

The horseshoe-shaped island, washed on the one side by the Moskva river and on the other, by the Bypass Canal, terminates at the spit. It was covered with granite in 1935 when the new Maly Kamenny, Maly Moskvoretsky and Maly Chugunny Bridges were built.

When the **Kamenny Most**, one of the first bridges over the Moskva river, was built at the end of the 17th century under the supervision of the *Starets Filaret* (*starets* is a title that was given to people viewed as spiritual leaders in Russia), it was regarded as the "seventh wonder of the world". The dry wooden arches of the bridge served as an excellent shelter for homeless people and thieves. The present bridge was built in its place in 1938.

In season, fruit vendors from the vicinity come to the city.

Branching off to the right from Bolshaya Polyanka Ulitsa is **Bolshaya Yakimanka Ulitsa**. At the bend of Bolshaya Polyanka Ulitsa your attention will be attracted by the festive-looking **Church of St Gregory Thaumaturgus**, built between 1667 and 1669. Near this pillarless five-domed church, the gate of Kadashevskaya Sloboda once stood.

The entire right side of Bolshaya Yakimanka Ulitsa is occupied by three modern buildings of unusual architecture – at least, unusual in Moscow. Built in 1982–85, they form a single cohesive group. The first one houses a shop for newlyweds.

The building in the centre, with huge and strange-looking cubes on top, is the **President Hotel**, a deluxe hotel owned by the Central Committee of the Communist Party. Formerly, guests were received here free of charge – or rather, at the expense of the state. Since the hotel has been renovated, however, all guests are expected to pay at the customary high rates.

On the ground floor of the next building is the **House of Toys** (*Dom Igrushki*), the biggest toy shop in Moscow which was a rival of the famous Detsky Mir (Children's World) Department Store in Lubyanka Ploshchad. The decor of the facades of the three buildings was designed to be in harmony with the nearby **Church of St John the Warrior**, an example of early 18th-century Baroque.

The street ends at the spacious **Kaluzhskaya Ploshchad**, formed by the crossing of the Garden Ring, passing under the square, and Leninsky Prospekt, leading into the southwestern part of the capital.

The 14-km (10-mile) **Leninsky Prospekt** is a busy arterial road leading ultimately to Kiev. This section contains the scientific centre of Moscow, with the capital's major research, medical and educational institutions being concentrated in the area. It ends in the new residential districts of Tyoply Stan and Troparyovo.

A familiar scene from many Muscovites' apartments.

THE TRETYAKOV GALLERY

Housed in an old-Russian style boyar mansion the **Tretyakov Gallery** (in Lavrushinsky Lane, not far from the Kremlin beyond the Moskva River) was founded by the collector and art patron Pavel Tretyakov and his brother Sergei, and has become the outstanding museum of Russian and Soviet art (open daily 10am–8pm except Monday). The gallery's original facade, which resembles either an ancient Russian *terem* (palace), or a portal of a church, was designed by the painter Viktor Vasnetsov.

In 1856 Pavel Tretyakov, a young merchant and industrialist, bought the works of Russian artists who were as young as he himself – Valery Yakobi, Mikhail Klodt. As the collection grew, he decided to establish a public museum of national art, the first of its kind in Russia.

Initially, the paintings were kept in the Tretyakov residence, but as time passed, new halls were added, designed for the sole purpose of exhibiting the paintings. In 1873 the collection was opened to the public. The project took almost 40 years of Tretyakov's life. In 1892 he presented his collection of 3,500 paintings to the city. Today, there are more than 50,000.

At first, Tretyakov bought the works of his contemporaries, preferably artists of democratic leanings – bright battle scenes by Vasily Vereschagin, the romantic *Princess Tarakanova* by Konstantin Flavitsky, *Bird-Catchers* by Vasily Perov. Then he filled a hall with spirited, inspired portraits by the old masters – Levitsky and Borovikovsky, the charming Rokotov, and several artists who were closer to Tretyakov's time – Tropinin, Venetsianov, Bryullov. Moscow had never seen such diversity.

Another major event for the gallery was the purchase of such major works as *Morning of the Execution of the Streltsy* by Vasily Surikov and *Ivan the Terrible and his Son Ivan* by Ilya Repin.

Vasily Perov (1833–82) portrayed peasants' lives with realism.

Other works by Repin (1844–1930) include *Portrait of the Composer Modest Mussorgsky*, *Barge Haulers on the Volga* and *The Zaporozhian Cossacks Writing to the Turkish Sultan*.

There, in that fairy-tale house in Lavrushinsky Lane, people got lost in the world of childhood tales, depicted by that kind sorcerer, Viktor Vasnetsov, in the epic forests of Ivan Shishkin, the delicate landscapes of Isaac Levitations, the portraits of soul-searcher and truth-lover Vasily Perov.

A world of icons: Ilya Ostroukhov took an active part in the creation of the gallery. An accomplished artist himself, he collected the icons which today form the bulk of Old Russian painting in the Tretyakov Gallery. There are ancient mosaics (10th–11th centuries), and the *Vladimir Mother of God* – perhaps the most famous icon in the world – a unique example of Byzantine 12th-century art.

There are works by Andrei Rublev (the famous *Trinity*), Dionysius, and artists of the Stroganov School. Icons were painted on old, dry planks of fir or limewood. Smaller icons were painted on a single board; larger ones required several boards joined by special splints. The functional side of the board was polished, after which a flax fabric was glued over the surface, to which a layer of chalk mixed with animal glue was applied. Only mineral paints were used. The icon was gilded with plate gold and covered with drying oil.

Another happy occasion for the gallery was the construction of the hall for Alexander Ivanov's *The Coming of Christ*, the gallery's largest painting.

In 1941 the gallery's treasures were evacuated to Siberia. In 1945, its doors again opened to the public, and more recently after extensive restoration.

Soviet and post-Soviet art is housed in the **New Tretyakov Gallery** at 10 Krymsky Val Street (daily 10am–7pm except Monday). The sculpture garden contains statues of Communist figures pulled down after the 1991 coup.

Tretyakov Gallery

Rooms 1 – 15	Painting and sculpture of the 18th and the first half of the 19th centuries
Rooms 16 – 31, 35 – 37	Painting and sculpture of the second half of the 19th century
Rooms 32 – 34, 38 – 48	Painting and sculpture of the late 19th and early 20th centuries
Rooms 49 – 54	Drawings and watercolours of the 18th to early 20th centuries
Rooms 55 – 62	Old Russian icon-painting of the 12th through 17th centuries

First Floor

Second Floor

Main Entrance

THE BOULEVARD RING

We continue our acquaintance with the city by going along the third city ring. The **Boulevard Ring**, which is actually a chain of 10 boulevards, emerged in the late 18th and the first half of the 19th century. The walls and towers of the White City, erected back in the 16th century, originally stood on this site. Late in the 16th century, Tsar Fyodor Ioannovich had over 7,000 masons from every part of Russia brought to Moscow to build the tsar's White City.

The construction work, supervised by the master builder Fyodor Kon from Zvenigorod, resulted in the emergence of an immense semi-circular brick wall, about 10 km (6¼ miles) long, up to 20 metres (63 ft) high and up to 6 metres (20 ft) thick. The wall had 27 towers, including 10 with gates.

In compliance with the master plan for the development of Moscow, adopted in 1775, the walls were pulled down and boulevards were laid in their place, while the gates were replaced by squares. Some squares still bear the names of the old gate towers. Mansions were built on both sides of the boulevards, and, in the early 20th century, tenement houses. But the foundations of the old walls have survived under the grass-covered central reservation of the present-day boulevards.

The Boulevard Ring does not resemble a ring at all, but a horseshoe which begins on the embankment of the Moskva river at the **Kropotkinskaya Metro Station** and ends where the Yauza flows into the Moskva river. Our tour starts at the Kropotkinskaya Metro Station.

It should be noted that the entire area adjoining the Boulevard Ring is regarded as a protected zone, which implies careful preservation of historical and cultural monuments.

The first boulevard starting in **Prechistenskiye Vorota Ploschad** is today known as **Gogolevsky Bulvar**. Its right side is lined with mansions dating from the 18th and the 19th centuries. Its left side is more recent, going back to the turn of the century. The first interesting edifice on the boulevard has an elaborate roof and a pointed pediment and was designed in 1901 (by Vasnetsov) as a picture gallery for Tsvetkov, the collector, whose paintings are now in the Tretyakov Gallery. During World War II, the building housed the Free French Mission. Today, this is the residence of the French military attaché. No. 6 used to belong to Tretyakov, the collector, and then to the millionaire Riabushinsky. In the late 1980s, the building was turned over to the Soviet Culture Fund. In the adjacent No. 10, built by Matvey Kazakov, the Naryshkins, a wealthy family, had their town estate in the 19th century.

A little further on we come to **Arbatskaya Ploshchad** (Metro Arbatskaya) where one of Moscow's most famous streets, **Old Arbat**, starts. On the right side is the Khudozhestvenny (Arts) Movie Theatre, one of Moscow's oldest.

Leading off to the right and ending at

the Kremlin's **Borovitskaya Gate** is **Znamenka Ulitsa**, a small but very old street (13th century), which takes its name from the Church of the Icon of the Mother of God, "The Sign". It is crossed by Malaya Znamensky Bulvar where the tsar's apothecary lived in the 17th century. Here, on Vagankovsky Hill, German apothecaries planted medicinal herbs. Not far away is the 18th-century Dormition Convent.

Nikitsky Boulevard: Beyond Arbat Square runs **Nikitsky Bulvar**. On the left side, at No. 7A, is the former townhouse of General Talyzin, where Gogol lived between 1848 and the time of his death. Today, fittingly, it houses a memorial library.

Opposite, No. 8A, the **House of the Press** (opened in 1920) saw such literary lights as Vladimir Mayakovsky and Ilya Ehrenburg. Today, the house belongs to the Union of Journalists.

The most architecturally attractive edifice on the boulevard is the former **Lunins's House** at No. 12, built in 1820 by the architect Domenico Gilardi. Its main building is decorated with eight Corinthian columns. The house was famous for its musical soirées. It is now the **Museum of Oriental Arts**.

Tverskoy Boulevard: Tverskoy (*Tver*) Bulvar, the next in sequence, begins at the square called **Nikitskiye Vorota** and ends at **Pushkinskaya Ploshchad** (Metro Pushkinskaya). It is the oldest of the boulevards. Pushkin, Lermontov and Tolstoy enjoyed strolling along the boulevard's central walk. In their day, it was one of the city's most select public gardens.

The beginning of the right side of the boulevard is occupied by the building of the **ITAR-TASS News Agency**. Further along are 19th-century mansions. In **Bogoslovsky Pereulok**, branching off to the left, stands the 17th- to 18th-century **Church of St John the Divine**, the oldest architectural monument on Tverskoy Bulvar. Not far from where the boulevard crosses **Tverskaya Ulitsa** on the right side is the "new" building of

Overlooking Pushkin Square.

the **Moscow Arts Theatre**, built in 1973.

Tverskoy Bulvar comes to an end at Pushkinskaya Ploshchad where several streets – Tverskaya, Chekhovskaya and Pushkinskaya – intersect. Under Pushkinskaya Ploshchad there are three Metro stations – **Tverskaya, Pushkinskaya** and **Chekhovskaya** – connected to each other by long underground passages.

Moscow's McDonald's: Tverskoy Bulvar is always swarming with people. This has been especially true since 1989, when the world's biggest **McDonald's restaurant** opened in the premises of the former Lira Café. At the time the queues stretched the entire length of Pushkinskaya Ploshchad and waiting times for the prized burgers ranged from two to four hours. The advent of several new branches has eased the situation.

From its crossing with **Bolshaya Dmitrovka Ulitsa** to the former **Petrovsky Gate** lies one of the shortest (some 300 metres/990 feet) and widest (about 125 metres/410 feet) parts of the boulevard. It was known from the early 19th

century as **Strastnoy Bulvar** and was named after the Strastnoy Convent (Convent of the Passion of Jesus) which at one time stood on the site of today's **Rossiya Movie Theatre**.

At the very end of the boulevard on the left side stands a **city hospital**. This imposing building with a portico supported by 12 Ionic columns stretches right up to the Petrovsky Gate. The building was erected in the late 18th century to the design of Matvei Kazakov and later rebuilt by Osip Bove. At one time the house belonged to the Princes Gagarin. In the early 19th century it housed the English Club, made famous by Leo Tolstoy's novel, *War and Peace*. In 1812 the French writer Stendhal stayed in this house. In 1833 it became the New St Catherine's Hospital. The English Club later moved to the mansion in Tverskaya Ulitsa which now houses the Museum of the Revolution.

At the intersection of Strastnoy Bulvar and Petrovka Ulitsa is **Ploshchad Petrovskikh Vorot**, one of the few squares

On Tverskoy Boulevard.

whose appearance has remained practically unchanged for 100 years.

From the crossing with Petrovka Ulitsa down to Trubnaya Ploshchad stretches **Petrovsky Bulvar**, named after the **Vysokopetrovsky Monastery** (Monastery of St Peter on the Hill). The boulevard was laid out in the late 19th century. At its start, on the right side is the former mansion of the aristocratic Tatishchev family.

On the same side, at the end of the boulevard, stands the building of the former Hermitage Hotel and Restaurant. The house was built in the early 19th century and again in the mid-1860s.

The Hermitage, once one of the best-known and most popular restaurants in Moscow, was established by the French chef, Olivier. It was frequented by celebrated writers, composers and various guests of honour who were all given the warmest reception. Both Fyodor Dostoyevsky and Ivan Turgenev were among its patrons. Pyotr Tchaikovsky held his wedding party in the White Room of the restaurant. After the revolution the building was converted into the **House of the Collective Farmer**.

The boulevard terminates at Trubnaya Ploshchad where several streets – Neglinnaya Ulitsa, Tsvetnoy Bulvar, Trubnaya Ulitsa, and Rozhdestvenka Ulitsa – come together. The square was named after the pipe (*Truba* means pipe in Russian) which was laid in the wall, leading from the Neglinnaya river to the White City.

Today there is no trace whatsoever of this conduit, but the Neglinnaya still flows under the square and the Tsvetnoy Bulvar. Before the revolution, the most popular pet market in town, *Ptichy Rynok*, was located here and next to it was a slum neighbourhood known as Grachevka where Chekov once lived.

Branching off to the left from Trubnaya Ploshchad is **Tsvetnoy Bulvar**, named after a flower market that used to be here. The round grey building, characteristic of its period, houses the **Mir Movie Theatre**, which is equipped for

A Georgian trader in the Central Market

wide-frame projection and multi-channel stereo sound – one of the first movie theatres of this type in Moscow. The next building, at No. 13, houses the **State Circus**, also known as the Old Circus. It was established in 1919 on the basis of Salamonsky's private circus.

Where market prices are set: Next to the circus is the **Central Market**. It was founded in the early 20th century, and the new building was built in the mid-1950s. It is Moscow's best-known market. You will see sellers from every part of the country and prices here determine the level of prices at the other Moscow markets. In its heyday the Central Market sold exotic produce like sturgeon, caviar and dried fruit from as far afield as the Caucasus and Central Asia.

After closing in the mid-1990s for much neeed refurbishment, it has reopened to sell more conventional ranges of meat and dairy produce, fruits, nuts, spices, vegetables and flowers.

Rozhdestvensky Boulevard: From Trubnaya Ploshchad, Rozhdestvensky

Bulvar, which was named after the former **Rozhdestvensky (Nativity) Convent**, rises steeply along the slope of Sretensky Hill. The first street to the right is **Rozhdestvenka Ulitsa**. It lies on the route of an old road leading from the Kremlin to the Nativity Convent.

A convent home for the homeless: At its start on the left side is the ensemble of the Nativity Convent, founded in the late 14th century on the high left bank of the Neglinnaya river. The ensemble includes the early 16th-century **Cathedral of the Nativity of the Most Holy Virgin**, the **Church of St John Chrysostom** (1677), nuns' cells with a belfry and an over-the-gate church, a typical example of 16th to 17th-century Russian architecture. The convent was lucky not to have been pulled down during the reconstruction of Moscow.

In the mid-1970s it was turned over to the Moscow Institute of Architecture, located nearby, for restoration and conversion to a museum of Russian art.

All that remained unresolved was the question of money for the restoration. Thus, for more than 20 years, the ancient ensemble was enshrouded in scaffolding and abandoned. In the early 1980s the derelict building was taken over by homeless squatters who established a kind of commune here. When the convent was handed back to the Russian Orthodox Church in the early 1990s, the young people were evicted and the nuns returned. With the financial assistance of various "patriotic" organisations, including the right-wing Nationalist group, Pamyat, the buildings are being restored.

At No. 11 is the **Moscow Institute of Architecture**. The building, from the mid-18th century, was part of Count Vorontsov's estate.

Sretensky Boulevard: Sretensky Bulvar, the shortest in the chain of Moscow boulevards (its length is only 214 metres/ 700 ft), lies between the **Sretensky Gate** and **Turgenevskaya Ploshchad** (Metro Turgenevskaya).

On the right side of the boulevard is a

Sretensky Gate at the turn of the century.

group of houses that are among the most beautiful in Moscow. These are tenement houses built in the early 20th century by the architect Proskurin with funds provided by the Rossiya insurance agency. They are not only distinguished by the original decor of their facades, but are also very comfortable inside. In the years of the Civil War the Russian Telegraph Agency (ROSTA) had its headquarters here.

At the Clean Pond: Sretensky Bulvar ends at Turgenevskaya Ploshchad. The square assumed its present appearance quite recently, after the old houses were pulled down and the rubble cleared away. Beyond the distinctive entrance of the **Chistiye Prudy Metro Station** opens the widest Moscow boulevard, **Chistoprudny Bulvar**, named after Chistiye Prudy, the rectangular pond in the centre. At one time the pond was known as *Poganiye Prudy* (Foul Pond), for it collected all the sewage from the slaughterhouses and meat shops in the neighbourhood. In 1703 the pond was cleaned

out on the orders of Prince Menshikov and since then it has been called *Chistiye Prudy* (Clean Pond). The pond lies in the floodlands of the **Rachka River**, a tributary of the Yauza. Today you will not see the river, however: it has been diverted underground.

In **Arkhangelsky Pereulok**, branching off to the right, is the **Church of St Gabriel the Archangel**, also known as the Menshikov Tower, built in the early 18th century in Russian baroque style. Until 1723 the tower was topped with a tall spire, but this was destroyed in a fire caused by lightning. The 79-metre (260-foot) high tower was the second tallest structure in Moscow after the Bell Tower of Ivan the Great.

The building at No. 19 on the opposite side of the boulevard, designed by Roman Klein in the early 20th century, once housed a popular movie theatre, the Coliseum, and earlier still, in the 1930s, the first Moscow Workers' Theater of the Proletkult. Since its reconstruction in the early 1970s, the build-

The Church of St Gabriel the Archangel.

ing has housed the **Sovremennik (Contemporary) Theatre**.

Chistoprudny Bulvar ends at its crossing with **Pokrovka Ulitsa** in **Ploshchad Pokrovskikh Vorot**, recalling the Pokrovsky Gate of the White City which once stood at this point.

Pokrovsky Boulevard: Beyond the square Pokrovsky Bulvar begins. On its left side is a building, erected in the late 18th century, which was formerly the Pokrovsky Barracks. Branching off to the left from this spot is narrow **Durasovsky Pereulok**, named after the Durasovs, the former owners of the palace at No. 11 which was built in the late 18th century by a disciple of Matvey Kazakov. Since 1932 the building has housed the **Kuibyshev Military Engineering Academy**. On the right side of the boulevard stood a private gymnasium for girls. Today the building houses Russian Encyclopedia Publishers.

Yauzsky Boulevard: Pokrovsky Bulvar ends at **Ploshchad Yauskie Vorota** and from here it becomes Yauzsky Bulvar, the narrowest of the Moscow boulevards. On its right-hand side is a monumental residential building with a high entrance gate. In front of the arch statues of a worker and a woman collective farmer stand on heavy pedestals. The building was erected in 1936 following the best traditions of the "Stalinist" style.

In the narrow **Petropavlovsky Pereulok**, branching off to the right, is the **Church of Ss Peter and Paul**, a monument of early 18th century Moscow baroque. Dominating **Serebryanichesky (Silversmith's) Pereulok**, named after the jewellers' and engravers quarter that existed here at one time, is the 17th/18th-century **Trinity Church** with a bell tower, which used to be the principal church in the quarter.

The boulevard becomes ever narrower on its way downhill towards its end at Ploshchad Yauskie Vorota.

At this spot there are three bridges – the **Bolshoi (Greater) Ustinsky Most**, the **Maly (Lesser) Ustinsky Most**, and the **Astakhovsky Most**. Beyond them lies a historical district of Moscow known as **Zayauzye**. The area between Yauzsky Bulvar and Solyanka Ulitsa was known as the **Khitrovka** after the rambling market that was situated here in the 19th century. The unemployed, who came here to find work at this unofficial job market, found accommodation in the numerous seedy doss houses which congested the area.

The writer, Maxim Gorky, wrote about the Khitrovka in his play *The Lower Depths*. The market also attracted criminal elements and other undesirables – among the items for sale were weapons and false passports.

Quite a few artisans also lived in this district, prominent among them the tailors. It is said that they were able to remedy seemingly hopeless situations, like mending dresses with burned-through holes with such skill that the holes became indiscernible. Such masters, known as "jobbers", charged surprisingly small sums for the "jobs" they did so well.

Trinity Church.

MONASTERIES AND CONVENTS

The Novodevichy Convent: Grand Duke Vassili III of Moscow made a solemn promise to found a convent on a bend in the Moskva River if he were to recapture the old Russian city of Smolensk from Lithuania. He did, and Smolensk was placed once again under the sceptre of Moscow. Three thousand roubles in silver were contributed from the ducal purse to the construction of the Novodevichy Convent.

Thus one of the most beautiful Moscow monasteries came into being in 1524. Sensibly, it was constructed on the southwestern approaches to Moscow, on the Smolensk Road, to honour the reintegration of the city into the Russian state. Immediately it became a kind of court convent, for its nuns came from the families of Moscow boyars, princes and tsars.

From among its oldest structures the **Cathedral of the Smolensk Icon of the Mother of God**, built in the 16th-century on the orders of Vassili III after the pattern of the Dormition Cathedral of the Moscow Kremlin, has survived. Its five domes, cut through with narrow window slits, rest upon a six-pillar base.

The cathedral's iconostasis is the most imposing of all the baroque iconostases in Moscow. Its wooden columns, decorated with an ornament in the form of a climbing grapevine, are made of whole tree trunks. The iconostasis was made on the orders of Tsar Boris Godunov. Its oldest icon is the **Smolensk Icon of the Mother of God "Hodegetria"**, dating from the first quarter of the 16th century. Many of the icons were produced by the famous Moscow icon-painter, Simon Ushakov.

The convent has an eventful history. In 1598 Tsar Boris Godunov was crowned here. In the late 17th-century Peter the Great imprisoned his power-seeking sister Sophia here: she had been at the head of the *streltsi* mutiny. It was also here that Peter the Great's first wife, the disfavoured Tsarina Eudoxia Lopukhina, spent the rest of her life in seclusion. The tombs of both are in the cathedral and its crypt is the burial place of the family of Tsar Ivan the Terrible. It was a tradition then to establish cemeteries on monastery grounds.

The Novodevichy Convent has two cemeteries. The small, older cemetery, with the graves of clergymen, princes, merchants, and heroes of the Patriotic War of 1812, is situated within the convent grounds. The new, larger one lies behind the southern wall of the convent. Since the 19th-century it has been the burial place for notable personalities in Russian history and culture, war heroes and eminent statesmen. Until recently the public was not admitted to this cemetery. The reason for this was prosaic enough: it was the reluctance of the Communist power elite to allow ordinary people to come near the graves of pre-socialist national heroes.

The writers Anton Chekhov, Vladimir

Mayakovsky, Nikolai Gogol and Alexei Ostrovsky, the composers Skriabin, Prokofiev and Shostakovich, the painter Serov, the sculptor Mukhina, the actress Yermolova, the directors Stanislavsky and Eisenstein, and also the former Soviet leader Khrushchev and several other Soviet politicians and scientists lie buried here.

The Donskoy Monastery: It was around a field church on the southern approaches to Moscow, which housed the **Don Icon of the Mother of God**, that Boris Godunov gathered his troops before embarking on his final battle with the Crimean Khan, Kazy Girei, who was on yet another raid into the Russian territory. Here, the **Lesser Cathedral** of the future monastery was later built on the orders of Tsar Fyodor Ioannovich, the last tsar of the Rurik dynasty, to commemorate the ensuing victory.

The foundation stone for the **New Cathedral**, built in Russian baroque style, was laid down a hundred years later, in 1684, in fulfillment of a pledge made by Yekaterina Alexeyevna, Peter the Great's sister. The cathedral is reminiscent of the palaces of ancient Rome. Its walls were painted with frescoes by the Italian artist Claudio. Almost simultaneously with the New Cathedral, new walls and towers were erected and the three-tier **Over-the-Gate Church of the Tikhvin Icon of the Mother of God** was built on top of the central entrance. Though the danger of an attack was non-existent, the fortress was built according to all the rules of the science of fortification. The monastery has recently been returned to the Russian Orthodox Church.

The St Daniel Monastery: The Danilov (St Daniel) Monastery was the first place of religious seclusion to be built in Muscovy. It was founded as early as the 13th century by Prince Daniil of Moscow, the youngest son of Alexander Nevsky and known as the founder of the Moscow Principality. Daniil is the only one of the Moscow princes to have been canonised by the Russian Church.

The present walls and towers of the

Aerial view of the Novodevichy Convent.

monastery were built in the late 17th century during the period of the monastery's heyday. **Danilovskaya Sloboda** grew and at the **Danilovskoye Cemetery** the **St Daniel Church** was built to the design of Matvey Kazakov. The oldest structure in the monastery grounds is the **Cathedral of the Holy Fathers of the Seven Ecumenical Councils** with the **Church of St Daniel the Stylite** (late 16th to early 17th centuries). The **Trinity Cathedral** was built in the mid-19th century to the design of the architect Osip Bove.

The monastery has a dramatic history. It was closed down and then reopened more than once. From the late 19th century onwards it was used as a reformatory for young offenders. After the revolution of 1917 it was closed down and later, in 1928, it was reopened to be used, under the guise of a reception centre for homeless children, as a prison for the children of people repressed by Stalin's regime. In 1985 the monastery was returned to the Russian Orthodox Church.

When the time came to choose the place to be used as the centre for the celebrations in honour of the Millennium of the Baptism of Rus, Patriarch Pimen chose St Daniel. Having fallen into utter disrepair, the cloister was completely restored in less than five years. Today, the monastery's most significant sacred possession, the reliquary containing the holy relics of the Orthodox Prince St Daniil, is kept in its main cathedral. The monastery has also become the residence of the Patriarch of Moscow and All Russia, whose offices have been transferred here together with the church's administration.

The New Monastery of the Saviour: The monastery was founded in 1462 in the reign of Ivan III, who unified the Russian lands round Moscow. The tsar needed more room in the Kremlin and so he ordered one of the Kremlin convents to be moved outside the city limits (today's Dinamovskaya Ulitsa, Proletarskaya Metro Station).

No 15th-century structures have sur-

The Danilov Monastery.

vived in the monastery. Its present stone walls and five towers date back to the 17th century. The main church of the monastery, the **Cathedral of the Transfiguration of the Saviour**, was built in 1645–51. Subsequently, it became the burial place of the boyar family Romanov, relatives of the tsar. The inner vaults of the cathedral were painted later in the 17th century by masters of the Armoury. Dominating the monastery ensemble is a 70-metre (230-ft) high bell tower.

The Krutitskoye Metropolitans' Residence: Towering over the high bank of the Moskva river are the domes and spires of the ensemble of the former Krutitskoye Metropolitans' Residence. The ensemble was given its name after the small hills (*krutitsy*) on which it stands. The Krutitskoye Metropolitans' Residence was founded in the 17th century on the site of a small 15th-century monastery. The 15th-century **Church of the Resurrection**, the mid-17th century five-domed **Cathedral of the Dormition,** with a hipped-roof belfry, and the Metropolitans' chambers have survived. The **over-the-gate Teremok**, faced in coloured tiles with carved white-stone columns and connected by a gallery to the Dormition Cathedral, is regarded as the gem of the Krutitskoye ensemble.

The Teremok was built in 1688–94 by Osip Startsev as a residence for the Moscow Metropolitans. Many of the structures of the ensemble are being restored.

The Simonov Monastery: As with all the other monasteries, this one, which once served as a mighty fortress, was built on the high bank of the river. Established back in 1379, it was named, together with the entire neighbourhood, after its founder, the **Monk Simon**. The monastery was part of the system of defensive fortresses built on the southern approaches to Moscow and, more than once, it saved the city from raids by Tatar-Mongol khans. In 1640 a new stone wall was built round it. In the 1930s, during the reconstruction of Moscow, most of its structures were pulled down and only three towers and the refectory buildings survived. Today the monastery grounds are occupied by the **Cultural Centre of the Likhachev Auto Works** – such was the ease with which the "proletarian" culture ousted the age-old culture of the Russian people.

The Estate in Kuzminki: The ensemble of the estate in Kuzminki emerged in the 18th and 19th centuries. Formerly the land on which it was built belonged to the Simonov Monastery. The estate was erected in the 18th century for the Stroganovs, a family of rich salt merchants. A large number of celebrated architects and sculptors – including Bazhenov, Gilardi, Kazakov, Voronikhin and Klodt – played a part in its construction.

The ancient forest is crossed by 12 radiating avenues. In the centre of the estate is the main pavilion with a 10-metre (33-ft) arch, the **Egyptian House**, decorated with sculptures of animals and ancient gods, **the stables**, decorated with sculptural pieces by Klodt, and the **Red Palace**. In the early 19th century the estate was bought by the Princes Golitsyn.

Left, restoration at the Danilov Monastery. Right, evening light, Kolomenskoye.

After the revolution the buildings were occupied by various public and state organisations whose presence caused great damage. In 1986 the ensemble was turned over to the History Museum and restoration work is now under way.

The rococo-style **Kuskovo Palace**, along the Shosse Entusiastov, was the former home of the Sheremetyev family and now has a collection of 18th-century ceramics.

Kolomenskoye: The name of this area goes back to the 13th century. It was the name of the village founded by settlers from the town of Kolomna who had fled under the onslaught of the hordes led by Khan Batu. The village soon became a property of the grand duke of Moscow and, subsequently, a royal estate.

Ivan the Terrible ordered an out-of-town palace to be built in Kolomenskoye. The structures that have survived date approximately from the 16th and 17th centuries. The gem of the ensemble is the hipped-roof **Church of the Ascension**, built in 1532. It was the first and most perfect hipped-roof church in Russia. The church served as one of Moscow's watchtowers. Inside the church is a 17th-century iconostasis.

Next to it stands the belfry of the 16th-century church of **St George the Victorious**. The front gate with an over-the-gate chapel has also survived. The clock above the gate was brought here from the Sukhareva Tower, which was destroyed during Stalin's reconstruction of the city. Near the northern gate the 17th-century church of the **Kazan Icon of the Mother of God** has survived. Another church to be seen here, the model for the magnificent Cathedral of the Protecting Veil in Red Square, is the five-domed **Church of St John the Baptist**, with its octagonal tower-like side chapel.

In 1926 a museum of wooden architecture was set up in the grounds of the ensemble. Peter the Great's house from Arkhangelsk, the entrance tower from St Nicholas Monastery in Karelia, and several other examples of wooden architecture were transferred here. The ensemble **Kuskovo Palace.**

is set in a natural park full of ancient trees. Specialists think one of the oaks is a contemporary of Ivan Kalita (14th-century). The park is a favourite recreation haunt for the residents of the capital's southeastern outskirts.

The Estate in Tsaritsyno (between the Lenino and Orekhovo Metro Stations): The history of this locality goes back to the 16th century when Tsarina Irina, the wife of Tsar Fyodor Ioannovich, had her estate here. It was then that the **Tsaritsyno Ponds** were dug. In the 17th century this area was the property of the boyar family Streshnev, and later of the Princes Golitsyn. In 1712 Peter the Great presented the estate, which was then called *Chornaya Gryaz* (Black Mud), to the Moldavian, Hospodar Kantemir. In 1775 Catherine the Great bought the estate and renamed it Tsaritsyno.

On the orders of the empress, the architect Vassili Bazhenov worked diligently on the estate for eight years. The palace that he built, however, did not meet with Catherine's approval because,

according to historians, the symbolism of the decor of the buildings reminded Catherine of the Freemasons, whom she hated. Bazhenov was disgraced and the palace pulled down.

Construction work was resumed in 1786, this time under the direction of another, no less famous architect, Matvey Kazakov, Bazhenov's principal rival. The work was interrupted by the unexpected death of the empress. To this day, the enormous ensemble, the creation of two great Russian architects, has stood unfinished.

The **Lesser Palace**, the **Opera House**, the **Cavaliers' Building**, the **fancy bridges** and the **Grapevine Entrance Gate** have partially survived. In 1988 a Russian Orthodox church, the first church to be built in Soviet times, was constructed near Tsaritsyno to commemorate the Millennium of the Baptism of Rus.

St Andronik Monastery of the Saviour (10 Andronevskaya Ploshchad, near the Ploshchad Ilyicha Metro Station) is

the oldest architectural monument in Moscow after the Kremlin. It was constructed around 1360 on the high left bank of the Yauza river by Aleksy, the first Russian metropolitan, who came to Moscow and ordered a church to be built on the spot where he first sighted the Kremlin.

The monastery was named after its first father superior, St Andronik, and the 10th-century icon of the Saviour. The main church, the **Cathedral of the Saviour**, was built in 1420–27 on the site of a wooden church over the common grave of the Russian warriors who fell in the Battle of Kulikovo. The cathedral was painted by Andrei Rublev and by Daniil Chyorny.

It was here that, shortly before his death, Andrei Rublev created his famous icon, *The Old Testament Trinity*, which is now kept in the Tretyakov Gallery, and it is here, within the walls of the monastery, that the earthly remains of the great master lie buried.

In the 16th and 17th centuries, the monastery became a centre of Russian culture where historical chronicles were written and the fundamentals of philosophy were elaborated.

Late in the 17th-century, after Peter the Great married Eudoxia Lopukhina, the Lopukhins, an influential boyar family, became patrons of the monastery. The festive-looking **Church of St Michael the Archangel**, designed in Moscow baroque style, was built in 1694 with funds provided by the Lopukhins. Later, the church became the Lopukhins' family burial place. Behind it stands still another church, the **Church of St Aleksy**, which is dedicated in honour of the founder of the monastery.

The Petrovo-Dalneye Estate (Ilyinskoye Highway, near the Tushino Metro Station): Petrovo-Dalneye, also known as **Petrovskoye**, is one of the most beautiful architectural ensembles among Moscow manors. It lies on the bank of the Moskva river. The manor house, built in the early 19th century in neo-Gothic style, belonged to the Golitsyns. The stable

buildings and a marvellous park have also survived.

The Ostankino Estate: In the 18th century the family estate of the Counts Sheremetev stood where the Ostankinsky District of the capital stands now. In 1792 Count Nikolai Sheremetev commissioned the Italian architects Camporesi and Blank to build a wooden palace here to house his **serf theatre**. It was the most popular serf theatre in late 18th-century Moscow. Its stage machinery made it possible to transform the auditorium into a ballroom almost instantaneously. The celebrated serf actress Parasha Kovaleva-Zhemchugova, whom Count Nikolai Sheremetev later married, performed at the theatre.

The numerous rooms of the palace are well-known for their unique decor featuring rich tapestry, tiled stoves, expensive mirrors, fanciful chandeliers and girandoles, and patterned parquet floors, all of which made the palace one of the most beautiful in Moscow.

Today the palace, boasting a fine collection of paintings, engravings and porcelain, functions as a museum of serf art. Near the old pond the **Trinity Church**, built in early baroque style in the 17th century, has survived.

The Izmailovo Estate: This estate, situated on a small artificial island, was from the 14th century the property of the boyar family Izmailov and, later on, of the Romanovs. It was the favourite out-of-town estate of Tsar Alexei Mikhailovich. Surviving structures in its central part include the **Cathedral of the Protecting Veil**, decorated with coloured tiles made from drawings by Polubes.

Next to it stands the **Church of the Nativity**. Both were built in the 1670s. The buildings that served as hospitals for veteran soldiers and single officers, participants in the Patriotic War of 1812, were added in 1840. The Eastern and Western Gates and a three-tier bridge tower have also survived.

This entire complex is associated with the name of Peter the Great, who staged his mock manoeuvres here.

Right. Rublev's Trinity.

THE GOLDEN RING OF RUSSIA

One wonders where this tourist route got its name. Here, in the central part of the Mid-Russian Plain, there are no gold mines nor has life ever been particularly opulent. Yet the ring of old Russian towns is pure gold in terms of their role in the development of Russian statehood, the advent of enlightenment and the arts; to this day, the towns of the ring are inhabited by a people who have until recently been known as Great Russians. It is here that the origins of the Great-Russian nation and the Russian state are to be found.

Each stopover on this route is a living chronicle, a museum of ancient Russian architecture. The art of building towns has a long history in Russia. Each city (and Russia was once famous for its cities) had its architectural *pièce de résistance*, its unique image.

Sergiyev Posad (Zagorsk), **Pereslavl-Zalessky**, **Rostov Velikii**, **Yaroslavl**, **Kostroma**, **Suzdal** and **Vladimir** – each is an architectural pearl and each conjures up myriad names and events in medieval Russian history. They have gone through many difficult periods in their lifetime. Ravaged by Mongol hordes, treacherous neighbours and Polish invaders, they rose from the ashes time after time, as if illustrating the celebrated Russian knack for survival. Their worst years, however, were during the era of "militant atheism" at the outset of Soviet power.

Names have changed: Churches were demolished, monasteries were closed, bells were broken. The towns lost their very names. Ancient **Sergiyev Posad** was renamed **Zagorsk** in 1930 in honour of a Communist activist killed during the Civil War. When the town got its ancient name back in 1990, many did not even know that such a name existed. A similar thing happened to the small mid-Russian town of **Bogorodsk** (1781) which, again in 1930, was given the name **Noginsk** in honour of one of Lenin's comrades-in-arms.

Another terrible blow was delivered to the ancient towns in Middle Russia by industrial development, which started with Lenin's GOELRO plan and continued in the years of Stalin's universal industrialisation. Industrial development at any price reduced this picturesque land, which was once famous for its endless forests, crystal-clear lakes, rivers and churches of white stone, to an ecological disaster area. Now there is a huge concentration of industrial enterprises in the area. **Vladimir Oblast** region, which is the smallest in Russia, has the country's second highest number of enterprises.

Sergiyev Posad (Zagorsk): Despite all this, the ancient cities survived, having preserved at least part of their matchless monuments and local colour and evoking the air of days long gone by. Gradually, Russia is becoming aware of its historical heritage. People are rediscovering their roots, both in history and in culture. Ancient names are being re-

Moscow and Surroundings

20 km / 12 miles

to St. Petersburg

Vysokovsk

Klin

KLINSKO-DMITROVSKAYA GRADA

Ya

Teryayevo

Solnechnogorsk

Volokolamsk

Chismena

Zelenograd

Sheremetiev Airpor

Novopetrovskoye

MOSKOVSKAYA VOZVYSHENOST

Istra

Kh

Dedovsk

Krasnogorsk

Arkhangelskoye

Zvenigorod

Odintsovo

Ruza

Moskva

Vnukovo Airport

Kubinka

Mozhaysk

to Borodino

Akulovo

Aprelevka

Sofino

to Minsk and Brest

Kievshy

Pakhra

Kuriyovo

Naro-Fominsk

Vereya

Atepchevo

Voronovo

Protva

Borovsk

Stolk

Lopasna

Balabanovo

Chekh

Obninsk

Nara

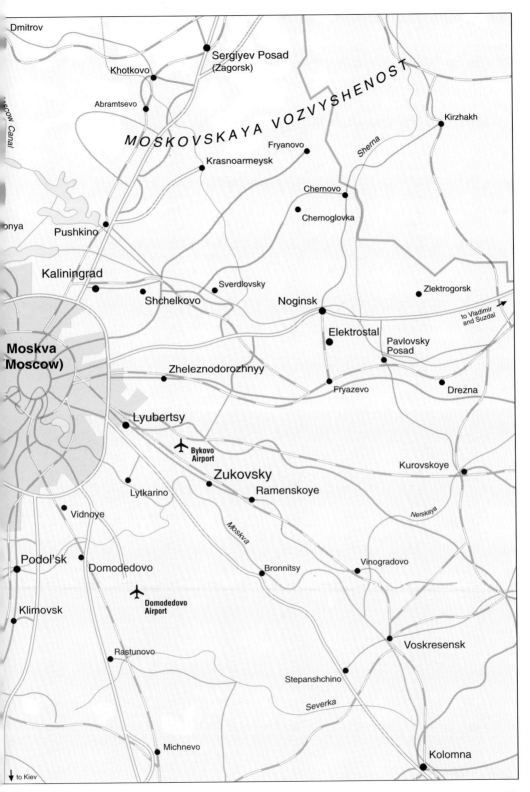

Dmitrov

Sergiyev Posad
(Zagorsk)

Khotkovo

Abramtsevo

MOSKOVSKAYA VOZVYSHENOST

Fryanovo

Kirzhakh

Krasnoarmeysk

Sherna

Chernovo

Chernoglovka

onya

Pushkino

Kaliningrad

Sverdlovsky

Zlektrogorsk

Shchelkovo

Noginsk

to Vladimir
and Suzdal

Elektrostal

Pavlovsky
Posad

**Moskva
(Moscow)**

Zheleznodorozhnyy

Fryazevo

Drezna

Lyubertsy

Bykovo
Airport

Zukovsky

Kurovskoye

Lytkarino

Ramenskoye

Nerskaya

Vidnoye

Moskva

Podol'sk

Domodedovo

Bronnitsy

Vinogradovo

Klimovsk

Domodedovo
Airport

Rastunovo

Voskresensk

Stepanshchino

Severka

Michnevo

Kolomna

↓ to Kiev

stored to towns and cities. The church is regaining control of its desecrated cathedrals. Once again, the mellow chimes of church bells call the Russian people to repentance.

An ancient centre of pilgrimage: The voyage around the Golden Ring starts and ends in Moscow. The road you are travelling on has seen endless columns of pilgrims including, at least twice a year, the Grand Prince, and later the tsar himself. All journeyed to one of the largest monasteries in Russia, the **Trinity-St Sergius Lavra**. The monastery, in Sergiyev Posad (Zagorsk), is one of the most interesting places in the vicinity of the capital, and lies 71 km (45 miles) to the northeast of Moscow. It was founded by the Venerable **Sergiy of Radonezh** in the 14th century; in 1744 it was awarded the honorary title of "lavra", which in translation from the Greek means "main, most important monastery". There were four such monasteries in Russia: Kievo-Pecherskaya Lavra, Aleksandro-Nevskaya Lavra in St Petersburg, Pochay-evo-Uspenskaya (on the Volyn) and the Trinity-St Sergius in Sergiyev Posad.

From monk's cell to national glory: For the Trinity-St Sergius, its many centuries of history started with a tiny monk's cell and a wooden church built by two brothers from Radonezh, Stefan and Varfolomei. The latter took his vows as Sergiy and became the first father superior of the monastery. Sergiy of Radonezh was closely involved with the struggle against the Mongols and the unification of Russia. It was he who gave the blessing to Prince Dmitry of Moscow and his troops on the eve of the battle in Kulikovo Field (1380), which was destined to become a crucial turning point in the history of the Russian state.

Sergiy was canonised after his death and proclaimed "guardian of the Russian land". He was buried in the Trinity Church of the monastery. To this day, pilgrims flock here to bow before his remains, still untouched by decay.

Two centuries later, the monastery resisted the Polish invaders with incred-

Scenes from the life of St Sergius.

244

ible valour and stubbornness. The citadel stood fast for 16 months. The 15,000-strong army of the Poles were helpless before the fortress, which was protected by some 3,000 monks. This militancy helped to enhance forever the reputation of the monastery.

The monastery also played an enormous cultural role. The Trinity school of "book writing" and colour miniatures dates to the 15th century. Valuable manuscripts formed a collection without parallel at the time. The artists Andrei Rublev and Daniil Chyorny, whose work is found widely along the Golden Ring, lived and worked here.

The architectural ensemble of the Trinity-St Sergius was completed by the late 18th century. Even though it comprises architectural monuments spanning several centuries, the ensemble itself is surprisingly unified. The oldest building in the monastery is the **Trinity Church** (1422–23), which stands over the grave of Venerable Sergiy of Radonezh.

The church was decorated by Andrei Rublev and Daniil Chyorny. It was for this church that Rublev painted his famous **Trinity**, the icon widely regarded as the masterpiece of medieval icon-painting in Russia (it is now in the Tretyakov Gallery in Moscow). The church served as the focus for further construction. To the east is the **Church of the Holy Spirit** (1476–77), which was built by Pskov masters. For a long time, this church served as a belfry and observation tower. In the centre of the grounds is the five-domed **Assumption Cathedral** (1559–85), which mainly repeats the forms of the Assumption Cathedral in the Moscow Kremlin. Near the northwest corner of the cathedral is a small, low building – **the crypt of Tsar Boris Godunov** and his family. The stone walls of the monastery date from the 16th and 17th centuries. Standing parallel to the south wall is the **Refectory Church of St Sergius** (1686–92). The highest structure in the "lavra" is the belfry (87 metres/285 ft), which was built in the middle of the 18th

Church of the Holy Trinity.

century and which was the last architectural component of the ensemble.

Today, Trinity-St Sergius is still a place of pilgrimage for Russia's Christians. Believers come here from all over the land to pay homage to the holy remains of "the guardian of the Russian land". This is the largest monastery today run by the Russian Orthodox Church (some 100 monks).

There is also a **Seminary** (founded in 1742) and a **Religious Academy** (founded in 1814). About 500 students attend the two establishments; some live in the monastery. In 1969 the town, then called Zagorsk, was opened to tourists. Today, it receives about 700,000 visitors a year. The monastery's **museum of history and art** has thousands of items: unique 14th- to 17th-century icons, masterpieces of applied art – wood, bone and stone carvings, embroidery, woven fabrics, folk costumes and jewellery.

Matryoshkas: Besides its reputation as the country's oldest centre of religion,

the town is also famous for its toys. It is here that the first **Russian Matryoshka doll** appeared early this century. You can buy one in any shop. As you leave for the next stop, Pereslavl-Zalessky (138 km/ 85 miles from Moscow), you'll be able to see the outlines of Sergiyev Posad for a long, long time on the horizon.

Pereslavl-Zalessky was founded in the 12th century by Prince Yury Dolgorukiy, the Long-Armed, the founder of Moscow. The town sprawls on the banks of **Lake Plescheevo**, which resembles a giant crystal dish. One of the most famous people born here was Grand Prince Alexander Nevsky, whose military fame resulted from his victory over Teutonic knights on the ice of Lake Chudskoye in 1242. The town also contributed to Russia's naval fame: it was on the waters of Lake Plescheevo that Peter the Great's "mock flotilla" sailed in 1689–93. The flotilla became the first school of shipbuilding and navigation in Russia. You can familiarise yourself with this page in history in the **Botik ("Little Boat") Museum Estate**, named after the first vessel built by Russian shipwrights under Peter's guidance.

During the reign of **Grand Prince Ivan Kalita**, **Goritsky Monastery** was founded in Pereslavl-Zalessky (1337–40). The gates of the monastery, which date to the 17th century, are a masterpiece of Russian art. The huge sevendomed **Assumption Cathedral** (1757) is the crown of the ensemble. Surprisingly, the church is painted in the realist tradition. In the centre of the town is the white-stone **Transfiguration Cathedral** (1152–57), which is the oldest surviving monument in the whole of northeastern Rus. Take a closer look at the Church of Peter the Metropolitan (1585). It is an interesting specimen of the tent-roofed churches that were so common in the 16th century.

Rostov Velikii: The next town on your tour is Rostov Velikii (the Great). It lies 203 km/126 miles from Moscow. Rostov has been compared to "a great marvel, a reflection of heaven on the ground". It **Old man in Pereslavl.**

has also been called "a symphony in stone" and the "eternal city" of Russia. It does indeed rise like some fairy-tale apparition out of the expanse of the Russian landscape beyond the waters of **Lake Nero**. By the end of the first millennium AD it was already a centre of power, with many inhabitants and great wealth. But real fame came when human hands created the 17th-century **Kremlin** (1670–83), which looks as if it had risen from the depths of the lake, so astounding is its glamour and glitter even to the contemporary eye. In the southeastern part of the Kremlin is the **Church of the Saviour-on-the-Porch** (1675), made particularly interesting by its interior: the walls, iconostasis and the arcade are covered with frescoes, the work of Timofei Yarets of Rostov.

The chimes of Rostov: The White Chamber next to the church resembles the Palace of Facets in the Moscow Kremlin. The **Hodigitira Church** (1693) stands near the northern wall. The town centre is dominated by the 16th-century **As-sumption Cathedral** and belfry (1682–87). The latter is a treasury of ancient masterpieces. In all, there are 13 bells with a total weight of 4,500 poods (a pood equals 16 kg or 35 lbs). The largest bell, the **Sysoi**, weighs 2,000 poods.

Rostov has long been famous for its mellow chimes. The velvet voice of the Sysoi alone can be heard more than 19 km (12 miles) away. Later, an individual *Kammerton* was picked for each bell, and music was written for the Rostov chimes. Recordings have been made to the joy of amateur fans and real connoisseurs of the bell-ringer's art.

In addition to its architectural magnificence and bell music, Rostov is also famous for its enamels. The first enamels were manufactured here in the 1780s. The process involves the application of easy-melting paints to a metal base. Today, the works of local artisans are known all over the world.

Yaroslavl (260 km/161 miles from Moscow) is one of the oldest towns in Russia. It was founded in 1010 by

The higher echelon of the Russian Orthodox Church.

Yaroslav the Wise. Situated on a well-fortified cape where the **River Kotorosl** meets the **Volga**, Yaroslavl controlled the movement of merchant ships along the great Volga. You could get as far as Rostov Velikii along the River Kotorosl; from Rostov, an intricate system of minor rivers and patches of dry land, the *voloki*, over which the boats were hauled, took the merchants to Vladimir.

Between 1218 and 1463, Yaroslavl was the centre of an independent principality; in 1468 it became part of Muscovy. In the 16th century Yaroslavl became the main trading post between Moscow and Arkhangelsk (the only port connecting Russia with Western Europe at that time). People said that Yaroslavl was an outpost of Moscow. For a long time, it had the second largest population in Russia.

Yaroslavl is full of historical and cultural monuments and for this reason is called the "Florence of Russia". Stonemasons came to the city in the 13th century, but the oldest buildings still standing date from the 16th century (the **Transfiguration Monastery**). The golden age came in the 17th century, when a new architectural school was born here. Most churches were built with the money donated by rich merchants. These include the masterpiece of the Yaroslavl school, the **Church of Elijah the Prophet** (1647–50), and the **Church of St John Chrysostom** in Korovniki. Both have a smart, dressy look which obviously appealed to the clients. In the 18th century, Yaroslavl gave Moscow the art of theatre. **The Yaroslavl Drama Theatre** bears the name of its founder, Fyodor Volkov.

Kostroma, another town founded by Yury Dolgorukiy (the Long-Armed) in 1152, lies 76 km (47 miles) from Yaroslavl. The town presents a unique opportunity to re-visit the past and is a favourite location for the motion-picture industry. The old town was built of wood and no two houses are alike. There is also a museum of wooden architecture.

One of the ancient structures surviv-

Suzdal, the pearl of the Golden Ring.

ing is the **Ipatievsky Monastery**, founded in the late 13th century. The mighty walls of the monastery protected a unique collection of books, which boasted the *Ipatievskaya Chronicle*, a genuine encyclopaedia of knowledge about ancient Rus. Also worth seeing is the newly restored **Monastery of the Epiphany** built at various times between the 14th and 19th centuries.

Suzdal: The pearl of the Golden Ring, Suzdal, lies 198 km/128 miles from Moscow. It is one of the oldest towns in the country, first mentioned in the chronicles in 1024. In the 12th century, under Yury Dolgorukiy, the town was the capital of the Rostov-Suzdal Principality. Later, when the capital moved to Vladimir, it remained important.

Suzdal suffered many destructive assaults, yet rose from the ashes every time. Wood and stone houses were built by the dozen, and several monasteries were founded.

In the 19th century, when a railroad was built between Moscow and Nizhni Novgorod, it passed Suzdal by. The town avoided becoming an industrial centre and kept its original image intact. There are over 100 architectural monuments of the 13th to 19th centuries crowded into a small area (only 9 square km/3.5 square miles). Suzdal is a unique museum town: in 1983, it received the Golden Apple Prize, which is awarded by an international jury for the preservation of local colour and for the excellence of its tourist facilities.

It's impossible to cover all of Suzdal's highlights, but look out for the **Nativity of the Virgin Church** (1222–25) with its matchless Golden Gate; the unforgettable ensembles of the **Saviour Monastery of St Euthymius** (founded in 1352) with the grave of Dmitry Pozharsky, the leader of the Russian army during the Polish invasion of 1610–12, and the belfry whose bells ring hourly; the **Deposition Monastery** (founded in 1204) and the **Intercession Convent** (1364), to which Vassili III, Ivan the Terrible and Peter the Great exiled their wives.

A winter evening in Suzdal.

Be sure to see the **Museum of Wooden Architecture and Peasant Life**. It includes the 18th-century **St Nicholas and Transfiguration churches**. Other wooden structures were later moved here from all over the district.

To take it all in, to breathe the atmosphere of days long gone, climb the steep bank of the **Kamenka river** in front of the Convent of the Intercession. You'll never forget the panorama of Suzdal. Naturally, your impressions will last longer fortified with a glass or two of *medovukha*, an alcoholic beverage made with honey only in Suzdal.

Thirty km (19 miles) further is the ancient town of **Vladimir**. Founded in 1104 by **Prince Vladimir Monomakh**, it played an enormous role in the development of the Russian state and national culture. For a long time, Vladimir was the capital of the Vladimir-Suzdal Principality. The town survived two terrible invasions – by the Mongols in 1238 and the Poles early in the 17th century. There are world-famous buildings of white stone here, dating from the 12th century.

The **Assumption Cathedral** was consecrated as the main cathedral of Kiev Rus in 1158, only to witness its destruction by the hordes of Batu Khan 40 years later. Here, on the bank of the Kliazma, some of Russia's greatest statesmen, including Alexander Nevsky and Dmitry Donskoy, were crowned and here too the regiments of Vladimir received the church's blessing on their way to fight the Teutonic Knights. The walls of the cathedral were decorated by the best artists of ancient Russia. The oldest frescoes date to the 12th and the 13th centuries. In 1408, Andrei Rublev and Daniil Chyorny worked here, covering over 300 sq. metres (3,200 sq. ft) of wall space with brilliant frescoes.

The Golden Gate of Vladimir, another unique monument, was erected in 1164, during the heyday of the Vladimir-Suzdal Principality. **St Dmitry's Cathedral**, made of carved white stone, was built in 1194–97 by Vladimir Prince Vsevolod in honor of his newborn son, Dmitry. Another famous place in Vladimir is the **Assumption Cathedral** in the **Princess' Convent** (1201), where the wives and daughters of princes were buried. These masterpieces of Russian art set the tone for the architectural ensemble of Vladimir, whose historic centre contains some interesting and colourful 19th and early 20th-century buildings.

The best place to end our tour of the Golden Ring is **Bogoliubovo**, 9 km (6 miles) away from Vladimir, near the residence of **Prince Andrei Bogoliubsky** who reigned in 1158–65. Here is probably the greatest creation of Vladimir architects – the **Intercession-on-the-Nerl Church** (1164). This gem must have seemed a supernatural wonder to anyone in the 12th century, standing as it did over the perilous waters of the flooded river. To this day the sight of the single-domed cathedral, stretching towards the sky and reflected in the waters of the Nerl, evokes admiration in anyone who sees it for the first time.

Left, procession at Sergiyev Posad. Right, church tower at Vladimir. Overpage, lunchtime shoppers.

INSIGHT GUIDES
Travel Tips

FOR THOSE
WITH MORE THAN
A PASSING INTEREST
IN TIME...

Before you put your name down for a Patek Philippe watch *fig. 1*, there are a few basic things you might like to know, without knowing exactly whom to ask. In addressing such issues as accuracy, reliability and value for money, we would like to demonstrate why the watch we will make for you will be quite unlike any other watch currently produced.

"Punctuality", Louis XVIII was fond of saying, "is the politeness of kings."

We believe that in the matter of punctuality, we can rise to the occasion by making you a mechanical timepiece that will keep its rendezvous with the Gregorian calendar at the end of every century, omitting the leap-years in 2100, 2200 and 2300 and recording them in 2000 and 2400 *fig. 2*. Nevertheless, such a watch does need the occasional adjustment. Every 3333 years and 122 days you should remember to set it forward one day to the true time of the celestial clock. We suspect, however, that you are simply content to observe the politeness of kings. Be assured, therefore, that when you order your watch, we will be exploring for you the physical—if not the metaphysical—limits of precision.

Does everything have to depend on how much?

Consider, if you will, the motives of collectors who set record prices at auction to acquire a Patek Philippe. They may be paying for rarity, for looks or for micromechanical ingenuity. But we believe that behind each $500,000-plus bid is the conviction that a Patek Philippe, even if 50 years old or older, can be expected to work perfectly for future generations.

In case your ambitions to own a Patek Philippe are somewhat discouraged by the scale of the sacrifice involved, may we hasten to point out that the watch we will make for you today will certainly be a technical improvement on the Pateks bought at auction? In keeping with our tradition of inventing new mechanical solutions for greater reliability and better time-keeping, we will bring to your watch innovations *fig. 3* inconceivable to our watchmakers who created the supreme wristwatches of 50 years ago *fig. 4*. At the same time, we will of course do our utmost to avoid placing undue strain on your financial resources.

Can it really be mine?

May we turn your thoughts to the day you take delivery of your watch? Sealed within its case is your watchmaker's tribute to the mysterious process of time. He has decorated each wheel with a chamfer carved into its hub and polished into a shining circle. Delicate ribbing flows over the plates and bridges of gold and rare alloys. Millimetric surfaces are bevelled and burnished to exactitudes measured in microns. Rubies are transformed into jewels that triumph over friction. And after many months—or even years—of work, your watchmaker stamps a small badge into the mainbridge of your watch. The Geneva Seal—the highest possible attestation of fine watchmaking *fig. 5*.

Looks that speak of inner grace *fig. 6.*

When you order your watch, you will no doubt like its outward appearance to reflect the harmony and elegance of the movement within. You may therefore find it helpful to know that we are uniquely able to cater for any special decorative needs you might like to express. For example, our engravers will delight in conjuring a subtle play of light and shadow on the gold case-back of one of our rare pocket-watches *fig. 7*. If you bring us your favourite picture, our enamellers will reproduce it in a brilliant miniature of hair-breadth detail *fig. 8*. The perfect execution of a double hob-nail pattern on the bezel of a wristwatch is the pride of our casemakers and the satisfaction of our designers, while our chainsmiths will weave for you a rich brocade in gold *figs. 9 & 10*. May we also recommend the artistry of our goldsmiths and the experience of our lapidaries in the selection and setting of the finest gemstones? *figs. 11 & 12.*

How to enjoy your watch before you own it.

As you will appreciate, the very nature of our watches imposes a limit on the number we can make available. (The four Calibre 89 time-pieces we are now making will take up to nine years to complete). We cannot therefore promise instant gratification, but while you look forward to the day on which you take delivery of your Patek Philippe *fig. 13*, you will have the pleasure of reflecting that time is a universal and everlasting commodity, freely available to be enjoyed by all.

Should you require information on any particular Patek Philippe watch, or even on watchmaking in general, we would be delighted to reply to your letter of enquiry. And if you send us

fig. 1: The classic face of Patek Philippe.

fig. 4: Complicated wristwatches circa 1930 (left) and 1990. The golden age of watchmaking will always be with us.

fig. 6: Your pleasure in owning a Patek Philippe is the purpose of those who made it for you.

fig. 9: Harmony of design is executed in a work of simplicity and perfection in a lady's Calatrava wristwatch.

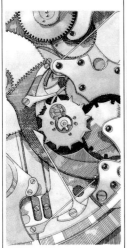

fig. 2: One of the 33 complications of the Calibre 89 astronomical clock-watch is a satellite wheel that completes one revolution every 400 years.

fig. 5: The Geneva Seal is awarded only to watches which achieve the standards of horological purity laid down in the laws of Geneva. These rules define the supreme quality of watchmaking.

fig. 7: Arabesques come to life on a gold case-back.

fig. 10: The chainsmith's hands impart strength and delicacy to a tracery of gold.

fig. 11: Circles in gold: symbols of perfection in the making.

fig. 3: Recognized as the most advanced mechanical regulating device to date, Patek Philippe's Gyromax balance wheel demonstrates the equivalence of simplicity and precision.

fig. 8: An artist working six hours a day takes about four months to complete a miniature in enamel on the case of a pocket-watch.

fig. 12: The test of a master lapidary is his ability to express the splendour of precious gemstones.

PATEK PHILIPPE
GENEVE

fig. 13: The discreet sign of those who value their time.

your card marked "book catalogue" we shall post you a catalogue of our publications. Patek Philippe, 41 rue du Rhône, 1204 Geneva, Switzerland, Tel. +41 22/310 03 66.

Let your message travel with Insight Guides

Getting Acquainted

The Place

Area: 1000 sq. km (390 sq. miles).

Population: 9 million (city 8.7 million). There are reckoned to be an additional 1 million unregistered "Muscovites" living in the city.

Natural Resources: crude oil, natural gas, coal, timber, manganese, gold, lead, zinc, nickel, potash, phosphates, mercury.

Major Industries: mining, metallurgy, fuels, building materials, chemicals, machinery, aerospace.

Language: Russian.

Religion: 82 percent Christian (primarily Russian Orthodox, but also Catholics, Baptists and Evangelicals); the remainder are Muslims, Jews and Buddhists.

Ethnic Groups: Russians 82 percent; Tatars 4 percent; Ukrainians 3 percent.

Time zone: GMT plus 3 hours.

Currency: rubles.

Weights & measures: metric.

Electricity: AC 220 volts in tourist hotels with a continental-type plug.

International dialling code: (7) 095.

Orientation

Moscow lies on a hilly plain 142 metres/450 ft above sea level. The area of the city is over 1,000 sq. km (390 sq. miles) making it one of the biggest cities in the world. The 109-km (68-mile) urban motorway ring encircles Greater Moscow and its diameter ranges from 35–40 km (22–25 miles). The conurbation now extends well beyond the motorway.

The River Moskva flows through the city from northwest to southeast and its width varies from 150–200 metres (450–600 ft). A total of 18 bridges span the river inside the city boundaries. The biggest tributary, the Yauza with its 17 bridges, joins the Moskva from the northeast. A navigable canal links the Moskva with the Volga. An extensive system of waterways connect Moscow with the Black Sea, the Caspian Sea, the Sea of Azov, the White Sea and the Baltic Sea.

With its central location, Moscow is also the country's major terminal for road, rail, river and international flights. The main approach roads into the city, important trade routes even in the Middle Ages, link into the concentric pattern of the city's road network. The main railway lines approach the city centre in a similar way.

The Climate

Moscow is in the temperate continental climatic zone. Summer lasts from mid-May to the end of August and the average temperature is 18°C (64°F), with a maximum of around 30°C (86°F). In the winter months, with snow falling and settling towards the end of December, the temperatures can fall as low as minus 30°C. Annual rainfall at 575 mm (22 inches) is low. Summer is the best time to visit Moscow, though July and August are the rainiest months. The winter months can be very cold but do have a certain charm that you can enjoy if you bring appropriate clothing.

The Economy

Moscow plays as pivotal a role in the Russian economy as it did in the former Soviet Union, more so in fact as foreign investment pours into the capital. There are currently more than 65 international banks in the capital including the World Bank and an office of the International Monetary Fund (IMF), while Russia's home-grown banking network has, with the Russian Chamber of Commerce and the Stock Exchange, once again taken up residence in the historic Kitai-Gorod.

Moscow is also Russia's insurance centre, the hub of terrestrial and satellite communications and the headquarters of the robust gas and oil industries. Once a cotton town, Moscow was transformed by the Communists into a centre specialising in machine building, motor manufacturing and engineering.

As privatisation begins to bite, many of the old enterprises are closing down or being hived off while the workforce is left to its own devices. Outside western and Russian businesses, most of the new employment opportunities are in construction and the service sector.

The Government

Russia today has a bewildering number of political parties and pressure groups. They range from the ultranationalist "Liberal Democrats", led by the maverick politician Vladimir Zhirinovsky, to pro-reform organisations like Grigory Yavlinsky's Yabloko. Since it was reinstated by Boris Yeltsin in 1993 the Communist Party has made a comeback, although Gennady Zyuganov's failure to defeat Yeltsin in the 1996 presidential race was a major blow.

As reports of Yeltsin's health became more alarmist, the rising political star was General Alexander Lebed, of the nationalist Congress of Russian Communities and Yeltsin's national security advisor.

Planning the Trip

What To Bring

Most of the things you'll need for your trip are readily available, especially in western owned supermarkets – but often at prohibitive prices. You'll need to take with you all prescribed medicines. It will also save time if you bring your own contraceptives, first aid items, laundry soap, specialist batteries for cameras, shavers etc., and an umbrella. In the winter you will also need waterproof shoes, a warm hat, scarf and gloves. Make sure you have photocopies of all documents including passport and visa.

Casual dress is perfectly acceptable for sight-seeing and eating out although most Russians dress formally in the more expensive restaurants.

Entry Regulations

Visas & Passports

A visitor to Russia must have a valid passport and a visa. The easiest way to obtain a visa is through a travel agent. A tourist visa is valid for a set number of days to a maximum of 30; the price varies depending on how quickly it is needed.

Changes to the visa are only possible in conjunction with an Intourist office; any extension must be negotiated after you arrive in Moscow. In order to obtain a visa the travel agency will require a valid passport, visa application form, three passport photographs and, if you do not have an invitation from relatives or friends (*see below*), confirmation of hotel reservations. Whether you apply individually from an embassy or through a travel agency, you should allow ample time as it may take up to a month for the paperwork to be processed. In theory this period can be shortened to 48 hours if an applicant is a business traveller or if he has a written invitation (telex and fax are also accepted) from a Russian host but things rarely work out this easily in practice.

If you go to Russia at the invitation of relatives or friends, you can get a visa for a private journey which presupposes that no hotel reservation is needed. Individual tourists should have their trip organised through their Russian hosts or a travel agency.

You should carry your passport and visa at all times while you are in Russia. Without it you might be prohibited entry to your hotel, your embassy and many other places.

Customs Regulations

On entering Russia you will have to fill in a customs declaration form, stating how much currency you have and any valuables (rings, watches, personal stereos etc.). This form is stamped by customs and you will not be allowed to leave Russia without it. On departure you will be asked to complete a second form before handing both forms to customs with your passport. You can convert any unspent rubles back into hard currency at a hotel exchange counter or at the bank at Sheremetyevo II airport.

Customs regulations have been revised several times in the past few years making for some confusion. You should study the current regulations carefully before you travel. You are prohibited from importing and exporting weapons and ammunition (excluding approved fowling-pieces and hunting-tackle), also drugs, syringes, etc., antiques and works of art.

You are allowed to bring in to Russia any amount of foreign currency and personal property you do not intend to offer for sale on the territory of the Russian Federation. You are not allowed to take any rubles out of Russia and it's a good idea to keep receipts for expensive gifts and souvenirs to avoid interminable questions at customs. Duty-free allowances on tobacco and alcohol are as for all countries outside the EU.

Customs officers are generally polite and reasonable but you must expect a careful examination of all your luggage.

Health

Do not drink Moscow tap water, bottled mineral water is readily available. To be on the safe side avoid ice in drinks.

Money

The Russian ruble used to be divided into 100 kopeks. Kopeks, however, are no longer in circulation. Ruble coins are nowadays a rarity. You will find the current exchange rates posted at all currency exchange offices. Rates fluctuate considerably due to inflation and price instability.

Currency Exchange Offices

These can be found all over the city, including hotels. Most deal exclusively in cash and major credit cards (e.g. AMEX, VISA), but not usually travellers' cheques. It's worth shopping around as commission rates vary from 1–5 percent. You will sometimes be asked to present your passport and visa as well as your customs declaration where all your money transactions should be recorded.

Eurocheques are accepted by all banks.

Credit Cards

Most tourist related businesses accept major credit cards: American Express, Diners Club, Visa, Eurocard and Mastercard. Cash dispensers are starting to appear on major streets in Moscow. If you have an AMEX card you can use those at Sadovokudrinskaya ulitsa 21A and at Sovincenter (Mezhdunarodnaya Hotel), Krasnoprenskaya naberezhnaya 12.

Black Market

Avoid changing money on the street, the rates are rarely favourable and you are likely to be tricked or robbed.

Although strictly illegal, you may be asked to pay in dollars for certain purchases, e.g. souvenirs bought from street vendors. You are within your rights to insist on payment in rubles but its probably best to play each situation by ear.

Public Holidays

New Year Holiday 1 & 2 January.
Orthodox Christmas Day 7 January.
International Women's Day 8 March.
Easter variable March/April.
Workers' Day/Spring holiday – 1 & 2 May.
Victory Day 9 May.
Sovereignty Day 12 June.
Constitution Day 12 December.

Religious holidays are now acknowledged officially, and they are now recognised by the many people who participate in religious services. The most important secular holiday is New Year, celebrated with much eating and drinking by all Russians.

Getting There

By Air

More than 30 international airlines connect Moscow with the rest of the world. Flights take about 9 hours from New York, 4 hours from London or Paris, 3 hours from Frankfurt, 2 hours from Stockholm, 6 hours from Delhi and 8 hours from Peking.

British Airways operates daily flights from London Heathrow and the new private Russian airline, Transaero, operates a cheaper service from London Gatwick to the Sheremetyevo I which takes an extra half an hour due to a 30 minute stop-over in Riga. It is also possible to fly daily with Scandinavian Airlines via Stockholm or with Finnair via Helsinki, or Lufthansa via Frankfurt.

Located 32 km (20 miles) northwest of the city centre, Sheremetyevo II is Moscow's International Airport and the main entry point to Russia. The airport still has great difficulty in handling the growing number of visitors as well as all those citizens travelling abroad for business or pleasure.

Tourists can expect waiting times of an hour or more to pass through passport and customs control. Aeroflot and Lufthansa have recently started a joint venture to modernise the airport and improvements can be expected. The Novotel caters for transit passengers. In the main arrival hall there is an exchange office, an Intourist service desk, a post office, a selection of duty-free stores, pharmacy, and information bureaux.

At Domodyedovo and at Vnukovo airports there are special Intourist lounges that should provide a little more comfort during waiting hours. If you continue on a domestic flight arrive at the check-in counter at least 40 minutes before the scheduled departure time, otherwise your seat might be taken.

The Central Air Terminal allows you to check in your luggage for internal flights and take an Aeroflot bus to the different domestic airports.

If you need assistance, contact:

Sheremetyevo information, tel: 155 0922.

Tourist information Sheremetyevo II, tel: 578 9101, 578 5614.

Tourist information Sheremetyevo I, tel: 578 5614.

Domodyedovo information, tel: 323 8565.

Vnukovo information, tel: 436 2967.

FROM THE AIRPORT TO TOWN

The only convenient way to reach Moscow from the airport is by taxi, by reserved hotel car, by Intourist bus or by reserved bus for tourists arriving in groups.

When hiring a taxi make sure you agree on a price in advance.

AIRLINE OFFICES

Aeroflot, Leningradskiy Prospekt 37, tel: 155 5045.

Air France, Korovy Val Ulitsa 7, tel: 237 2325, 237 3344, 237 6777. Monday–Friday 9am–1pm and 2–6pm.

Air India, Korovy Val Ulitsa 7, ground floor, tel: 237 7494, 236 4440. Monday–Friday 9.00am–1pm and 2–5.15pm, Saturday 10am–3pm.

Alitalia, Pushechnaya Ulitsa 7, tel: 923 9840. Monday–Friday 9am–5pm, Saturday 9am–2pm.

Austrian Airlines, Krasnopresnenskaya nab. 12, Floor 18, tel: 253 8268, 253 1670, 253 1671. Monday–Friday 9am–1pm and 2–5.30pm, Saturday 9am–1pm.

British Airways, Krasnopresnenskaya nab. 12, Floor 19, tel: 253 2492. Monday–Friday 9am–5.30pm.

Finnair, Kamergersky Per. 6, tel: 292 8788, 292 3337. Monday–Friday 9am–5pm.

Japan Airlines, Kuznetsky Most Ulitsa 3, tel: 921 6448, 921 6441. Monday–Friday 9am–6pm.

KLM, Royal Dutch Airlines, Krasnopresnenskaya nab. 12, Floor 13, tel: 253 2150/51. Monday–Friday 9am–5pm.

Lufthansa, German Airlines, Olimpiysky Prospekt 18/1, Hotel Penta, tel: 975 2501. Monday–Friday 9am–5.30pm, Saturday 9am–1pm.

Delta, Krasnopresnenskaya nab. 12, Floor 11, tel: 253 2658/59. Monday–Friday 9am–5pm.

LOT, Polish Airlines, Korovy Val Ulitsa 7, Office 5, tel: 238 0003, 238 0313. Monday–Friday 9am–6pm, Saturday 9am–5pm.

SAS, Scandinavian Airlines, Kuznetsky Most Ulitsa 3, tel: 925 4747. Monday–Friday 9am–5.30pm

Swissair, Krasnopresnenskaya nab. 12, Floor 20, tel: 253 8988, 253 1859. Monday–Friday 9am–5pm.

These airlines and others also have offices in Sheremetyevo II Airport. Tickets can be booked direct with the airline and at the Mezhdunarodnaya, Rossiya and Cosmos Hotels. For further information about international airlines tel: 156 8019.

AEROFLOT

Many countries within the Commonwealth of Independent States (CIS) have now started their own airlines but for the forseeable future at least, Aeroflot will be a formidable competitor. Foreigners are still reluctant to travel on Aeroflot internally because of its poor safety record while the prices of the international airline remain uncompetitive and the service inferior.

Aeroflot Information Sheremetyevo II: tel: 575 8816.

Moscow: Leningradskiy Prospekt 37, tel: 155 5045; ticket information, tel: 926 6278.

By Sea

Although Moscow is connected to five seas, by river and canal, and is therefore an international seaport, tourists arriving in Russia by sea arrive at the larger coastal ports and continue from there by train or plane to Moscow.

Several Russian ports accept international passenger liners. St Petersburg on the Baltic Sea is connected with London, Helsinki, Gothenburg, Stockholm and Oslo. Odessa on the Black Sea is on the itinerary of liners from Marseilles, Istanbul, Naples, Barcelona, Malta, Piraeus, Varna, Alexandria and Constanta.

Additional information about sea routes, schedules and bookings can be obtained from Intourist or other travel agencies.

There are two River Terminals in Moscow, connecting the capital with cities as far away as Astrakhan, Perm, Rostov on Don, Ufa, Kazan, Kuibyshev, Saratov, Volgograd, Kasimov and Ryazan:

The Northern River Terminal: Leningradskiy Prospekt 1, tel: 459 7476.

The Southern River Terminal: Yuri Andropov Prospekt 11, tel: 118 7811.

By Rail

Within European Russia railways are the most important means of passenger transportation. Railways connect the largest CIS cities (Moscow, St Petersburg, Kiev, Minsk) with Western European capitals. Travellers who can spare the time can travel in comfortable first-class sleeping-cars, the pride of the Russian Railways. From Western Europe the train takes about three days to Moscow, with a change of gauge at the border.

The most popular among rail routes between the west and Russia is the Helsinki–St Petersburg route (departure 1pm, arrival 9pm) and Helsinki–Moscow (departure 5pm and arrival 9.30 next morning).

There are also transcontinental rail routes, such as those from Moscow to Vladivostok and from Moscow to Peking. They demand an adventurous spirit and a willingness to spend a week on the train contemplating the endless Siberian and Transsiberian (Baikal) landscapes. Food for the trip should be bought in advance since the buffet facilities at stations are little more than basic.

Of the nine railway stations in Moscow, the most important are:

- Byelorusskiy Vokzal, Ploshchad Tverskaya Zastava; trains for Western Europe, Poland, Belarus and Lithuania.
- Rizhskiy Vokzal, Rizhskaya Ploshchad; trains for Riga, Latvia.
- Kievskiy Vokzal, Ploshchad Kievskovo Vokzala; trains to the Ukraine, Budapest, Prague and Bucharest.
- Leningradskiy Vokzal, Komsomolskaya Ploshchad 3; trains to Helsinki, Talinn, Novgorod, Murmansk, Tver and St Petersburg.
- Yaroslavskiy Vokzal, Komsomolskaya Ploshchad 5, for the Trans Siberian Express, Siberia and the Far East.

The high-speed *Aurora Express* from Moscow to St Petersburg takes five hours for the 650-km (410-mile) journey and is a good alternative to flying.

By Road

The restrictions which applied to motorists from western Europe during the Soviet era have now been lifted and it is possible to enter from the country any crossing point.

The main road routes are as follows:

Poland: Teraspol-Brest (7am–9pm). This is the quickest route to Moscow passing through Minsk and Smolensk (1,054 km/630 miles); Medyka-Shegini (October–May, 7am–9pm).

Romania: Siret-Porubnoe (8am–8pm) and Albita-Lesheny.

Slovak Republic: Michalovce-Uzhgorod.

Hungary: Zahony-Chop. This route will take you to Moscow via Lvov, Kiev and Orel.

Finland: Vaalimaa-Torfyanovka (7am–midnight) and Nujamaa-Brusnichnoe (8am–9pm). This route is for those coming via St Petersburg.

If you intend to continue within European Russia you can drive to the Caucasus and the Black Sea, ferrying the car across to Yalta or Odessa and crossing the Ukraine to Slovakia or Poland.

Since crossing the border into Turkey is now possible, you can also exit or enter via Anatolia. Whether this route remains open, however, depends on the changing political conditions in the Caucasus.

Hotels, motels, campsites, petrol stations and breakdown services are located at regular intervals along the main roads. The Intourist agencies will also supply information to motorists.

Sovinteravtoservice are the specialists for car travel in the CIS. They solve nearly every problem a foreigner is likely to experience on Russian roads. Write or phone for detailed information: Institutski Pereulok 2–1, Moscow, tel: 288 9056.

During the past few years marked changes have taken place in the quality of services along Russian roads. But you should still be cautious. Diverting from the highways is possible at your own risk, but not advisable as accommodation and petrol stations are few and far between. You may find that you are only allowed to stay at prebooked hotels or campsites along your planned route. We recommend that you organise your journey through a recognised travel agency.

Details of cars must be entered on the visa. Motorists who present their national driving licence at the border will be asked to complete a driving licence insert so that the information on the licence can be understood by the Russian authorities. Visitors intending to stay in Russia for longer than one month should obtain an international driving licence. All foreign cars must show a nationality plate.

There is no obligatory Third Party Liability and the Green Card or international insurance certificate does not apply, although at the border it is possible to obtain cover for short stays through the state insurance company Ingosstrakh, Piatnitskaya Ulitsa 12, Moscow, tel: 231 1677.

There are no scheduled international bus lines to Moscow, but private tour bus operators run a variety of coach tours and packages from the UK, Germany and Finland.

Tour Operators

Intourist

Intourist, the former state travel agency, was privatised at the beginning of 1993. The company cooperates with travel agencies abroad, which act as agents on its behalf. It continues to offer services in all the large Russian cities and runs numerous hotels, motels, campsites and restaurants. A few small, independent firms have sprung up during the past few years, but Intourist remains by far the largest travel company in Russia.

Intourist organises local sightseeing trips as well as special interest tours for history, art and nature lovers. The company also arranges car hire.

Intourist Moscow Ltd: Ulitsa Petrovka 13/15, tel: 927 1179

INTOURIST OFFICES ABROAD

United Kingdom: London: 219 Marsh Wall, Isle of Dogs, London El4 9FJ, tel: 0171 538 8600.

Canada: Montreal: 1801 McGill College Avenue, Suite 630, tel: 849 6394.

United States: New York: 630 Fifth Avenue, Suite 868, tel: 212-757 3884.

Australia: Sydney: Underwood House, 37–49 Pitt Street, tel: 277 652.

TRAVEL AGENTS

United States: Four Winds Travel, 175 Fifth Avenue, New York, NY 10010. Russian Travel Bureau Inc, 245 East 44th Street, New York, NY 10017.

United Kingdom: Martin Randall Travel, 10 Barley Mow Passage, London W4 4PH, tel: 0181-742 3355. Page & Moy, 136–140 London Road, Leicester LE2 1EN, tel: 01533-542 000 Progressive Tours, l2 Porchester Place, London W2 2BS, tel: 0171-262 1676. Regent Holidays UK Ltd, 15 John Street, Bristol BS1 2HR, tel: 01272-211 116. Scotts Tours, 48a Goodge Street, London W1P 1FB, tel: 0171-580 4843.

Useful Addresses

Russian Missions Abroad

Australia, Griffis, 78 Canberra Avenue, Canberra, tel: 295 9033.

Canada, 285 Charlotte Street, Ottawa, tel: 235 4341.

New Zealand, Carory, 57 Messines Road, Wellington, tel: 476 6113.

United Kingdom, Embassy: 5 & 13 Kensington Palace Gardens, London, tel: (71) 229 3628/29. Consulate: 9 Coates Crescent, Edinburgh, tel: 225 7098

United States, Embassy: 2650 Wisconsin Avenue NW, 20007 Washington DC, tel: 298 5700/72.

Consulate: 2790 Green Street, San Francisco, tel: 928 6878 or 9 East 91st Street, New York, NY 10128, tel: 348 0926

Chambers of Commerce

International Trade Centre, 1–2 Mezhdunarodnaya, tel: 923 4323.
Chamber of Commerce of the Russian Federation, Ilinka ulitsa 6, tel: 921 0811.
Moscow Chamber of Commerce, Malaya Dmitrovka 13, tel: 299 7612.
British-Russian Chamber of Commerce, 1904 World Trade Centre, Krasnopresnenskaya Naberezhnaya 12, tel: 253 2554.
American-Russian Trade and Economic Council, Tarasa Shevchenko ulitsa 3, tel: 243 5470.

Courier Services

DHL, tel: 941 8732.
Federal Express, tel: 253 1641.
TNT, tel: 156 577.
UPS, tel: 430 7069
All offer worldwide courier service from Moscow.

Practical Tips

Tipping

Tipping is still an accepted practice. Waiters, porters, taxi drivers, especially in Moscow and St Petersburg, have always appreciated tips. 10 percent is the accepted rule.

However, do not tip guides, interpreters or other Intourist personnel. If you want to show your gratitude, they will appreciate a small souvenir or gift.

Religious Services
RUSSIAN ORTHODOX

Most churches are now open for services. The main Sunday service usually starts around 10am.
The Church of Assumption, Novodevichy Convent, Novodevichy Proyezd 1.
Trinity Cathedral, Daniilovsky Monastery, Daniilovsky val ulitsa.

ANGLICAN

St Andrew's Church, Voznesensky pereulok 9, tel: 143 3562.

AMERICAN PROTESTANT

Ulofs Palme ulitsa 5, tel: 143 3562.

CATHOLIC

Chapel of Our Lady of Hope, Kutuzovsky Prospekt 7, tel: 243 9621.

GERMAN EVANGELICAL

German Embassy, twice a month, tel: 238 1324.

BAPTIST

Seven Day Adventist and Baptist churches, Maly Vuzovsky Pereulok 3, tel: 297 0568.

MUSLIM

Vypolzov Pereulok 7, tel: 281 3866.

JEWISH

Choral Synagogue, Bolshoy Spasoglinishchevsky Pereulok 8, tel: 923 9697.

SOCIETY OF EVANGELIC CHRISTIAN BAPTISTS

Maly Vuzovsky Pereulok 3, tel: 297 0568.

GREEK ORTHODOX

Arkhangelsky Pereulok 15a, tel: 923 4605.

Many former churches and religious meeting places are being reconverted to religious use. Information can be obtained from:
Moscow Patriarchate, Chistoprudny pereulok 5, tel: 201 3416.
Armenian Religious Community, Sergei Makeyav ulista 10, tel: 255 5019.
Religious Board of the Buddhists of Russia, Ostozhenka ulitsa 49, tel: 245 0930.
Jewish Religious Community Council, Bolshoy Spasoglinishchevsky Pereulok 10, tel: 925 4280.
Muslim Religious Society, Vypolzov Pereulok 7, tel: 281 4904.

Photography

Photographic equipment is easily obtained and there are quick film-developing services. There is a Kodak at the **Passage Department Store**, Petrovka ulitsa 10, at GUM, Red Square 3 and a **Fuji Film Centre** at

Noviy Arbat ulitsa 17. Most hotels sell photographic equipment.

You should not take photographs of military installations. The interpretation of what constitutes a military installation rests with the officials – be cautious, ask your guide or interpreter.

Media
Newspapers & Magazines

Kiosks located in major hotels carry the main western daily newspapers (usually one day late).

The most important newspapers for any foreigner in Moscow are the (Tuesday–Saturday) *Moscow Times* (Pravdy ulitsa 24, tel: 257 2550) and the *Moscow Tribune* (Leninsky Prospekt 45, tel: 135 1114).

Where in Moscow is a bi-monthly listings magazine and is a Canadian-Russian publication (Dm. Ulyanova ulitsa 19, tel: 126 4526). *Moscow News* (Tverskaya ulitsa 16, tel: 207 1747) is an informative English-language weekly published in Moscow. *Travel to Russia* is a bimonthly illustrated magazine, published in Russian, German, English and French that carries tips and information about the fast-changing travel conditions in the country.

There are any number of Russian-language dailys – *Komsomolskaya Pravda*, *Trud*, *Nezavisimaya Gazeta* etc. *Pravda* and *Izvestia* still exist but the latter now writes from a liberal ideological standpoint. *Pravda*, once the official newspaper of the Party, has been resurrected from bankruptcy several times and is always in the news.

Radio

There are three official stations and more than eight commercial stations in Moscow, one of the most popular is the French, Radio Nostalgie. Radio Moscow broadcasts news in English every hour on the hour.

Television

More than 40 satellite TV channels can now be received in Moscow with the proper TV and satellite dish. Many large hotels and even some restaurants offer CNN International.

Postal Services

Post offices are usually open between 8am and 10am–7.45pm, but routine postal services are also available in the larger hotels.

Not all post offices accept international mail above the size of a standard letter. Postal delivery is quite slow – it may take up to three weeks for a letter from Moscow to reach Western Europe, or a month to reach the US. Visitors wishing to send more valuable packages should use an international courier company (*see above*).

Main post office (Glavpochtamt): Ulitsa Myasnitskaya 26a, open 8am–7.45pm. The address of the international post office is Varshavskoe Shosse 37, tel: 114 4645; open daily 9am–8pm.

Cables

Cables to addresses within Russia can be sent from any post office or by phone. International cables can be sent from most post offices, but not by phone.
Central Telegraph office: Tverskaya ulitsa 7.

Communications

Telephone

If you are calling Russia from abroad be prepared to try often; the lines are not good and are always busy. The country code for Russia (from UK) is 007. Moscow's code is 095; St Petersburg's is 812.

Local calls may be made from hotels and the old telephone boxes. Your hotel service bureau will also book international calls from Moscow but you may have to wait up to 48 hours to be connected. It is now possible to make long distance calls from all private phones, Inter-City Pay Phone Centres and card phones in some hotels. Telephones are also available at the Central Telephone and Telegraph Office in Tverskaya Street, but you may have to wait for a few hours even though there are direct lines to the US and Canada.

When making an international call, dial 8 +10 + the country code:
Australia 61.
UK 44.
US and Canada 1.

Useful Telephone Numbers

Time: 100.
Information (Spravochnaya): 09.
Moscow city information: 05.
Telegrams by phone: tel: 927 0202.
Booking of international calls: tel: 8190.
Taxi: tel: 927 0000.
Metro information: tel: 222 2085.
Tram and Trolleybus information: tel: 923 8753.

Telex & Fax

All official institutions and major business representatives have telex numbers and the majority of them now also have a fax machine. Moscow has a public fax and telex service at Tverskaya ulitsa 7 (tel: 924 9004) where you can register a number by which you can be reached if you plan to stay in the city for a long period. Any incoming message will be forwarded either by phone or by local mail. It is the only way to beat the slow mail service. The telex access codes for Russia are 871 from the US and 64 from Europe.

Emergencies

All Russian cities have the same emergency telephone numbers which can be dialled free of charge from public telephones. Officials responding to these calls will speak very little English, so a minimal knowledge of Russian may be needed to make yourself understood.

Fire (Pozharnaya okhrana): 01
Police (Militsia): 02
Ambulance (Skoraya pomoshch): 03
Gas Emergency (Sluzhba gaza): 04

Medical Services

Visitors from the US, Canada, European countries and Japan need no health certificate. It is a good idea to take your own medicines although there are pharmacies selling foreign medicines where you can find most things you need. Emergency medical services for tourists are free of charge but you will have to pay for drugs and in-patient treatment. Doctors at the major hotels speak foreign languages.

The following hospitals offer western levels of service, but charge accordingly:

The European Medical Centre, 2-ya Tverskaya-Yamskaya 10, tel: 251 6099.
American Medical Centre, 2-ya Tverskaya-Yamskaya 10, tel: 956 3366.
Athens Medical Centre, Michurinsky Prospekt 6, tel: 143 2503.

Dentist

Dentists are available at the American Medical Centre (*see above*).
Medstar, Lomonosovsky Prospekt 43, tel: 143 6377 offers a complete dental service with European-trained personnel and equipment.

Eye Care

Svyatoslav Fyodorov's clinic, tel: 484 8120, is world famous for curing shortsightedness with laser microsurgery.
Optic Moscow Shop, Arbatskaya ulitsa 30, tel: 241 1577.

Pharmacies

There are now western style pharmacies all over the city, mostly open Monday–Saturday, 10am–8pm
American Medical Centre drugstore, Shmitovsky proezd, tel: 956 3366.
Drugstore at Sadko Arcade, Krasnogvardeysky proezd 1, tel: 253 9592.
Pharmacy central enquiry office, tel: 927 0561.

Getting Around

Public Transport

Metro

The quickest and most convenient form of transport in Moscow is the Metro, which links the city centre with the suburbs and carries nine million passengers a day. Construction started before World War II and the system is still expanding. At the last count there were 150 stations and 243 km (150 miles) of track.

Not only is the service efficient but, from an architectural point of view, the stations are tourist attractions in their own right. These underground palaces were designed by the country's best architects and famous artists are responsible for the decor. No expense was spared, as can be seen from the marble columns, art deco chandeliers and Socialist Realist artwork. In 1995 commercial advertising was accepted for the first time in an effort to help offset rising costs.

The Metro runs from 6am–1am and there are trains at approximately 3-minute intervals. The fares increase sharply every few months, but still remains relatively cheap for foreigners. Tokens may be bought from the ticket offices in the entry halls. Most major hotels are near a Metro station (marked "M").

Trams, Trolleybuses & Buses

The tram system only operates in the outlying districts. They run from 5.30am–1am. Trolleybus and bus services run between 6am and 1am. Most maps show bus routes, but it is usually quicker to take the metro.

Taxis

There are two types of taxi: taxis for personal use which run day and night and taxi-buses or the *marshrut* taxi, which operate the same route from 9am–9pm. The telephone number for taxis is 927 0000 or 927 2108, but it is probably more convenient to hail one in the usual way.

Moscow's taxis are usually yellow with a narrow chequered band round the sides. All taxis are metered but there is no official tariff at the moment, and fares vary considerably. Agree on a price beforehand. Many private car owners operate an unofficial taxi service, but their activities have been curtailed by the new currency regulations. It is safer, though not always cheaper, to get a hotel to book a cab for you. Never get into a cab which already has a passenger.

River Trams

Between May and September you can travel up and down the Moskva River by boat. There are two routes: one runs from the International Trade Centre to the Novospassky Bridge, stopping every few minutes; the other leaves from the Kiev Railway Station Pier and goes to the Rowing Basin in Kuntsevo. They leave three times a day: 11.30am, 2.30pm and 5.30pm. If

you like travelling on the river, you can also take the Raketa hydrofoil from Gorky Park to the Novospassky Bridge.

Private Transport

Car Rental

Both Intourist and western hotels offer car rental with or without a driver.

Intourservice, Varvarka ulitsa 6, tel: 296 5852, offers chauffeured limousines and so does Mosrent, Zemeldelchesky Pereulok 14/17, tel: 248 3607. Other car rentals are **Avis**, Berezhkovskaya naberezhnaya 12, tel: 240 9863 and **Hertz**, Prospekt Mira 49/11, tel: 284 4391.

Filling Stations

Finding a filling station in Moscow isn't easy as they are often hidden away on side roads. Russian cars use 73 or 93-octane fuel while Western cars use 95 octane. Without a voucher the 95-octane fuel is not available. Vouchers valid for 10 litres (2 gallons) of fuel can be obtained from your embassy. The following stations sell diesel fuel and 95-octane fuel:

Andropova Prospekt 6, tel: 116 9511. Kashirskoye Shosse 105/23, tel: 324 0233.

There are two private filling stations in Moscow:

Grant, Malaya Gruzinskaya ulitsa 38, tel: 252 2350 (open Monday to Friday, 9am–6pm)

Nefto-Agip, Leningradskoye shosse 63, tel: 458 4957 24 hours (English spoken)

Service Stations

You'll find an up-to-date and comprehensive list of specialist dealers and repair shops in the Moscow Business telephone Guide, available in the large western hotels, e.g. National, Metropol.

Spare parts are available from Kalinka Stockmann, Lyusinovskaya ulitsa 70/1, tel: 954 8374; CLИVИDIK workshop, Kievskaya ulitsa 8, tel: 240 2092; Kuntsevo (Opel), Gorbunova ulitsa tel: 448 8550; the Road Service Station, 165 Mozhaiskoye Shosse, tel: 446 1740 or the Road Service Station at km 22, Varshavskoye Shosse, tel: 388 6409

Accidents

Report to the GAI, Sadovaya Samotechnaya Ulitsa 1, tel: 924 0705.

For a towing service and emergency repair, telephone AVTO.SOS, tel: 256 0636 or 256 6402 (24 hours, daily).

Insurance

To drive in Moscow it is advisable to take out additional Russian car insurance. Claims are paid only in the currency in which you pay for the policy. Contact:

Ingosstrakh, Pyatnitskaya Ulitsa 12, tel: 231 1677.

Rules of the Road

Russia is a signatory to the International Traffic Convention. Rules of the road and road signs correspond in general to international standards. The basic rules, however, are worth mentioning.

1) Traffic drives on the right.
2) It is prohibited to drive a car after consuming even the smallest amount of alcohol. If the driver shows a positive alcohol test, the consequences may be very serious. It is also prohibited to drive a car under the influence of drugs or medication.
3) The driver must have an international driving licence and documents verifying his right to drive the car. These papers must be in Russian and are issued by Intourist.
4) Vehicles, except for those rented from official travel agencies such as Intourist and Mir, must carry the national registration code. All must have a national licence plate.
5) The use of the horn is prohibited within city limits except in emergencies.
6) The use of seat belts for the driver and front seat passenger is compulsory.
7) The speed limit in populated areas (marked by blue coloured signs indicating "town") is 60 kph (37 mph); on most arterial roads the limit is 90 kph (55 mph). On highways different limits apply and these are shown on road signs.
8) You can insure your car in Russia through Ingosstrakh, the national insurance company.

Main Roads

Moscow's main roads all have the same identification (white letter on a blue background: A – the Boulevard Ring (Bulvarnoye Koltso); B – Garden Ring (Sadovoye Koltso); K – Motorway Ring. The radial roads: M-1 – Kutuzovsky Prospekt heads west towards Minsk, Brest and Warsaw; M-4 – Varshavskoye Shosse heads south towards Kharkov, Simferopol and Yalta; M-8 – Entuziastov Shosse heads northeast to Vladimir and Suzdal; M-9 – Prospekt Mira to Sergiev Posad (Zagorsk); M-10 Leningradsky Prospekt to St Petersburg.

The speed limit in the left-hand lane of these roads and all the other main trunk roads is 80 kph (50 mph). The speed limit on all other roads is 60 kph (37 mph).

House Numbers

The system for house numbering in Moscow is quite different to the rest of Europe. The apartment blocks themselves are numbered, not the entrance doors. On the radial roads from the city centre, the blocks on the right-hand side are even numbers. On the ring roads and roads which run parallel, the numbers go from right to left as seen from the city centre. Even numbers are always on the right-hand side.

Street Glossary

Shosse = Highway.
Ulitsa (Ul.) = Street.
Ploshchad (Pl.) = Square.
Pereulok (Per.) = Lane, small street.
Naberezhnaya (Nab.) = Embankment.
Most = Bridge

Where to Stay

Hotels

When you check into a Russian hotel you will be given a guest card which you should carry at all times. Each hotel has a service bureau which will assist you in all small matters, from medical help to calling a taxi or obtaining theatre and concert tickets, restau-

rant reservations or arranging international telephone calls.

Most visitors to Moscow arrive with a confirmed hotel reservation. If, however, you need accommodation during the peak tourist season, when many hotels are fully booked, try the Alexander Blok (botel), Krasnopresnenskaya naberezhnaya 12, tel: 255 9278 or one of the large Intourist Hotels, e.g. Intourist, Rossiya and Izmailovo.

The hotel day is from noon to noon. Exceptions are seldom made especially in hotels that cater for large groups.

Payment should be made in roubles or by credit card.

Hotels are listed in the following categories (in brackets after the hotel name): de Luxe, A, B, 1, 2.

Aerostar Hotel (de Luxe), Leningradsky Prospekt 37, tel: 213 9000. Canadian/Russian hotel with excellent seafood restaurant. Moderately expensive.

Belgrade Hotel (B), Smolenskaya Ulitsa 8, tel: 248 1676. Tiny rooms but convenient location.

Budapest Hotel (B), Petrovskiye Linii 2/18, tel: 924 8820. Good value, not far from Kremlin. Cable TV.

Cosmos Hotel (A), Prospekt Mira 150, tel: 217 0785. Monstrous 3,500-bed monument to Soviet times. Lots of restaurants.

Intourist Hotel (A), Tverskaya ulitsa 3/5, tel: 956 8400. Central. Double rooms only. Medium price range.

Izmailovo Hotel (A), Izmailovskoye Shosse 71, tel: 166 0109. Five blocks adding up to 8,000 beds. Comfortable. About 5 miles (9 km) from city centre.

Metropol Hotel (de Luxe), Teatralny Proyezd 1/4, tel: 927 6000. This is the place to stay if you can possibly afford it. It has been beautifully renovated and is elegant, luxurious and expensive.

Mezhdunarodnaya Hotel I and II (de Luxe), Krasnopresnenskaya naberezhnaya 12, tel: 253 1391 (I) and 253 1394 (II). Built in the 1970s but still one of the best hotels. Prices reflect that status.

National Hotel (de Luxe), Okhotny Ryad ulitsa 14/1, tel: 258 7000. Close to Kremlin and noted for famous guests from Lenin to H. G. Wells. Has been splendidly refurbished.

Novotel Hotel Airport (de Luxe),

Sheremetievo-2, tel: 926 5900. Airport hotel with usual Novotel standards.

Olympic Penta (de Luxe), Olimpiysky Prospekt 18/1, tel: 971 6101. Built for 1980 Olympics, and has good fitness centre. Now German-run.

Orlenok Hotel (A), Kosygina ulitsa 14, tel: 939 8844. In pleasant suburb. Attracts business people.

Pullman Iris Hotel (de Luxe), Korovinskoye Shosse 10, tel: 488 8000. French-run 200-room hotel convenient for airport and beside eye clinic.

Rossiya Hotel (A), Varvarka ulitsa 6, tel: 298 5400. Claims to be the biggest hotel in the world (more than 5,000 rooms). Its best feature is its location – on Red Square. Inexpensive compared with other joint venture establishments.

Salyut Hotel (B), Leninsky Prospekt 158, tel: 438 01265. Not central but clean and comfortable. 2,000 beds.

Savoy Hotel (de Luxe), Rozhdestvenka ulitsa 3. tel: 929 8500. This was the first Western-Soviet joint venture into the hotel business. First class standards.

Slavyanskaya/Radisson, Berezhkovskaya Bab 2. Tel: 941 8020. Brand-new luxury hotel. Boasts a 24-hour coffee shop.

Solnechny Hotel (A), includes a camping site, 21st km on Varshavskoye Shosse, tel: 382 1465.

Sputnik Hotel (1), Leninsky Prospekt 38, tel: 938 7057. Basic accommodation in southwest suburb.

Ukraina Hotel (B), Kutuzovsky Prospekt 2/1, tel: 243 2895. A Stalin wedding cake. Centrally located with clean, spacious rooms with wooden floors. Relatively inexpensive.

Varshava Hotel (B), Leninsky Prospekt 1/2, tel. 238 4101. Cheap accommodation for business visitors.

Private Accommodation

You can rent an apartment or arrange bed and breakfast through the following agencies:

BI-Servis, Paveletskaya Ploshchad, tel: 928 5323

New Solutions, Volodrskaya ulitsa 38, tel: 915 6722

Vita Agency, Staraya Basmannaya ulitsa 15, tel: 265 4948

Ya-Servis, Pyatnitsky pereulok 8, tel: 231 0053

Russia does not have an extensive system of youth hostels. Some big cities have youth hotels belonging to Sputnik, the Bureau of International Youth Tourism. During the summer months, when demand exceeds hostel capacity, Sputnik falls back on unused, inexpensive university dormitories. For information write to: Sputnik International Youth Travel Bureau, 4, Ulitsa Chalpygina.

An American owned alternative is (recommended):

Travellers Guest House Moscow, Bolshaya Pereyaslavskaya ulitsa 50, floor 10, tel: 971 4059

Campgrounds

Mozhaysky at Mozhayskoye Shosse 165 is situated 16 km (10 miles) west of the city; **Butovo Camping**, Bolshaya Butovskaya ulitsa 5, tel: 548 7900 is 25 km (15 miles) south of the city centre.

Eating Out

What to Eat

The Russians love hearty meals. For breakfast there is a choice of bread, coffee with milk, tea with lemon, or cocoa, sour cream, yoghurt, milk pudding, soft-boiled eggs or omelettes, hot sausages or *tefteli* (meat balls), butter and marmelade.

The main meals consist of three or four courses. On offer for the first course are egg dishes, sliced meat or sausage, aspic (with meat, mushrooms or fish), cucumber, prawns, fish salads, brawn, various kinds of fish or black caviar. This is followed by soup. Popular from the selection available are: *schi* (cabbage soup), *borsch* (beetroot and meat soup with sour cream), *rassolnik* (kidney soup with gherkins), meat ball soup; in summer also: *botvinya* (cold soup with smoked fish, radish, beetroot and cucumber) or *akrshka* (cooked meat, smoked sausage,

hard-boiled eggs, finely-sliced onion and fresh cucumbers with *kvas*, served ice-cold).

For the main dish there is a choice of beef and pork joints, chicken, duck, game, mushroom dishes, fish (e.g. salmon, sturgeon, pike-perch, sterlet) with potatoes, beet, cucumbers, vegetables, salad, etc.

For dessert there are cakes, biscuits, semolina or buckwheat *blihschiki* (pancakes) with sweet sauces, curd or apples, stewed fruit, *kisyel* (a dish made from fruit juice or fresh berries, dried fruit and potato flour).

Russian cooking is enriched by the different regional specialities from the former Soviet Union, all of which are available in Moscow. Favourite Ukrainian dishes include *galushki* (pastry with a meat or curd cheese filling) and *varenyky zvyshneyu* (curd dumplings with red cherries served with sugar and sour cream). *Chicken Kiev* (or Kiev Cutlet), known throughout the world, is prepared with different spices and garlic. Loved by everyone in the Ukraine is *salo* (salted raw lard spiced with garlic) served with black bread. *Kolbasa* (different kinds of smoked sausages) is very also popular.

With the advent of perestroika Georgian food came to the rest of the former USSR. The Georgian cuisine is famous for its *shashlyk*, *tsyplyata tabaka* (roast chicken), *basturma* (specially fried meat), *suluguni* (salted cheese) and *satsyvi* (chicken). It can be served with *lavash* (special kind of bread) or with *khachapuri* (roll stuffed with cheese).

In Moscow you can also find restaurants serving Armenian-Turkish Dolma dishes (minced meat in tomatoes, cucumbers, paprika etc.), as well as *chebureki* (meat pasties) from the Crimea and *pelmeni* (ravioli) from Siberia. Central Asian cuisine is represented by a variety of pilaws or rice dishes.

Where to Eat

Many new restaurants have opened throughout Moscow. For the more popular establishments it is advisable to book a table in advance in the evenings. Waiters at all restaurants will expect a 10 percent cash tip. The restaurants in the major hotels accept credit cards (American Express, Visa, Carte Blanche, Mastercard).

Moscow is, naturally, the place for Russian cuisine (also Georgian, Ukrainian or Uzbek). There are also European (mostly Italian and French), American, Indian, Chinese and Japanese restaurants. There are also plenty of fast-food buffets where you can grab a quick bite to eat.

Most restaurants have menus in English.

Many restaurants don't take food orders after 10.30pm, although there are an increasing number of establishments that stay open until midnight or later.

The best source for up-to-date information on wining and dining in Moscow is the listings magazines e.g. *Where in Moscow*.

The following restaurants represent a broad selection of varying cuisines. If you just want to have a late-night drink in a bar or a pub, the best place to head is one of the big hotels.

1001 Nights, Leninsky Prospekt 146, tel: 438 9544. Arabian cuisine and music.

Aist, Malaya Bronnaya ulitsa 1/8, tel: 299 5628. Food from across the former Soviet Union.

Alexander Blok, Krasnopresnenskaya Naberezhnaya 12, tel: 255 9278. T restaurant, on a ship, serves typical American food.

Ambassador, Prechistenka ulitsa 29, tel: 201 4014. Traditional Russian and European cuisine.

Aragvi, Tverskaya ulitsa 6, tel: 229 3762. Georgian food.

Art-Cafe Nostalgie, Chistoprudny bulvar 12, tel: 916 9478. International cuisine with wide selection of expensive French wines.

Atrium, Leninsky Prospekt 44, tel: 137 3008. Russian *nouvelle cuisine*.

Azteca, Ulitsa Novoslobodskaya 11, tel: 972 0511. Rated by the Mexican embassy as one of the best Mexican restaurants in the world.

Dalva, Tverskaya ulitsa 24, tel: 299 8506. Azerbaijani and Lebanese food.

Borodino, Aerostar Hotel, Leningradsky Prospekt 37, tel: 213 9000. Selection of steak and fresh seafood dishes.

Boyarsky Zal, Metropol Hotel, Teatralny Proyezd 1, tel: 927 6063. Traditional Russian cuisine using old recipes, pleasantly served in luxurious surroundings.

Cafe Margarita, Malaya Bronnaya ulitsa 28, tel: 299 6534. Homemade pastries and a view of the Patriarch's Pond.

Capriccio, Ulitsa Goncharny Proyezd 8, tel: 912 6620. Fresh pasta and other Italian specialities.

Central, Tverskaya ulitsa 10, tel: 229 0241. Elegant old dining room, Russian food.

Club Royal, Ulitsa Begovaya 21, tel: 945 1410. Smart atmosphere, standard Russian and European fare.

Dinastiya, Zubovsky Bulvar 29, tel: 246 4396. Traditional Chinese eatery near Park Kultury metro.

Don Quixote, Pokrovsky Bulvar 4, tel: 917 4757. Spanish specialities include paella, tapas and seafood dishes; also good selection of Spanish wines.

Dorian Grey, Kadashevskaya naberezhnaya 6, tel: 237 6342. Haute cuisine Italian and European restaurant, specialising in seafood.

El Gaucho, Bolshoy Kozlovsky pereulok 3, tel: 923 1098. Argentinian restaurant serving steaks and grills.

El Rincon Espanol, Hotel Moskva, Okhotny Ryad ulitsa 7, tel: 292 2893 and Bolshoy Dmitrovka ulitsa 13/8, tel: 292 7223. Bar-restaurants, Spanish food.

Exchange, Radisson Slavyanskaya Hotel, Berezhkovskaya naberezhnaya 2, tel: 941 8020. Authentic steak house in American owned hotel

Farkhad, Bolshaya Marfinskaya ulitsa 4, tel: 218 4136. Authentic Azerbaijani food, but bring your own alcohol. Arabian atmosphere.

Guria, Komsomolsky Prospekt 7, tel: 246 0378. Russians still queue to get into this cheap and cheerful Georgian restaurant.

Iberia, Ulitsa Rozhdestvenka 10, tel: 928 2672. Nothing to do with Spain, this is an elegant Georgian restaurant with Gypsy-style violin music.

Japanese Noodles, Ulitsa Arbat 31, tel: 241 0886. Busy restaurant in colourful Arbat setting.

Khram Luny, Bolshoy Kislovsky pereulok 1, tel: 291 0401. The "Temple of the Moon" is a Chinese restaurant specialising in regional cuisines.

Kolkhida, Sadovaya-Samotechnaya ulitsa 6, str. 2, tel: 299 6757. Good Georgian food. Quiet ambiance.

La Cantina, Tverskaya ulitsa 5, tel: 926 3684. Friendly Tex-Mex, very

crowded in the evening.

Maharaja, Ulitsa Pokrovka 2, tel: 921 9844. A wide range of traditional Indian dishes at reasonable prices.

Manila, Vavilova ulitsa 81, tel: 132 0055. Filipino and Russian food.

McDonald's, Pushkinskaya Ploshchad, tel: 200 1655. Moscow's most successful fast-food outlet.

Mei-Hua, Rusakovskaya ulitsa 2/1, tel: 264 9574. Chinese restaurant.

Moosh, Oktyabrskaya ulitsa 2/4, tel: 284 3670. Armenian food and music.

Moscow-Bombay, Glinishchevsky pereulok 3, tel: 292 9731. European as well as Indian cuisine in a relaxing atmosphere with Indian music and dancing.

Olimp, Luzhnetskaya naberezhnaya 24, near Luzhniki Stadium, tel: 201 0148. Floor show.

Patio Pasta, Tverskaya-Yamskaya 1, tel: 251 5861. Open noon-midnight the best feature of this fast-food restaurant is the excellent salad bar.

Patio Pizza, Tverskaya ulitsa 4, tel: 292 0891. A busy pizzeria open till late outside the Hotel Intourist.

Pekin in Moscow, Bolshaya Sadovaya ulitsa 1/2, tel: 209 1865. Good Chinese food.

Pivnushka, Leninsky Prospekt 28, tel: 952 5567. German beer restaurant with show at weekends.

Pizza Hut, Kutuzovsky Prospekt 17 and Tverskaya ulitsa 12, tel: 243 1727. Pizza's galore.

Praga, Arbat ulitsa 2, tel: 290 6171. Russian and Czech food, with live entertainment.

Razgulyai, Spartakovskaya ulitsa 11, tel: 267 7613. Russian food, music at weekends.

Robin Hood, Bolshaya Gruzinskaya ulitsa 42, tel: 254 0738. The speciality, despite the name, is Russian cuisine using traditional recipes.

Ruslan Cafe, Vorontsovskaya ulitsa 32/36, tel: 912 0632. Russian food, gypsy music at weekends.

Russkaya Izba, Ilyinskoye village close to Archangelskoye, tel: 561 4244. Traditional Russian food.

San Marco, Arbat ulitsa 25, tel: 291 7089. Fresh spaghetti and lobsters in a cosy atmosphere.

Savoy, Rozhdestvenka ulitsa 3, tel: 929 8600. The classic Western restaurant in Moscow.

Silla, *Valery Bryusov*, Krymskaya naberezhnaya, tel: 956 6527. Chinese

and Korean specialities on board ship.

Sirens, Ulitsa Bolshaya Spasskaya 15, tel: 208 1412. European sea food and some rather exotic specialities including sauteed frogs legs and Florida sea turtle soup.

Skazka, Tovarishchevsky Pereulok 1, tel: 911 0998. Expensive traditional Russian food, gypsy music.

Stanislavskogo 2, Leontevskiy pereulok 2, tel: 291 8689. French and Russian food.

Starlite diner, Bolshaya Sadovaya ulitsa 16, tel: 290 1638. Open 24 hours daily, this popular eatery serves such American dishes as chicken pot pie and turkey dinner.

Strastnoy 7, Strastnoy Bulvar 7, tel: 299 0498. Luxurious dining.

U Nikitskikh Vorot, Bolshaya Nikitskaya ulitsa 23/9, tel: 290 4883. Bistro with live entertainment, good food.

U Pirosmani, Novodevichy Proyzed 4, tel: 247 1926. Georgian food and wine, violin and piano music.

U Yuzefa, Dubininskaya ulitsa 11/17, tel: 238 4646. The only Jewish restaurant in Russia.

Uzbekistan, Neglinnaya ulitsa 29, tel: 924 6053. Central Asian food.

Villa Peredelkino, Chobotovskaya 1st Alleya 2A, tel: 435 1211. Lovely Italian restaurant.

Victoria a.k.a. Hard Rock Cafe, Zelyoni Theatre, Gorky Park, tel: 237 0709. Owned by a rock-star, Russian-Armenian food.

Yakimanka, Bolshaya Polyanka ulitsa 2/10, Str.1, tel: 238 8888. Uzbek restaurant.

Yar, Leningradsky Prospekt 32, tel: 250 7449. Russian cuisine in a recreation of a famous pre-Revolutionary restaurant patronised by Rasputin.

Zaidi-Poprobui, Prospekt Mira 124, kor 11, tel: 286 7503. Typical Russian cuisine.

Drinking Notes

Everyone assumes they know what Russians drink: bottles of vodka and tea from the samovar. But wines from Georgia, Azerbaijan and the Crimea can also be found in Moscow, as well as "Soviet Champagne", excellent local beers (such as Moskovskaya), Caucasian brandies and *kvas*, a fermented yeast drink you can buy from stalls on the street.

As for vodka, it can come in a variety of flavours such as *limonaya* (lemon), *okhotnichnaya* (juniper berries, ginger and cloves), *starka* (apple and pear leaves) and *pertsovka* (with hot peppers).

Attractions

Opera & Ballet

Russia is renowned for its culture and Moscow for its world famous Bolshoi Theatre, with a tradition dating back to the 18th century. The current artistic director, Vladimir Vasilyev has promised to introduce a breath of fresh air into productions which became rather stale under the notoriously autocratic Yury Grigorovich.

The repertoire, however, remains firmly rooted in the traditional classical ballets like *Swan Lake* and *Giselle*, which is what the ticket-buying western public demands. Technical levels remain high and the Bolshoi continues to produce internationally acclaimed stars so you can expect to enjoy your evening. You can also see opera and ballet produced to a high standard at several other Moscow venues (*see* below).

Bolshoi Opera and Ballet Theatre, Teatralnaya Ploshchad 1, tel: 292 0050.

Stanislavsky and Nemirovich-Danchenko Musical Theatre (opera and ballet), Bolshaya Dmitrovka ulitsa 17, tel: 229 8388

Helicon-Opera, Bolshaya Nikitsakya ulitsa 19, tel: 291 1323

Kremlin Palace of Congresses (ballet), tel: 917 2336

Moscow Operetta Theatre, Bolshay Dmitrovka ulitsa 0, tel. 292 0377

Hermitage (operetta), Karetny Ryad ulitsa 3, tel: 209 2076

Chamber Music Theatre (small scale opera), Leningradsky Prospekt 71, tel: 157 4707

Concert Halls

Apart from the opera houses, the most important venue for classical music is the Moscow Conservatory. Tchaikovsky was one of the founding professors here (there is a statue of him outside) and the international piano competition which bears his name takes place here every five years.

The Great Hall of the Conservatory, Bolshaya Nikitskaya ulitsa 13, tel: 229 8183.

Rossiya Concert Hall (major rock concert venue in the Hotel Rossiya), Moskvoretskaya naberezhnaya 1, tel: 298 1124.

Tchaikovsky Concert Hall, Triumfalnaya Ploshchad 4, tel: 299 3957.

Olympic Village, (ballet and rock concerts) Ulitsa Pelshe 1, tel: 437 5650

Shalyapin House Museum (occasional recitals in the White Hall), Novinsky Bulvar 25, tel: 205 6236

Skryabin House Museum, Ulitsa Vakhtangova 11, tel: 241 1901

Theatres

Theatre performances usually begin at 7pm. There is no admission once the performance has started.

Moscow Academic Art Theatre, (MKhAT) Kamergersky pereulok 3, tel: 229 5370.

Maly Theatre, Teatralnaya Ploshchad 1, tel: 924 4083.

Vakhtangov Drama Theatre, Arbat ulitsa 26, tel: 241 0728.

Mossovet Theatre, Bolshaya Sadovaya ulitsa 16, tel: 299 2035

Sovremennik, Chistoprudny Bulvar 19a, tel: 921 6473

Staislavsky Drama Theatre, Tverskaya ulitsa 23, tel: 299 7621.

Mayakovsky Theatre, Bolshaya Nikitskaya ulitsa 19, tel: 290 4232.

Satirikon Theatre, Sheremetevskaya ulitsa 8, tel: 218 1019.

Central Children's Theatre, Teatralnaya Ploshchad 2, tel: 292 0069.

Sats Children's Musical Theatre, Prospekt Vernadskovo 5, tel: 930 5243.

Central Puppet Theatre, 3 Sadovaya-Samotechnaya Street, tel: 299 6313

Moscow Puppet Theatre, 26 Spartakovskaya Street, tel: 261 2197.

Lenin Komsomol Theatre, Ulitsa Malaya Dmitrovka 6, tel: 299 0708.

Mime Theatre, Izmailovsky Bulvar 39, tel: 163 8150.

Romen Gypsy Theatre, Leningradsky Prospekt 32, tel: 250 7353.

Old Circus, Tsvetnoy Bulvar 13, tel: 200 6889.

Circus, Vernadskovo Prospekt 7, tel: 930 2815.

Cinemas

Cinemas open at 9 or 10am and show films all day long. All Russian cinemas show films with monotonous voice-over dubbing. Modern western films are now widely available.

Americom House of Cinema (English language films), Radisson Slavyanskaya Hotel, Berezhkovskaya naberezhnaya 2, tel: 941 8890

Illuzion (showing old films), Kotelnycheskaya naberezhnaya 1, tel: 227 4353

Kinocenter (the best for Russian films), Druzhinnikovskaya ulitsa 15, tel: 205 7306

Moskva, Triumfalnaya Ploshchad 1, tel: 251 5860.

Khudozhestvenny, Arbatskaya Ploshchad 14, tel: 291 9624.

Art

Tretiakov Art Gallery, Lavrushinsky pereulok 10, tel: 233 1050. Open: daily 10am–8pm except Monday.

New Tretiakov Art Gallery, Krymsky Val ulitsa 10, tel: 230 7788Open: daily 10am–8pm except Monday. (See floor plan page 274-275.)

Pushkin Museum of Fine Arts, Volkhonka ulitsa 12, tel: 203 9578. Open: Tuesday–Saturday 10am–8pm, Sunday 10am–6pm.

Museum of Private Collections, Volkhonka ulitsa 14, tel: 203 7998. Open: Wednesday–Friday 10am–4pm, Saturday and Sunday noon-6pm.

Andrei Rublev Museum of Early Russian Art, Andronevskaya Ploshchad 10, tel: 278 1429. Open: May-September, Monday and Tuesday 1-8pm, Thursday–Sunday 11am–6pm; October-April, daily except Wednesday 11am–6pm.

Church of the Intercession in Fili, 1812 goda ulitsa 6, tel: 148 4552. Open: May-September, Friday–Sunday 11am–6pm, Monday and Thurs 11am–8pm.

Museum of Arts of Eastern Peoples, Nikitsky Bulvar 12a, tel: 291 9614. Open: Tuesday–Sunday 11am–8pm.

All-Russia Museum of Decorative, Applied and Folk Art, Delegatskaya ulitsa 3, tel: 923 1741. Open: Monday, Wednesday, Saturday, and Sunday 10am–6pm, Tuesday and Thursday 12.30-8pm.

Folk Art Museum, Leontevsky pereulok 7, tel: 290 2114. Open: Tuesday and Thursday 10am–8pm, Wednesday, Friday, Saturday, Sunday 10am–5pm.

Art & Architecture

Shchusev Architecture Museum, Vozdvizhenka ulitsa 2, tel: 291 1978. Open: daily except Monday and Friday 11am–7pm.

Donskoy Monastery, Donskaya Ploshchad 1, tel: 232 0766. Open: May-September, daily except Monday and Friday, 10am–6pm; October-April 10am–5pm.

Ostankino Palace Museum of Serf Art, Ostankinskaya ulitsa 5, tel: 283 4645. Open: May-September, daily 11am–5pm; October–April 10am–4pm.

Kolomenskoye Museum Reserve, Andropova Prospekt 39, tel: 115 2768. Open: September-April 11am–5pm; May-August Wednesday and Thursday, 1-8pm, Friday–Sunday 11am–5pm.

Kuskovo Estate and Museum of Ceramics, Yunosti ulitsa 2, tel: 370 0160. Open: April-September, daily except Monday and Tuesday 10am–7pm; October–March, 10am–4pm.

House Museums

Glinka Museum, Fadeeva ulitsa 4, tel: 972 3237. Open: Tuesday and Thursday 10am–8pm, Wednesday, Friday, Saturday and Sunday 10am–6pm.

Dostoyevsky Apartment, Dostoyevskovo ulitsa 2, tel: 281 1085. Open: Thursday, Saturday, Sunday 11am–6pm, Wednesday and Friday 2-9pm.

Lermontov House-Museum, Malaya Molchanovka ulitsa 2, tel: 291 5298. Open: Wednesday and Friday 2-5pm, Thursday, Saturday, Sunday 11am–5pm.

Chekhov House-Museum, Sadovaya-Kudrinskaya ulitsa 6, tel: 291 6154. Open: Tuesday, Thursday, Saturday and Sunday 11am–5pm, Wednesday and Friday 2-6pm.

Pushkin Apartment, ulitsa Arbat 53, tel: 241 4212. Open: Wednesday–Sunday 11am–5pm.

Tolstoy Estate-Museum, Ulitsa Lva Tolstovo 21, tel: 246 9444. Open: Tuesday–Sunday 10am–6pm.

Vasnetsov House-Museum, Vasnetsova pereulok 13, tel: 281 1329.

Open: Wednesday–Sunday 10am–5pm

Shalyapin House-Museum, Novinsky Bulvar 25, tel: 252 2530. Open: Tuesday–Thursday, Saturday and Sunday 10am–4,30pm

Gorky House-Museum, Ulitsa Kachalova 6, tel: 290 0535. Open: Wednesday and Friday noon-8pm, Thursday, Saturday and Sunday 10am–6pm.

Mayakovsky Museum, Lubyansky proyezd 3, tel: 921 9387. Open: Friday–Tuesday 10am–5pm, Thursday 1pm-8pm.

Science & Technology

Politechnical Museum, Novaya Ploshchad 3, tel: 923 0614. Open: Tuesday–Sunday 10am–6pm.

Planetarium, Sadovaya Kudrinskaya ulitsa 5, tel: 254 0153. Open: Wednesday–Monday 11.30am–6pm.

Zoological Museum, Bolshaya Nikitskaya ulitsa 6, tel: 203 8923. Open: Tuesday–Sunday 10am–5pm.

Zoo, Bolshaya Gruzinskaya ulitsa 1, tel: 255 3580. Open: May-August 9am–7pm; September 9am–6pm; Oct-March 9am–5pm; April 9am–6pm.

Space Museum, Kosmonavtov Alleya, Prospekt Mira, tel: 286 3714. Open: Tuesday–Sunday 10am–7pm.

Historical

Novodevichy Convent, Novodevichy Proyezd 1, tel: 246 8526. Open: daily 10am–5pm, except Tuesday.

Church of the Trinity in Nikitniki, Nikitnikov pereulok 3, tel: 298 5018. Open: Monday, Friday, Saturday, Sunday 10am–5pm, Wednesday and Thursday noon-7pm.

St Basil's Cathedral, Red Square, tel: 298 3304. Open: daily 10am–5pm, except Tuesday.

Kremlin Museums – Cathedral of the Assumption, Cathedral of the Annunciation, Archangel Cathedral, Church of the Deposition of the Robe, Patriarch's Palace, Armoury and Diamond Fund, tel: 229 2036 or 921 4720. Open: daily except Thursday, 10am–5pm.

The House of the Boyar Romanovs, Ulitsa Varvarka 10, tel: 298 3706. Open: Thursday–Monday 10-5, Wednesday 11am–6pm.

Old English Court, Ulitsa Varvarka 6, tel: 298 3961 . Open Tuesday, Saturday and Sunday 10am–6pm, Wednesday–Friday 11am–7pm.

Central Museum of the Revolution, Tverskaya ulitsa 21, tel: 299 6724.

Open: Tuesday–Sunday 10am-5.30pm.

Moscow History Museum, Novaya Ploshchad 12, tel: 924 8490. Open Tuesday, Thursday, Saturday and Sunday 10am–6pm, Wednesday and Friday noon-8pm.

Military

Museum of the Armed Forces, Sovetskoy Armii ulitsa 2, tel: 281 4877. Open: Wednesday–Sunday 10am–4.30

Battle of Borodino Panorama Museum, Kutuzovsky Prospekt 38, tel: 148 1965. Open: daily except Friday, 10.30am–4pm.

Exhibition Venues

All-Russian Exhibition Centre, tel: 181 9504 (Metro VDNKh). Open: 10am–9pm.

Central Exhibition Hall (Manezh), Manezhnaya Ploshchad 1 tel: 202 9304. Open: Monday, Wednesday–Sunday 11am–8pm.

Exhibition Hall of Artists of the Russian Federation, Kutsnetsky Most ulitsa 20, tel: 228 1844. Open: Tuesday–Friday 1-8pm, Saturday and Sunday noon-7.30pm.

Central House of Artists, Krymsky Val 9, tel: 238 9634. Open: Tuesday–Sunday 11am–5pm.

Parks

Gorky Park, Krymsky Val ulitsa 9, tel: 237 0707 (Metro Park Kultury). Open daily 10am–10pm. This famous park covers an area of 240 hectares (593 acres) and incorporates the Recreation Park, Neskuchny Garden, a children's park and Sparrow Hills. Amusements include open air theatres, fairgrounds, boat hire, cafe and restaurant facilities, skating rink, tennis courts.

Izmaylovsky Park, Narodny Prospekt 17, tel: 166 7909 (Metro Izmaylovsky Park). Open daily 10am–9pm. One of the largest green spaces in Europe, the park incorporates the ruins of the 17th-century royal estate at Izmaylovo village and a famous flea market near the metro station. There are sports facilities, a lake, children's amusements and cafes.

Sokolniki Park, Sokolnichesky Val ulitsa 1, tel: 268 5430 (Metro Sokolniki). Open 24 hours. The park, meaning falconers, was laid out in the 1840s and has always been a favourite with Muscovites. There are ponds and tree-lined allees, bicycle rentals and cafe facilities.

Botanical Garden, Botanicheskaya ulitsa 4, tel: 219 5344 (Metro Botanichesky Sad). Open Friday–Sunday 8am–5pm. Founded in 1945 the garden includes 12,000 plants, an arboretum, rose garden, aviary and ponds.

Serebryany Bor Forest Park, 1-ya Liniya 1a, tel: 947 7926 (Metro Polezhayevskaya). Open 24 hours. Moscow's "beach", there are woodland beaches here which can become very crowded on summer weekends.

Nightlife

Moscow has a nightlife but to enjoy it to the full, you need plenty of spare cash as well as staying power. At least nowadays there is no unofficial curfew and, as many restaruants stay open until midnight you'll even be able to get a bite to eat after a night out at the theatre if you wish. Remember, however, that the metro begins to shut down at around 12.30am.

Nightclubs abound, but are tailored to suit the needs and appetites of Russia's new business elite who are very reach indeed. Most clubs charge an entry fee and you may need to show your passport to security. Many clubs are a happy-hunting-ground for Moscow's very persistent prosititutes and the music and entertainment is often bland. Moscow's clubbers tend to dress formally and you'll be lucky to get in anywhere without collar and tie. Casinos are another feature of Moscow after dark, although the mayor Yury Luzhkov has recently announced his intention to close many of them down on the grounds that they are a front for Mafia activities. If you just want to put your feet up after a long day's sightseeing, most hotels have late-night bars, some staying open to 4am or even later. But drinks are rather expensive.

Nightclubs

Night Flight, Tverskaya ulitsa 17, tel: 229 4165. Every night 9pm-5am.

Pilot, Trekhgorny Val ulitsa 6, tel: 252 2764. Thursday–Sunday 11pm-6am.

Zhar-Ptisa, Kudrinskaya ploshchad 1, tel: 255 4228. Open 9pm-6am

Hermitage, Karetny Ryad 3, tel: 299 1160. Friday–Sunday 10pm-6am,

techno and occasional live bands.

Tabula Rasa, Berezhkovskaya naberezhnaya 28, tel: 240 9289. Daily 6pm-6am, live music, restaurant and dance floor.

Krisis Genre, Ostrovskovo pereulok 22, tel: 243 8605. Daily noon-1am, cellar bar with live music and low prices.

Arbat Blues Club, Filippovsky pereulok 11, tel: 291 1546. Friday and Saturday 8.30pm-5.30am, rock and blues

B.B. King, Ulitsa Sadovaya-Samotechnaya 4, tel: 299 8206. Open daily to 2am Friday and Saturday to 5am, local jazz bands.

Shopping

Moscow's shopping hours are coming more into line with those of the west, especially in the large malls. Standard opening hours elsewhere are Monday–Saturday 10am–7pm, many smaller shops take a lunch break from 2–3pm.

What to Buy

Folk art souvenirs are still the most popular purchase with foreigners. There is also a wide choice of embroidered table cloths, towels and shawls, hand-painted Palekh laquer boxes, or trays from the village of Zhostovo, Zhel porcelain, lovely carved wooden toys, samovars, and of course Matryoshka nest dolls. Art books can also be a good buy – there are several very good English language book shops in Moscow.

There is no shortage of private art galleries and antique shops but be aware of very strict customs regulations.

Where to Shop

The best areas for shopping are Arbat ulitsa, Tverskaya ulitsa, Red Square (GUM department store), ulitsa Petrovka (Passazh and TsUM department store), ulitsa Kuznetsky Most and the Radisson Slavyanskaya Hotel complex. At weekends you can sometimes pick up a bargain at Izmaylovsky Park flea market.

Souvenirs

Russkie Uzory, Petrovka ulitsa 16. Complete range of folk art souvenirs, including embroideries, etc.

Russky Souvenir, Kutuzovsky Prospekt 9. Applied art.

Arbatskay Lavka, Ulitsa Arbat 27. Brightly painted Russian wooden toys.

Art Showroom, Bolshaya Polyanka ulitsa 56.

Salon Iskusstva, Bolshaya Yakimanka ulitsa 52. Handicrafts and paintings.

Jewellery

Rostov Finift, Ulitsa Vozdvizhenka 5. Finift, a type of enamel, earrings, bracelets, rings etc.

Yantar, Gruzinsky Val ulitsa 14. Amber.

Samotsvety, Ulitsa Arbat 35. Semi-precious stones.

Diamond Hill, Ulitsa Pokrovka 10. All precious gems.

Tsentryuvelir, Ulitsa Novy Arbat 6. Diamond watches, rings etc.

Univers, TsUM department store, Ulitsa Petrovka 2. Jewelry by Russian designers.

Zhemchug, Olimpiysky Prospekt 22. Pearls.

Antiques & Art Galleries

Alpha-Art, Ulitsa Krymsky Val, 10. Central House of Artists – Moscow's largest auction house, specialising in Russian painting and graphics of the 19th and 20th centuries.

Antikvariat, Ulitsa Bolshaya Yakimanka 52. Painting, porcelain, jewelry.

Vostochnaya, Ulitsa Khmelyova 10. Paintings and graphics by local artists – also early 20th-century carpets from the Trans-Caucasus.

Mars, Ulitsa Malaya Filevskaya 32. Paintings graphics and sculptures by artists from Russia and the CIS.

Department Stores

GUM, 3 Red Square.

TsUM, Petrovka ulitsa 2.

Sadko Arcade, Krasnogvardeysky proyezd 1 (in Expocenter).
St George Street (in Radisson Slavyanskaya Hotel), Berezhkovskaya naberezhnaya 2.
Moskva Department Store, Leninsky Prospekt 54.
Petrovsky Passage, Petrovka ulitsa 10.
Sovincenter, Krasnopresnenskaya naberezhnaya 12.

Bookshops

The following bookshops usually have foreign-language books:
Dom Knigi (House of the Book), Novy Arbat ulitsa 26.
Biblio Globus, Ulitsa Myastnitskaya 6.
Zwemmers, Kuznetsky Most ulitsa 18.
Inostrannaya Kniga, Malay Nikitskaya ulitsa 16.
Moskniga, Tverskaya ulitsa 18.

Food Shops

Danilovsky Food Market, Mytnaya ulitsa 78.
Stockmann's, Zatsepsky Val ulitsa 4-8.
Arbat Irish House, Ulitsa Novy Arbat 11.
Yeliseevsky Gastronom, Tverskaya ulitsa 14.
Garden Ring, Bolshaya Sadovaya ulitsa 1.
Privat-Bordo, Rossiya Hotel, south side, Ulitsa Varvarka 6.
Progress, Zubovsky Bulvar 7.
Vienna Trade House, Prospekt Mira 1.

Sport & Leisure

Moscow has dozens of sporting complexes, stadia and other facilities, some built for the 1980 Olympics.

All the big Moscow sports complexes such as the Dynamo Stadium, Leningradsky Prospekt 36 (tel: 212 7092) and Luzhniki Sports Complex, Luzhnetskaya naberezhnaya 24 (tel: 201 0955), host wide range of sports events, from soccer to athletics. Check with the hotel service counter.

Participant

Bowling

Both the Cosmos Hotel and the Mezhdunarodnaya Hotel have bowling alleys open to the public.

Cross-country Skiing

Available at the larger Moscow parks: Izmaylovsky, Sokolniki and Gorky.
For downhill skiing and sledging go to Sparrow Hills.

Fitness

The Chaika Sports Complex on Prechistenskaya naberezhnaya 3-5, tel: 202 0474 has a gym, sauna and tennis courts. All the Moscow parks are ideal for jogging. The Radisson Slavyanskaya, the Cosmos, the Rossiya and the Mezhdunarodnaya Hotels all have swimming pools, saunas and gyms for their guests.

Golf

Tambo Golf Club, Dovzhenko ulitsa 1, tel: 147 6254.

Horse Riding

There is horse riding at the Hippodrome at Begovaya ulitsa 22 (tel: 945 4516), the Urozhay Riding Centre at Sokolniki Park, Poperechny prosek 11 (tel: 268 5922) and the Equestrian Sports Centre in the Bittsa Forest Park (tel: 318 0744).

Skating

In Gorky Park, at the Young Pioneer Stadium (Metro Dinamo), on the TsSKA skating rink (Central Army Sports Club), Leningradsky prospekt 39a and on the Patriarch's Pond. You can hire skates at the Olimpiysky Sport Hall, Olimpiysky Prospekt 16, tel: 284 6466.

Squash

The Indian and the American Embassies have courts open to members and their friends.

Swimming

The Cosmos Hotel has an indoor swimming pool open to non-residents. There is an indoor Olympic pool at Prospekt Mira 18, tel: 404 3136.

Language

Russian is one of the 130 languages used by the peoples of the former USSR. It is the mother tongue of some 150 million Russians and the state language of the Russian Federation. By talking to anybody in Russian, you will be understood by most people.

From a linguistic point of view, Russian belongs to the Slavonic branch of the Indo-European family of languages; English, German, French, Spanish and Hindi are its relatives.

Historically Russian is a comparatively young language. The appearance of the language in its present shape, based on the spoken language of the Eastern Slavs and the Church-Slavonic written language, is attributed to the 11th to 14th centuries.

Modern Russian has absorbed numerous foreign words and they form a considerable group within the Russian vocabulary. Very few tourists will be puzzled by Russian words like *telefon, televizor, teatr, otel, restoran, kafe, taxi, metro* or *aeroport*.

The thing that usually intimidates people on their first encounter with Russian is the alphabet. In fact it is easy to come to terms with after a little practice, and the effort is worthwhile if you want to make out the names of streets and shop signs.

The Russian (or Cyrillic) alphabet was created by two brothers, philosophers and public figures, Constantine (St Cyril) and Methodius; both were born in Solun (now Thessaloniki in Greece). Their purpose was to facilitate the spread of Greek liturgical books in Slavonic speaking countries. Today the Cyrillic alphabet, with different modifications, is used in Ukrainian, Byelorussian, Bulgarian, Serbian and in some other languages.

It is important that you reproduce the accent (marked here with the sign

' before each stressed vowel) correctly to be understood well.

Alphabet

printed letter	sounds as in	Russian name of letter
А а	a, archaeology	a
Б б	b, buddy	be
В в	v, vow	v
Г г	g, glad	ge
Д д	d, dot (the tip of the tongue close to the teeth, not the alveoli)	de
Е е	e, get	ye
Ё ё	yo, yoke	yo
Ж Ω	zh, composure	zhe
З з	z, zest	ze
И и	i, ink	i
Й й	j, yes	jot
К к	k, kind	ka
Л л	l, life (but a bit harder)	el'
М м	m, memory	em
Н н	n, nut	en
О о	o, optimum	o
П п	p, party	pe
Р р	r (rumbling, as in Italian, the tip of the tongue is vibrating)	er
С с	s, sound	es
Т т	t, title (the tip of the tongue close to the teeth, not the alveoli)	te
У у	u, nook	u
Ф ф	f, flower	ef
Х х	kh, hawk	ha
Ц ц	ts (pronounced conjointly)	tse
Ч ч	ch, charter	che
Ш ш	sh, shy	sha
Щ щ	shch (pronounced shcha conjointly)	
ъ	(the hard sign)	
Ы ы	y (pronounced with the same position of the tongue as when pronouncing G,K)	y
ь	(the soft sign)	
Э э	e, ensign	e
Ю ю	yu, you	yu
Я я	ya, yard	ya

Numbers

1	adín	один
2	dva	два
3	tri	три
4	chityri	четыре
5	pyat'	пять
6	shes't'	шесть
7	sem	семь
8	vósim	восемь
9	d'évit'	девять
10	d'ésit'	десять
11	adínatsat'	одиннадцать
12	dvinátsat'	двенадцать
13	trinátsat'	тринадцать
14	chityrnatsat'	четырнадцать
15	pitnátsat'	пятнадцать
16	shysnátsat'	шестнадцать
17	simnátsat'	семнадцать
18	vasimnátsat'	восемнадцать
19	divitnátsat'	девятнадцать
20	dvátsat'	двадцать
21	dvatsat' adin	двадцать один
30	trítsat'	тридцать
40	sórak	сорок
50	pidisyat	пятьдесят
60	shyz'disyat	шестьдесят
70	s'émdisyat	семьдесят
80	vósimdisyat	восемьдесят
90	divinósta	девяносто
100	sto	сто
101	sto adin	сто один
200	dv'és'ti	двести
300	trísta	триста
400	chityrista	четыреста
500	pitsót	пятьсот
600	shyssót	шестьсот
700	simsót	семьсот
800	vasimsót	восемьсот
900	divitsót	девятьсот
1,000	tysicha	тысяча
2,000	dve tysichi	две тысяч и
10,000	d'ésit' tysich	десять тысяч
100,000	sto tysich	сто тысяч
1,000,000	milión	миллион
1,000,000,000	miliárd	миллиард

Pronouns

I/We
ya/my
я/мы

You
ty (singular, informal)
vy (plural, or formal singular)
ты /вы

He/She/They
on/aná/aní
он/она/они

My/Mine
moj (object masculine)
mayá (object feminine)
mayó (neutral or without marking the gender)
maí (plural)
мой/моя/моё/мои

Our/Ours
nash/násha/náshe/náshy (resp.)
наш/наша/наше/наши

Your/Yours
tvoj etc. (see My)
vash etc. (see Our)
твой/ваш

His/Her, Hers/Their, Theirs
jivó/jiyó/ikh
его/её/их

Who?
khto?
Кто?

What?
shto?
Что?

Forms of Greetings

Forms of Address: Modern Russian has no established and universally used forms of address. The old revolutionary form *tavárishch* (comrade), still used amongst some party members, lacks popularity with the rest of the population.

One way is to say: *Izviníte, skazhíte pozhálsta...* (Excuse me, tell me, please...) or *Izvinite, mózhna sprasít'...* (Excuse me, can I ask you...).

If you want to look original and to show your penetration into the depths of history of courteous forms, you can appeal to the man *súdar'* (sir), and to the woman *sudárynya* (madam). Many people want to restore these forms of address in modern Russian society. If you know the name of the father of the person you talk to, the best and the most neutral way is to use these both when addressing him (her): "Mikhál Sirgéich" to Mr Gorbachev and "Raísa Maxímavna" to his spouse.

In business circles you can use forms *gaspadín* to a man and *gaspazhá* to a woman. The English forms of address "Mister" or "Sir" are also acceptable.

You can hear common parlance forms *Maladói chilavék!* (Young man!) and *Dévushka!* (Girl!) to a person of any age and also *Zhénshchina!* (Woman!) to women on the bus, in a shop or at the market. These forms should be avoided in conversation.

Hello!
zdrástvuti (neutral, often accompanied

by shaking hands, but it is not necessary)
Здравствуйте!
alo! (by telephone only)
Алло!
zdrástvuj (to one person, informal)
Здравствуй!
priv'ét! (informal)
Привет!

Good afternoon/Good evening
dóbry den'/dobry véchir
Добрый день/Добрый вечер

Good morning/Good night
dobrae útra/dobraj nóchi (= Sleep well)
Доброе утро/Доброй ночи

Good bye
dasvidán'ye (neutral)
До свиданья
chao! (informal)
Чао!
paká! (informal, literally means "until")
Пока!

Good luck to you!
shchislíva!
Счастливо!

What is your name?
kak vas (tibya) zavút?/kak váshe ímya ótchistva? (the second is formal)
Как вас (тебя) зовут?/Как ваще имя и отчество?

My name is... /I am...
minya zavut... /ya...
Меня зовут... /Я...

It's a pleasure
óchin' priyatna
Очень приятно

Good/Excellent
kharashó/privaskhódna
хорошо/отлично

Do you speak English?
vy gavaríti pa anglíski?
Вы говорите по-английски?

I don't understand/I didn't understand
ya ni panimáyu/ya ni pónyal
Я не понимаю/Я не понял

Repeat, please
pavtaríti pazhálsta
Повторите, поΩалуйста

What do you call this?

kak vy éta nazyváiti?
Как вы это называете?

How do you say...?
kak vy gavaríti...?
Как вы говорите...?

Please/Thank you (very much)
pazhálsta/(bal'shóe) spasíba
ПоΩалуйста/(Большое) спасибо

Excuse me
izviníti
Извините

Phrases
Getting Around

Where is the...?
gd'e (nakhóditsa)...?
Где находится...?

beach
plyazh
...пляΩ

bathroom
vánnaya
...ванная

bus station
aftóbusnaya stántsyja/aftavakzál
...автобусная станция/автовокзал

bus stop
astanófka aftóbusa
...остановка автобуса

airport
airapórt
...аэропорт

railway station
vakzál/stántsyja (in small towns)
...вокзал/станция

post office
póchta
...почта

police station
...milítsyja
...милиция

ticket office
bil'étnaya kássa
...билетная касса

marketplace
rynak/bazár
...рынок/базар

embassy/consulate
pasól'stva/kónsul'stva
...посольство/консульство

Where is there a...?
gd'e z'd'es'...?
Где здесь...?

currency exchange
abm'én val'úty
...обмен валюты

pharmacy
apt'éka
...аптека

(good) hotel
(kharóshyj) atél'/(kharoshaya) gastínitsa
...(хороший) отель (хорошая) гостиница

restaurant
ristarán
...ресторан

bar
bar
...бар

taxi stand
stayanka taxí
...стоянка такси

subway station
mitró
...метро

service station
aftazaprávachnaya stantsyja/aftasárvis
...автозаправочная станция

newsstand
gaz'étnyj kiósk
...газетный киоск

public telephone
tilifón
...телефон

hard currency shop
val'útnyj magazín
...валютный магазин

supermarket
univirsám
...универсам

department store
univirmák
...универмаг

hairdresser
parikmákhirskaya
…парикмахерская

jeweller
yuvilírnyj magazin
…ювелирный магазин

hospital
bal'nítsa
…больница

Do you have…?
u vas jes't'…?
У вас ес…

I (don't) want…
ya (ni) khachyu…
Я (не) хо чу…

I want to buy…
ya khachyu kupít'…
Я хочу купить…

Where can I buy…?
gd'e ya magú kupít'…?
Где я могу купить…?

cigarettes
sigaréty
…сигареты

wine
vinó
…вино

film
fotoplyonku
…фотоплёнку

a ticket for…
bilét na…
…билет на…

this
éta
…это

postcards/envelopes
atkrytki/kanv'érty
…открытки/конверты

a pen/a pencil
rúchku/karandásh
…ручку/карандаш

soap/shampoo
myla/shampún'
…мыло/шампунь

aspirin
aspirín
…аспирин

I need…
mn'e núzhna…
Мне нуΩно…

I need a doctor/a mechanic
mn'e núzhyn dóktar/aftamikhánik
Мне нуΩен доктор/автомеханик

I need help
mn'e nuzhná pómashch'
Мне нуΩна помощь

Car/Plane/Train/Ship
mashyna/samal'yot/póist/karábl'
маъшина/самолёт/поезд/корабль

A ticket to…
bil'ét do…
билет до…

How can I get to…
kak ya magu dabrátsa do…
Как я могу добраться до…

Please, take me to…
pazhalsta atvizíti minya…
ПоΩалуйста, отвезите меня…

What is this place called?
kak nazyváitsa eta m'ésta?
Как называется это место?

Where are we?
gd'e my?
Где мы?

Stop here
astanavíti z'd'es'
Остановите здесь

Please wait
padazhdíti pazhalsta
ПодоΩдите, поΩалуйста

When does the train [plane] leave?
kagdá atpravl'yaitsa poist [samalyot]?
Когда отправляется поезд (самолёт)?

I want to check my luggage
ya khachyu prav'érit' bagázh
Я хочу проверить багаΩ

Where does this bus go?
kudá id'yot état aftóbus?
Куда идёт этот автобус?

Shopping

How much does it cost?
skól'ka eta stóit?
Сколько это стоит?

That's very expensive
eta óchin' dóraga
Это о чень дорого

A lot, many/A little, few
mnóga/mála
много/мало

It (doesn't) fits me
eta mn'e (ni) padkhódit
Это мне (не) подходит

At the Hotel

I have a reservation
u minya zakázana m'esta
У меня заказана комната

I want to make a reservation
ya khachyu zakazát' m'esta
Я хочу заказать место

A single (double) room
adnam'éstnuyu (dvukhmestnuyu) kómnatu
одноместную (двухместную) комнату

I want to see the room
ya khachyu pasmatrét' nómer
Я хо чу посмотреть номер

Key/Suitcase/Bag
klyuch/chimadán/súmka
ключ /чемодан/сумка

At the Restaurant

Waiter/Menu
afitsyánt/minyu
официант/меню

I want to order…
ya khachyu zakazat'…
Я хочу заказать

breakfast/lunch/supper
záftrak/ab'ét/úzhyn
завтрак/обед/уΩин

the house specialty
fírminnaya blyuda
фирменное блюдо

mineral water/juice
minirál'naya vadá/sok
минерал'ьная вода/сок

coffee/tea/beer
kófe/chai/píva
кофе/ чай/пиво

What do you have to drink (alcoholic)?
shto u vas jes't' vypit'?
Что у вас есть выпить?

Ice/Fruit/Dessert
marózhynaya/frúkty/disért
моΩо еное/фрукты/дессерт

Salt/Pepper/Sugar
sol'/périts/sákhar
соль/перец/сахар

Beef/Pork/Chicken/Fish/Shrimp
gavyadina/svinína/kúritsa/ryba/kriv'étki
говядина/свинина/курица/рыба/ креветки

Vegetables/Rice/Potatoes
óvashchi/ris/kartófil'
овощи/рис/картофель

Bread/Butter/Eggs
khleb/másla/yajtsa
хлеб/масло/яйца

Soup/Salad/Sandwich/Pizza
sup/salát/butyrbrót/pitsa
суп/салат/бутерброд/пицца

a plate/a glass/a cup/a napkin
tar'élka/stakán/cháshka/salf'étka
тарелка/стакан/чашка/салфетка

The bill, please
shchyot pazhalsta
Счёт, поΩалуйста

Well done/Not so good
fkúsna/ták sibe
вкусно/так себе

I want my change, please
zdáchu pazhalsta
Сдачу, поΩалуйста

Money

I want to exchange currency (money)
ya khachyu abmin'át' val'yutu (d'én'gi)
Я хочу обменять валюту (деньги)

Do you accept credit cards?
vy prinimáiti kridítnyi kártachki?
Вы принимаете кредитные карточки ?

Can you cash a traveller's cheque?
vy mózhyti razminyat' darózhnyj chek?
Вы моΩете разменять дороΩный чек?

What is the exchange rate?
kakój kurs?
Какой курс?

Time

What time is it?
katóryj chas?
Который час?

Just a moment, please
adnú minútachku
Одну минуточку

How long does it take?
skól'ka vrémini eta zanimáit?
Сколько времени это занимает?

Hour/day/week/month
chas/den'/nid'élya/m'ésits
час/день/неделя/месяц

At what time?
f kakóe vrémya?
В какое время?

At 1/at 8am/at 6pm
f chas/ v vósim utrá/f shés't' chisóf v'échira
в час/в восемь утра/в шесть часов вечера

This (last, next) week
eta (próshlaya, sl'édujshchiya) nid'elya
эта (прошлая, следующая) неделя

Yesterday/Today/Tomorrow
fchirá/sivód'nya/záftra
вчера/сегодня/завтра

Sunday
vaskris'én'je
воскресенье

Monday
panid'él'nik
понедельник

Tuesday
ftórnik
вторник

Wednesday
sridá
среда

Thursday
chitv'érk
четверг

Friday
pyatnitsa
пятница

Saturday
subóta
суббота

The weekend
vykhadnyi dni
выходные дни

Signs & Inscriptions

вход/выход/входа нет
fkhot/vykhat/fkhóda n'et
Entrance/Exit/No Entrance

туалет/уборная
tual'ét/ubórnaya
Toilet/Lavatory

Ж (З) / М (М)
dlya zhén'shchin/dlya mushchín
Ladies/Gentlemen

зал оΩидания
zal azhidán'ya
Waiting hall

занято/свободно
zánita/svabódna
Occupied/Free

кассх
kassa
Booking office/cash desk

медпункт
mitpúnt
Medical Services

справочное бюро
správachnae bzuro
Information

вода для питья
vadá dlya pit'ya
Drinking Water

вокзал
vakzál
Terminal/Railway station

открыто/закрыто
atkryta/zakryta
Open/Closed

Russian	Transliteration	English

запрещается/опасно
zaprishchyaitsa/apásna
Prohibited/Danger

продукты/гастроном
pradúkty/gastranóm
Grocery

булочная/кондитерская
búlachnaya/kan'dítirskaya
Bakery/Confectionery

закусочная/столовая
zakúsachnaya/stalóvaya
Refreshment room/Canteen

самообслуживание
samaapslúzhivan'je
Self-service

баня/прачечная/химчистка
bánya/práchichnaya/khimchístka
Bath-House/Laundry/Chemical Cleaning

книги/культтовары
knígi/kul'taváry
Books/Stationery

мясо/птица
m'ása/ptítsa
Meat/Poultry

обувь
óbuf'
Shoe-store

овощи/фрукты
óvashchi/frúkty
Green-Grocery/Fruits

универмаг/универсам
univirmák/univirsám
Department store/supermarket

ткани/цветы
tkani/tsvity
Fabrics/Flowers

Translation Services

Translation services are available through Intourist or one of the local co-operative translation bureaux:
Inlingua, 2/1 Semyonovskaya Nab., tel: 360 0874.
Interpret, 1st Kadashevsky Per., tel: 231 1020.

Further Reading

Recommended Titles

History & Politics

A History of the Soviet Union, by G. Hosking. Fontana/Collins, 1990.
The Russian Chronicles, Preface by Dmitry Obolensky. Garamond, 1990
Memoirs, by M. Gorbachev. Doubleday, 1996.
The Other Russia, by Michael Glenny and Norman Stone. Faber & Faber, 1990.
Against the Grain, by Boris Yeltsin. Jonathan Cape, 1990.
Ten Days that Shook the World, by John Reed. Penguin, first published 1919.
The Gulag Archipelago, by Alexander Solzhenitsyn. Collins Harvill, 1988.

Art

Russian Art of the Avant Garde, by J.E. Bowlt. Thames & Hudson, 1988.
The Kremlin and its Treasures, by Rodimzeva, Rachmanov and Raimann. Phaidon, 1989.
Moscow Treasures and Traditions, with introduction by W. Bruce Lincoln. Soviet Ministry of Culture/Smithsonian Institution 1990.
Moscow Revealed, by John Freeman and Kathleen Berton. Doubleday 1991.
Three Centuries of Russian Painting, by S. Chekhonina, O. Chekhonin. Kitezh, St Petersburg, 1994.

Travel, Geography & Natural History

Among the Russians, by Colin Thubron. Penguin, 1983.
Journey for our time, the journals of the Marquis de Custine, edited and translated by Phyllis Penn Kohler. George Pilot 1980.

Literature

The Fiance and Other Stories, Anton Chekhov. Penguin, 1986.
The Master and Margarita, Mikhail Bulgakov.
Doctor Zhivago, by Boris Pasternak.
Children of the Arbat, by Anatoli Rybakov. Hutchinson, 1988.

War and Peace and *Anna Karenina*, by Leo Tolstoy.
Gorky Park, by Martin Cruz Smith
Mother Russia, by Robert Littell.

Other Insight Guides

The 190-title *Insight Guides* series includes companion books on Russia, St Petersburg, Eastern Europe, Baltic States, Poland, Hungary, Budapest, Czech & Slovak Republics, and Prague.

Insight Pocket Guides

Insight Pocket Guides to *Moscow* and *St Petersburg* are designed for visitors keen to make the most of a short stay. In each case, a local "host" provides timed itineraries and recommends places to see and things to do. Each book has a full-size fold-out map.

Insight Compact Guides

Insight Compact Guides to Moscow and *St Petersburg* are the perfect on-the-spot guides. This series packs an astonishing amount of information into an extremely portable format, with text, photographs and maps all carefully cross-referenced.

Index

A

N

O

S

285

The Insight Approach

The book you are holding is part of the world's largest range of guidebooks. Its purpose is to help you have the most valuable travel experience possible, and we try to achieve this by providing not only information about countries, regions and cities but also genuine insight into their history, culture, institutions and people.

Since the first Insight Guide – to Bali – was published in 1970, the series has been dedicated to the proposition that, with insight into a country's people and culture, visitors can both enhance their own experience and be accepted more easily by their hosts. Now, in a world where ethnic hostilities and nationalist conflicts are all too common, such attempts to increase understanding between peoples are more important than ever.

Insight Guides:
Essentials for understanding
Because a nation's past holds the key to its present, each Insight Guide kicks off with lively history chapters. These are followed by magazine-style essays on culture and daily life. This essential background information gives readers the necessary context for using the main Places section, with its comprehensive run-down on things worth seeing and doing. Finally, a listings section contains all the information you'll need on travel, hotels, restaurants and opening times.

As far as possible, we rely on local writers and specialists to ensure that the information is authoritative. The pictures, for which Insight Guides have become so celebrated, are just as important. Our photojournalistic approach aims not only to illustrate a destination but also to communicate visually and directly to readers life as it is lived by the locals.

Compact Guides
The "great little guides"
As invaluable as such background information is, it isn't always fun to carry an Insight Guide through a crowded souk or up a church tower. Could we, readers asked, distil the key reference material into a slim volume for on-the-spot use?

Our response was to design Compact Guides as an entirely new series, with original text carefully cross-referenced to detailed maps and more than 200 photographs. In essence, they're miniature encyclopedias, concise and comprehensive, displaying reliable and up-to-date information in an accessible way.

Pocket Guides:
A local host in book form
However wide-ranging the information in a book, human beings still value the personal touch. Our editors are often asked the same questions. Where do *you* go to eat? What do *you* think is the best beach? What would you recommend if I have only three days? We invited our local correspondents to act as "substitute hosts" by revealing their preferred walks and trips, listing the restaurants they go to and structuring a visit into a series of timed itineraries.

The result is our Pocket Guides, complete with full-size fold-out maps. These 100-plus titles help readers plan a trip precisely, particularly if their time is short.

Exploring with Insight:
A valuable travel experience
In conjunction with co-publishers all over the world, we print in up to 10 languages, from German to Chinese, from Danish to Russian. But our aim remains simple: to enhance your travel experience by combining our expertise in guidebook publishing with the on-the-spot knowledge of our correspondents.